Palgrave Frontiers in Philosophy of Religion

Series Editors
Yujin Nagasawa
Department of Philosophy
University of Birmingham
Birmingham, UK

Erik J. Wielenberg
Department of Philosophy
DePauw University
Greencastle, IN, USA

Palgrave Frontiers in Philosophy of Religion is a long overdue series which will provide a unique platform for the advancement of research in this area. Each book in the series aims to progress a debate in the philosophy of religion by (i) offering a novel argument to establish a strikingly original thesis, or (ii) approaching an ongoing dispute from a radically new point of view. Each title in the series contributes to this aim by utilising recent developments in empirical sciences or cutting-edge research in foundational areas of philosophy (such as metaphysics, epistemology and ethics).

More information about this series at
http://www.palgrave.com/gp/series/14700

Ciro De Florio • Aldo Frigerio

Divine Omniscience and Human Free Will

A Logical and Metaphysical Analysis

Ciro De Florio
Department of Philosophy
Università Cattolica del Sacro Cuore
Milan, Italy

Aldo Frigerio
Department of Philosophy
Università Cattolica del Sacro Cuore
Milan, Italy

Palgrave Frontiers in Philosophy of Religion
ISBN 978-3-030-31299-2   ISBN 978-3-030-31300-5 (eBook)
https://doi.org/10.1007/978-3-030-31300-5

© The Editor(s) (if applicable) and The Author(s) 2019
This work is subject to copyright. All rights are solely and exclusively licensed by the Publisher, whether the whole or part of the material is concerned, specifically the rights of translation, reprinting, reuse of illustrations, recitation, broadcasting, reproduction on microfilms or in any other physical way, and transmission or information storage and retrieval, electronic adaptation, computer software, or by similar or dissimilar methodology now known or hereafter developed.

The use of general descriptive names, registered names, trademarks, service marks, etc. in this publication does not imply, even in the absence of a specific statement, that such names are exempt from the relevant protective laws and regulations and therefore free for general use.

The publisher, the authors, and the editors are safe to assume that the advice and information in this book are believed to be true and accurate at the date of publication. Neither the publisher nor the authors or the editors give a warranty, expressed or implied, with respect to the material contained herein or for any errors or omissions that may have been made. The publisher remains neutral with regard to jurisdictional claims in published maps and institutional affiliations.

Cover illustration: Eshma/Alamy Stock Photo

This Palgrave Macmillan imprint is published by the registered company Springer Nature Switzerland AG.
The registered company address is: Gewerbestrasse 11, 6330 Cham, Switzerland
Printed by Markono Print Media Pte Ltd

In many examples of this book, the players are Emma and Thomas, who are, by the way, my children. And this book is lovingly dedicated to them.

Ciro De Florio

Preface

If you hold this book in your hands, unless in exceptional, and frankly speaking weird, cases, it is highly likely that you have recently decided to start reading it.[1] We do hope that nobody forced you to do so. You may have picked up this volume for various reasons: out of curiosity or interest, driven by a sudden passion or just to mock the authors. You could have chosen to do something different instead, like finally reading Proust's *Recherche*, going for a walk or, more wisely, boiling an egg. A series of alternatives, some more intriguing than others, was laid out in front of you, and you have stepped upon the path of events which has led to you reading these introductory words.[2]

Now, imagine that yesterday, while you were not even thinking about this book, someone had *already* known that you would choose to read it. Let us take a further step: imagine that some three hundred years ago someone already knew that three hundred years later, a person who looks exactly like you would choose to read a book on philosophy instead of enjoying a good walk.

That being said, if someone had already known that you would make such a choice, then in that far remote past it was already true that you

---

[1] Of course, you can argue that you are reading it on your tablet, e-reader or any other device. Plato's philosophic intuition is not necessary to state that this is not the point here.
[2] By the way, we appreciate that very much.

would choose to read this book. Consequently, the acts of egg-boiling, walking around or even reading Proust's *Recherche* have never been *true* alternatives: you would not have been able to decide against reading this book, even if you had wanted to, because otherwise what had been true for centuries (three or more) would instantly and mysteriously become false. Hold on: if you do not have alternatives, you are not free at all. In other words, not only are you not free to read a book, but, even worse, someone has in some way *already* predicted any action of yours. To be honest, we too cannot act differently while we are writing these words. Our free will, the mastery of our own destiny, and the responsibility we take for our actions or the lack thereof—all vanish in a beautiful cognitive illusion: it seems that we are free, while actually we are not.

Not so fast. In the previous argument, we have assumed that there is an individual who knows, in an ineffable way, what will happen in the future; but if this is not the case, so our freedom is safe. If this "individual" existed, well, it could be a problem. The point is that, according to the monotheistic tradition, such a "Someone" does exist: it is God. Things are therefore getting quite complicated: how is it possible to reconcile the existence of an omniscient god, who infallibly knows the outcome of history, with the free will of humans?

The present book deals with this question. Unfortunately for us—and for you too—it is not "one long argument" we are going to discuss here. The book takes into consideration the overarching discourse regarding these issues, the criticism against them, as well as their theoretical adequacy. Eventually, it suggests our own proposal, but we do not recommend skimming through the chapters in order to find out who the killer is. Before we set on our journey, some attention has to be dedicated to a few preliminary issues, in order to avoid the avoidable misunderstandings.

From a theoretical point of view, theology deals with God and the questions related to this topic. This is not a book of theology, though. No presupposition of faith can be found on the following pages. For this reason, we believe that it is a book of philosophy of religion, which is the rational investigation on the content of religious beliefs. Those readers conforming to atheism or agnosticism may want to continue reading the following chapters under a certain *very big* condition: if God exists or existed. Believers, on the other hand, can disregard the if-clause (or affirm the antecedent, by modus ponens). Nonetheless, we assume that this volume can be interesting for theologians too, as far as the mere rational investigation of the nature of God without, for instance, any reference to the Scriptures is concerned.[3]

This book contains several references to great ancient philosophers and theologians: from Aristotle to Saint Augustine and William of Ockham. We do not strive for historical fidelity or exegetical accuracy. Our aim is not to meticulously investigate the exact sayings of some particular author. The works of the great ancient thinkers are useful to identify the very general theoretical models, which are going to be discussed as such. However, we believe that historians of philosophy may also be interested in the contemporary reception of the topics, which have been addressed on by the subjects of their research.

Lastly, a brief remark about logic. This volume contains a good deal of formal analysis, which relies on various frameworks of logic. We are convinced that "there is no mathematical substitute for philosophy" (Kripke 1976, p. 416) and that the *amount* of philosophy at the beginning of a theorem is as much as at the end of it. However, we firmly believe that logic offers an incomparable and irreplaceable possibility for conceptual characterization, precision and accuracy; microscopy is not a living being nor it is biology, but it is impossible to carry out substantial research in biology without the right microscopy. In fact, within the context of our field, logic also has a heuristic function, which enhances the philosophical intuition.

There are no prerequisites to reading this book. We have included a chapter which introduces all the terminology we need. At the same time, a good deal of curiosity and passion for conceptual problems, and for the theoretical artefacts that for ages human beings have been designing in order to solve them, is essential for engaging with the topic.

---

[3] In particular, it could be of some interest for theologians who agree with the approach, say, of Crisp and Rea (2009).

One would hope to incur exclusively the debts of an intellectual kind. In these years we did contract a lot of them. In particular, we would like to thank Georg Gasser, who suggested some years ago that we should deal with issues regarding the philosophy of religion. Our profound gratitude is extended to Andrea Aguti, Marco Benasso, Daniele Bertini, Patrick Blackburn, Andrea Bottani, Claudio Calosi, Massimiliano Carrara, Pablo Cobreros, William Craig, Damiano Costa, Richard Davies, Vincenzo Fano, Riccardo Fedriga, Sergio Galvan, Alessandro Giordani, Simone Gozzano, David Jakobsen, Giorgio Lando, Winfried Löffler, Anna Marmodoro, Ulrich Meyer, Vittorio Morato, Matteo Morganti, Paola Müller, Peter Øhrstrøm, Elisa Paganini, Edmund Runggaldier, Marco Santambrogio, Alfredo Tomasetta, Giuliano Torrengo and Jacek Wawer. Then we want to thank Giulia De Florio for her invaluable linguistic assistance. We take full responsibility for the contents of this volume.

Finally, we would like to thank the editorial team at Palgrave Macmillan, expecially Brendan George and Lauriane Piette, for their very helpful editorial assistance and guidance.

Milan, Italy Ciro De Florio
Milan, Italy Aldo Frigerio

References

Crisp, O.D., and M.C. Rea. 2009. *Analytic theology: New essays in the philosophy of theology*. Oxford: Oxford University Press.

Kripke, S.A. 1976. Is there a problem about substitutional quantification? In *Truth and Meaning*, ed. Gareth Evans, and John McDowell, 324–419. Oxford: Oxford University Press.

Contents

1 **The Battle for Free Will**   1
   1.1 Fatalism and Determinism   3
   1.2 Logical Fatalism   6
      1.2.1 Bivalence   9
      1.2.2 Necessity of the Past   11
      1.2.3 Truth and Free Will   13
   1.3 How to Avoid the Battle   15
   1.4 From Logic Fatalism to Theological Fatalism   18
   References   25

2 **Metaphysics and Logic of Time**   27
   2.1 Ontology of Time   28
   2.2 Dynamics of Time: A- and B-Theory   32
   2.3 Dynamics and Ontology   37
   2.4 Intermezzo: Persistence and Scientific Image of the World   39
   2.5 Topology of Time: Closed and Open Universe   42
   2.6 Temporal Logic   47
      2.6.1 Linear Time   49
      2.6.2 Branching Time   50

	2.6.3	Peircean Semantics	53
	2.6.4	Thin Red Line Model	58
References			66

3 Extreme Measures — 69

- 3.1 Open Theism — 70
  - 3.1.1 A Different Concept of God — 71
  - 3.1.2 The Openness of the Future — 77
  - 3.1.3 To What Openness Is the Open Theist Committed? — 82
  - 3.1.4 Theological Difficulties — 85
  - 3.1.5 Conclusions on Open Theism — 91
- 3.2 Theological Determinism — 92
  - 3.2.1 Non Theological Compatibilism — 94
  - 3.2.2 Theological Compatibilism — 100
- References — 111

4 God Knows the True Future: Ockhamism — 115

- 4.1 Introduction — 115
- 4.2 The Ockhamist Solution — 120
- 4.3 The True Future — 124
- 4.4 Soft Facts — 125
- 4.5 Metaphysics of Time and Ockhamism — 134
  - 4.5.1 Presentism and Truth — 136
  - 4.5.2 TSB Revisited — 142
  - 4.5.3 Eternalist Ockhamism — 144
  - 4.5.4 Presentist Ockhamism? — 146
  - 4.5.5 Growing Block and Spotlight Ockhamism — 148
- 4.6 Conclusion: Is There Really an Ockham's Way Out? — 150
- References — 151

5 Molinism — 155

- 5.1 Conditionals of Freedom — 156
- 5.2 The Structure of the Molinist World — 162
  - 5.2.1 Local TRL — 162

	5.2.2	Many Worlds and Normal TRL	165
	5.2.3	What Answer to the Fatalist Argument?	171
	5.2.4	CFs as Counterfactuals?	174
5.3	The Costs of Molinism	179
	5.3.1	The Truth-Making Principle	181
	5.3.2	Liberalizing TSB	184
5.4	The Costs That the Molinist Does Not Have to Pay	191
	5.4.1	Adams' and Hasker's Arguments	191
	5.4.2	What Does Not Work in Adams' and Hasker's Arguments	195
	5.4.3	Adams' Argument	201
	5.4.4	Hasker's Argument	202
5.5	Conclusion	204
References	205

6 The Timeless Solution — 209

- 6.1 How the Timeless Solution Works — 210
- 6.2 Some Objections — 216
- 6.3 Timeless God and Eternalism — 222
- 6.4 A-Theory and Timeless God — 226
  - 6.4.1 The Semantic Debate — 227
  - 6.4.2 Assessing the Semantic Debate — 229
  - 6.4.3 The Metaphysical Debate — 231
- 6.5 Fragmentalism and Timeless God — 240
  - 6.5.1 Perspectival Semantics — 240
  - 6.5.2 Perspectival Semantics and Eternalism — 249
  - 6.5.3 Fragmentalism — 250
  - 6.5.4 God's Knowledge and Fragmentalism — 254
- 6.6 Conclusion — 256
- References — 257

Conclusions — 261

Index — 265

List of Figures

Fig. 2.1	Emma's case	61
Fig. 3.1	Kinds of theological determinism	101
Fig. 4.1	**TRL** schema	127
Fig. 4.2	Butterfly schema	129
Fig. 4.3	Butterfly schema (again)	145
Fig. 5.1	Emma's case (again)	163
Fig. 5.2	Molinist universe	170
Fig. 5.3	Molinist loop	196
Fig. 6.1	Boethius picture of eternity	212
Fig. 6.2	Foreknowledge and prophecy	221
Fig. 6.3	The closure of possibilities	241
Fig. 6.4	The failure of retrogradation	244
Fig. 6.5	Evaluation of φ at t from perspective t'	246
Fig. 6.6	Evaluation of $\mathbf{F}\varphi$ at t from perspective t	247
Fig. 6.7	Evaluation of $\mathbf{F}\varphi$ at t from perspective t'	247

1

The Battle for Free Will

A horrible fate was prophesied first to Laius and then to his son, Oedipus: he would kill his own father and marry his own mother Jocasta. All the efforts (at times cruel and even inhuman) of the characters involved ended up in failure. The Fate was obviously right and Oedipus, somehow unintentionally, stained himself with the terrible deeds he eventually perpetrated. One of the reasons why Greek tragedy is so dramatically effective lies in the idea of *ineluctability* that imbues all the characters' lives; it scares us because we basically feel ourselves free. We tend to believe that most of our actions, if not all of them, are the *consequence* of our choices, which in their turn determine our story. The decision to go to university by train or by car is my decision, which has some—yet minimal—consequences.

Moreover, not only our self-perception of human beings but the whole universe of social bonds, ethical norms and political institutions depends on the presupposition—more or less explicit and more or less vague— that human beings are free and therefore *responsible* for their actions. We deserve praise or, on the contrary, blame for what we have freely chosen. It is not by chance that, in many judicial systems, punishability depends on the concept of responsibility, that is, of freedom of the accused. If we want to be slightly more technical, we can express such self-perception by claiming that we perceive our future as *partially* open; that is, we think that we have in front of us multiple possible actions among which we can freely choose the one we want to take. It is also clear that we cannot entirely determine our future: many events do not depend on us. And yet, we deeply believe that many future aspects are neither unavoidable nor impossible. They have been traditionally called future contingents.[1]

Our intuition of being free is deeply rooted; consequently, we are inclined to abandon other beliefs that contrast with this feeling. However, the history of thinking is full of representations, firstly mythical and poetical then theoretical, that deny the *actual* man's free will. In fact, the tragic heroes of the Greek tragedy feel free and masters of their actions, and they ignore that they are just pawns at Fate's mercy. The tragedy affects us so much because of this discrepancy between our illusion of free will and the actual absence of it. Not by chance, according to the Stoic ethics—one of the first elaborations on ethics that explicitly takes into account the absence of free will in human beings—happiness lies precisely in getting rid of such cognitive distortion: the wise man knows that he is not free, therefore he tunes his desires with what will inevitably happen.

The theoretical stance according to which men are not free (in any informative acceptations of the term) is usually called *fatalism*. It denies that future contingents exist, thus maintaining that there is one inevitable future. This view may be accepted or argued for in various ways: by appeal to logical, metaphysical or theological laws. This book is dedicated to the logic-metaphysical analysis of the problem of theological fatalism. In short, theological fatalism claims that, since God predicts today what we will do tomorrow and since God's knowledge is infallible, tomorrow we will do nothing but what God has predicted that we would do, and therefore we are not free to choose between two or more alternatives. In other words, theological fatalism "is the thesis that infallible foreknowledge of

---

[1]One may wonder whether future contingents that do *not* depend on the free action of human beings may exist. We will deal later with this issue.

a human act makes the act necessary and hence unfree. If there is a being who knows the entire future infallibly, then no human act is free".[2]

In this introductory chapter, we shall deal with logical fatalism, which is at the basis of the most ancient philosophical analysis of the problem, included in the well-known chapter nine of Aristotle's *De Interpretatione*. Logical fatalism does not draw our impossibility to do otherwise from an omniscient God who predicts everything, but from some logico-semantical principles, quite intuitive at a first glance. We start from logic fatalism because it shows interesting intersections with theological fatalism. The plan of this chapter is as follows. In the next section, a few comments are devoted to the relationship between fatalism and a cognate notion: *determinism*. Then, in Sect. 1.2, we will present a version of the argument for logical fatalism, singling out, in Sect. 1.3, the main critical points and hinting at a few general strategies for solving them. Finally, in Sect. 1.4, we will make a theoretical switch from logical to theological fatalism, thus arriving at the threshold of the main topic of our investigation.

1.1 Fatalism and Determinism

Fatalism can be defined, *prima facie*, as the philosophical position, or better, the intuition, according to which future is fixed and inevitable; therefore free actions by agents do not exist. We can obviously toy with a certain idea of freedom, but actually we are not masters of our own destiny.

The idea that the history of the world is fixed and that each event is nothing but the necessary product of a determined cause-effect relation is at the basis of a concept similar to fatalism: *determinism*.

---

[2]Zagzebski, Linda, "Foreknowledge and Free Will", The Stanford Encyclopedia of Philosophy (Summer 2017 Edition), Edward N. Zalta (ed.), https://plato.stanford.edu/archives/sum2017/entries/free-will-foreknowledge/.

Pierre Simone de Laplace gives a well-known definition of determinism:

> We may regard the present state of the universe as the effect of its past and the cause of its future. An intellect which at a certain moment would know all forces that set nature in motion, and all positions of all items of which nature is composed, if this intellect were also vast enough to submit these data to analysis, it would embrace in a single formula the movements of the greatest bodies of the universe and those of the tiniest atom; for such an intellect nothing would be uncertain and the future just like the past would be present before its eyes. (De Laplace 1902, p. 4)

In a precise moment (we can call it t_0), the state of the universe is entirely determined by the laws of nature and by the state of universe in the preceding moment. Consequently, if we perfectly knew all the information about the state of the universe and the dynamics of the system, we could infallibly foresee the state of the universe in ten seconds as well as in thirty million years. In other words, the dynamic of evolution of the universe is described by a function: once the arguments are provided, the value is univocally determined. One can wonder whether the same holds also toward the past. Laplace—as we have seen in the quotation—did think so. In order for the projection to work toward both the future and the past, a two-way function is necessary. Otherwise, it would be admissible a state of the world at t_0 as the product of the laws of development and of the state at t_{-1}, as well as the product of the laws of development and the *alternative* state at t_{-2}. From the origin of modern science up to the so-called Quantum Revolution, determinism has been—more or less explicitly—at the basis of the scientific view of the world. However, it is a purely metaphysical hypothesis which concerns the general structure of the dynamic of reality.

Bernstein (2002, pp. 67–69) maintains that fatalism and determinism are two independent, though intertwined, theses. In a nutshell, determinism presumes a series of causal and nomic assumptions. Indeed, we can affirm that we consider the world deterministic because of the existence of laws, which are in their turn deterministic, that is, founded on a deterministic interpretation of the cause-effect relation. In a world without any causal regularity, it would be difficult to bring up determinism. However, according to Bernstein, even a universe made by a sequence of nomically non-related events can be fatalist, that is, each future event becomes inevitable.

For reasons that will be clear shortly, we prefer to speak of "necessitism" instead of "fatalism". The two notions distinguished by Bernstein can be defined as follows:

Necessitism A universe is necessitist if the course of events is given and does not admit alternatives or ramifications; the future, as well as the past, are written. Such a stance has to do with the *topology* and *ontology* of time (see Chap. 2).[3]

Determinism In a determinist world, the present state of the world and its laws of evolution determine univocally all the states of the world following the present one.

While necessitism does not imply determinism, the opposite is the case: a determinist world is also a necessitist one. Determinism provides an explicative account of why future facts are inevitable: they are inevitable because they are the effects of a determinist dynamic. For this reason, when we refer in this book to the models in which the future is closed and inevitable, we will mainly mean determinist models and not simply necessitist models, given that the necessity of the events within necessitism remains unsupported if determinism is not accepted.

Where, then, is fatalism's place? In our opinion, fatalism is a particular way to conceive necessitism, that is, it is *necessitism with respect to the choices of free agents*. In other words, in a world without free agents, it is quite meaningless to talk about fatalism (rather, we should speak about necessitism or determinism). So, while necessitism implies fatalism (*modulo* the existence of agents), the other way round does not hold inevitably. A universe where the agents do not possess free will—because they are possibly determined by biological or other kinds of factors—

---

[3]A necessitist universe should not be confused with a necessary universe; the latter is as it is and cannot be otherwise. On the contrary, it is strictly contingent that a necessitist universe has got that particular structure.

but where not all the future events necessarily derive from the present state is conceivable: there can be, for instance, quantum events that are really indeterministic. To put it another way, it is possible to conceive a non-determinist and non-necessitist world, in which it is not necessary for some events to happen, but it could be a fatalist world, because the human agents' acts would be determined.

Despite the fact that the abovementioned view is our working hypothesis, there is another intuition beneath it: the idea that fatalism is not a categorical negation of the agents' free will, but the inevitability of some future events, which are *existentially relevant* for the agent themselves. If we think about Oedipus' tragedy, his free will is not denied in a "metaphysical" sense; rather, it is claimed that his freedom of action is *irrelevant* in order to prevent some inevitable events from happening. Therefore, fatalism does not present itself as a hypothesis on the non-existence of free will, but as a hypothesis on its irrelevance (with respect to certain meaningful events). It is clear that a precise analysis of such an intuition requires a great deal of conceptual work (for example, we need some criteria to establish under which conditions an event becomes relevant), but compared to the distinctions that have been previously made, we can maintain that a fatalist universe, in this second meaning, envisages some forks (the protagonists can actually choose), but the undertaken courses of actions eventually converge on one state of the world, which is indeed inevitable.[4]

1.2 Logical Fatalism

In the previous section, reasons of the metaphysical kind have been taken into consideration in order to be fatalist: if we believe in determinism (possibly under the influence of a certain interpretation of the image of the world provided by science), then we are fatalist too. Determinism, obviously, is a philosophically challenging hypothesis that can be attacked

---

[4]Put in more technical terms, we affirm that these universes dictate the existence of convergent histories and, consequently, the branching also towards the past. As we shall see in the book, there are valid reasons to consider such structures as problematic.

from more than one side. Logical fatalism, instead, has challenged (and still does) just philosophers. According to logical fatalism, fatalism (i.e. the lack of free will) is due to purely logical reasons. In order to deny the freedom of human beings, we do not need to bring about complicated metaphysical views of reality; some very plausible logical principles are enough. It goes without saying that, if logic fatalists are right, then their stance is much stronger than the metaphysical counterpart: logical principles are not easily dismissible, and revising them usually gets a high-priced theoretical toll. As we soon will see, things are not so smooth, and the allegedly "pure" logical principles are in fact much thicker and therefore easier to be attacked. We will start by telling a story.[5]

> Today, 23 October 2018, Emma and Thomas are arguing about the future colonization of Mars. Emma believes that in 2070 there will be human bases on Mars, whereas Thomas does not. Emma and Thomas believe in contradictory propositions (one denies the other) and therefore one of them is right: in 2070 it will be true that there exist bases on Mars or, on the contrary, the red planet will still be desolate and without human settlements. But then, one of them today is already right about their prediction: either Emma's prediction or Thomas' one is right. Assume that Emma is right (as we shall see, the argument is perfectly symmetric—Thomas can be right as well); therefore, it is true in 2018 that in 2070 there will be human settlements on Mars. Let us think it over for a second. If Emma is right in 2018, that is, if it is true in 2018 that in 2070 there will be human settlements on Mars, then this holds for each instant of time. In 2012, it was already true that in 2070 there would be human settlements on Mars, as well as in 244 BC. Back then, we did not have any idea about the colonization of other planets, but this does not affect the argument, since here the truth is at stake, and not the knowledge of this truth. But if it has always been true that in 2070 there will be human colonies on Mars, the existence of colonies on Mars in 2070 has never been put under discussion and their non-existence has never been an option. Therefore, if Emma is right, it is *unavoidable* that there will be bases on Mars in 2070. But if it is unavoidable, then humans cannot decide not to launch the space programme; we—better, our grandchildren—are necessitated to

---

[5] Readers will forgive us for such an unorthodox version of Aristotle's naval battle.

colonize Mars, against the idea of free will. The argument can be extended to any proposition concerning the future; future contingents do not exist, everything is *already* predetermined. Fatalism, there it is.

The story we have just told does have a ring of plausibility. Actually, by making the argument more explicit, we can show that some passages are not trivial at all. In our discussion we will focus precisely on them:[6]

1. There will be Martian colonies in 2070 or there will not be Martian colonies in 2070.
2. If there will be Martian colonies in 2070, then it was always true that there will be Martian colonies in 2070; if there will not be Martian colonies in 2070, then it was always true that there will not be Martian colonies in 2070.
3. If it was always true that there will be Martian colonies in 2070, then there was never a time at which anyone or anything could prevent the construction of the colonies; if it was always true that there will not be Martian colonies in 2070, then there was never a time at which anyone or anything could bring about human colonies.
4. Thus, either no one (or nothing), at any time, could prevent the Martian colonies or no one (or nothing), at any time, could bring about the Martian colonies.
5. Thus, either the occurrence of the Martian colonies is necessary (that is, no one and nothing has the power, at any time, to prevent the colonies) or the nonoccurrence of the Martian colonies is necessary (that is, no one and nothing has the power, at any time, to bring about the occurrence of the colonies).
6. Thus, in general, fatalism is true.

There is an incredible amount of literature on the subject of Aristotle's naval battle: on both the correct interpretation and reconstruction of the argument and on Aristotle's actual strategy to avoid fatalism.[7] In the following subsections, we will not deal with such questions; instead,

---

[6] See Bernstein (2002, p. 70).
[7] Øhrstrøm and Hasle (2007, pp. 6–114) and Crivelli (2004, ch. 7) are great starting points.

we will analyse the fundamental points on which the arguments rest and will see which logic and metaphysical presuppositions can be traced down. The "thorny" passages are 1, 3 and 5, because they deal with the questions of *bivalence*, the *necessity of the past* and the *definition of freedom*. Moreover, we shall see that the definition of truth assumed in the argument will turn out to be relevant.

1.2.1 Bivalence

A common refrain claims that classical logic endorses the principle of bivalence, according to which every declarative proposition[8] has one truth value, either true or false. The principle of bivalence can be "broken up" into at least three independent logic-semantic principles:

(i) **Principle of non-inflation.** There exist only two truth values: True or False. In other words, the primitive semantic properties of the truth bearers are only two. Let us notice that this principle does not specify the ways the truth bearers assume a truth value. In order to do that, two other principles are required:

(ii) **Principle of minimal determinatedness (or no-gluts).** Each proposition has *at most* one truth value. In other words, propositions that instantiate two (or more) truth values do not exist. Let us notice that this principle is independent from the first one; even if there exist three truth values (true, false and indeterminate), the principle of no-gluts rules out the possibility for truth bearers to be, say, simultaneously true and indeterminate or false and true or false and indeterminate.

(iii) **Principle of maximal determinatedness (or no-gaps).** Each proposition has *at least* one truth value. Propositions lacking any truth value

---

[8] *Proposition* and *sentence* are often used in literature with two different meanings: the term "sentences" refers to linguistic entities, while the term "propositions" refers to the meaning of these entities. As this distinction is not relevant for the aims of this book, we will not follow this convention: we will be very sloppy in using these two terms, which are to be considered as synonymous in this book except in some particular cases, apparent from the context, in which we come back to the traditional distinction between these two terms.

do not exist. Moreover, this principle is independent from the first and the second principles. It might occur that a sort of overlapping of truth values takes place, that is, there are some gluts and principle (ii) is violated, but principle (iii) is satisfied. Let us notice that claiming that there are propositions whose truth value is indeterminate (*contra* (i)) and that there are propositions which do not have a truth value are two different things. In the former case, the evaluation function links such proposition to the truth value $\mathbb{I}$, whereas in the latter, the evaluation function is not defined for all the propositions of the domain.

Premise 1 of the fatalist argument is not in fact a formulation of the principle of bivalence. Instead, it states that between two contradictory propositions, one, and one maximum—given the principle of non-contradiction—must be true. In other words, 1. expresses a form of excluded middle:

EM For each proposition p, either p or $\neg p$ is true.[9]

A bit of logic work has to be done to draw the **EM** from the principle of bivalence; it is sufficient to assume that the negation behaves *normally*, that is, that the negation of a truth is a falsity and that the negation of a falsity is a truth: $T(p) \leftrightarrow F(\neg p)$ for each proposition p. Now, according to the principle of bivalence we know that p can be either true or false, but not both. Let us assume that it is true. It follows that $\neg p$ must be false. But if $T(p)$ then $F(\neg p) \vee T(\neg p)$.[10] Similarly, if $F(p)$ then $F(\neg p) \vee T(\neg p)$. But the antecedents of these two implications consume all the logical space available, that is—according to the principle of bivalence—

---

[9] In this introductory chapter, we tried to limit the logic symbols. However, some exceptions have to be made. As we have stated in the Preface, the use of logic-mathematical models should help *clarify* the instances at stake.

[10] It is a mere introduction of disjunction: if ψ follows from φ, then from φ follows that $\psi \vee \theta$, where θ is any closed formula. The correctness of this rule can be easily recognized if we consider that the truth of a disjunct is enough to make the disjunction true.

they do not admit other cases. It follows that $F(\neg p) \vee T(\neg p)$; since the negation behaves normally, we have $T(p) \vee T(\neg p)$. □

Let us go back to our argument. The idea is that the principle of bivalence holds for *all* the propositions, including (and especially, we would say) for the future tensed propositions. This seems to be a quite well-established assumption in a general non-epistemic conception of truth. That is, the truth value of propositions is something totally independent from our epistemic access to them. A future tensed proposition could be unknowable and nonetheless it still could possess a truth value. We shall soon see that the classic Aristotelian answer to the dilemma of future contingents lies in the negation of the validity of premise 1.

1.2.2 Necessity of the Past

At a closer look, the argument, in its premise 3, leverages another principle which is unlikely to be classified as "logic" or "logico-semantical". In order to understand it, let us think about a seemingly trivial aspect of our life. This morning Emma could decide to go to university by car or by train. Before she decided, the future was open and all the possibilities of choice lay ahead. She decided to go by train; now, in her office, while mulling over her decision and what happened, she certainly cannot intervene into what has already been. In other words, the past does not seem to be changeable. Furthermore, the impossibility to change what happened does not seem to depend on her lack of capacity; rather, it appears to be a structural, metaphysical limit. Even God—many people claim—cannot change the past. Obviously, Emma could have chosen something different from what she eventually chose. But once she has gotten on the train this fact cannot be altered; it becomes part of the design of the Universe and that is all. In short, it is the metaphysical commitment that lies behind the popular saying: "Do not cry over spilt milk".

Let us see how the necessity of the past plays a fundamental role in the argument in favour of logic fatalism. Let us assume, according to the argument, that 23 October 2018 Emma is right and that in 2070 Martian colonies will exist. Then, let us ask ourselves if between 2018 and 2070 somebody *could* prevent the settlement of human colonies on

Mars. Well, if somebody could stop the colonization (maybe with an administrative order by a future President of the United States of the World), this would imply that the proposition "In 2070 there will be colonies on Mars" becomes false. But this proposition was true in 2018 and stopping the building of settlements would trigger a modification of the past. A feature of the world in 2018, that is, that it was true that in 2070 there will be Martian colonies, would change according to a decision taken in the future. But for the reasons mentioned in the previous section this seems to be metaphysically impossible.

Philosophers have conceived for situations like the above mentioned one the concept of *accidental necessity*; the building of the colonies is not a logically (or metaphysically) necessary event. On the contrary, it is contingent, since we can easily admit possible worlds where people colonize Mars and possible worlds where Mars remains desolate. Analogously, it is contingent that Emma decides to get the car or the train to go to university. But once she makes her choice, then there is no turning back and that event becomes accidentally necessary. This passage had already been clearly pointed out by Aristotle:

> Now, that what is should be whenever it is, and that what is not should not be whenever it is not, is necessary, but it is not necessary that everything which is should be, nor that what is not should not be: for, that everything which is should be of necessity when it is is not the same as that everything which is should unqualifiedly be of necessity, and similarly with what is not. (*De Interpretatione*, 19a23–19b4)

Therefore, all the past, being the past, is necessary. It has been and cannot not be anymore. It could not have existed if the world had taken another road. However, among the past events we should include also the truth of the future tensed propositions: if it was true that in 2070 there will be Martian colonies, then it is now necessarily true that in 2070 the colonies will be. But if this is necessarily true, then it is unavoidable, that is, no action can modify such an outcome. Since the argument is still at a general level, there are true propositions for any future state of affairs. So, every aspect of the world is fixed, unchangeable and unavoidable. To sum up in one word: fatalism. Such a conclusion seems to be drawn by two logic-metaphysical principles, which are hardly negotiable: the principle of bivalence and the principle of necessity of the past. Actually, as we shall see in the next section, the argument brings about other two important questions worth being investigated: the implication between truth and ontology of time and the definition of free will.

1.2.3 Truth and Free Will

The last delicate passage of the argument is premise 5: since future facts are unavoidable, it derives that free will does not exist. To justify this passage, it is time to provide the definition of free will according to the *libertarian* account. Generally speaking, an agent is free to take an action p if the following conditions are respected:

(a) The agent has to be the *cause of action*; she must exercise a kind of control over it. Involuntary body actions—like the heart beating—are not free actions, because the agent is not the cause of the heart beating.
(b) The agent has to be *able to do otherwise*; in other words, the agent must face a real choice: if she is free to take the car or the train, the two possibilities must be genuine.

Such conditions seem to be consistent. If the fatalist argument is correct, condition (b) can never be satisfied: there are no alternatives to our actions. Martian colonies are to be built and we are not really free not to build them. However, this is not everyone's opinion. There exist alternative accounts of free will which try to make *compatible* (hence the term *compatibilism*) determinism and a sufficiently solid notion of free will. In particular, according to many philosophers there are senses in which it is plausible to ascribe free will to the agents, even though, in fact, they cannot do otherwise. It is evident that in such a train of thought the challenge is to preserve some of the fundamental intuitions that go along with the definition of free will: first of all, the moral responsibility.

Needless to say, the topic of free will is extremely wide and we cannot even superficially account for it. However, our task does not imply that we must provide a general overview of the topic. In Chap. 3, we shall take into account compatibilism in order to discuss the strategies for rebutting theological fatalism by rethinking the concept of human freedom. Since these are quite radical manoeuvres (that is why we call them "extreme measures"), if not differently indicated, we will refer to free will in the *libertarian* or *incompatibilist* sense.

Finally, let us spend some words on the truth of the future tensed propositions. In our version of the argument of the naval battle, we assumed that either Thomas or Emma is right about their hypothesis on Martian colonies. But what does it truly mean that there will be colonies on Mars? More precisely, what are the truth conditions of a future tensed proposition? To answer this question, we have to consider our idea of truth.[11] Common sense, science and most parts of philosophy agree on the very general intuition according to which a proposition is true because it states how the things really are.[12] In a symmetrical way, we can also state that a proposition is true because there is something (for instance, a fact) that makes it true (hence the appropriate term of *truth-maker*).

Truth-makers are entities, existing in the world, which make propositions true. It is easy to guess that the ontology of the truth-makers, that is, which kind of entities they are, is still a debatable point.[13] Apart from the metaphysical options about truth-makers, in this introductory part we can state that a proposition is true because there is a fact (or a state of affairs) that makes it true: the proposition that snow is white is true because it is a fact that snow is white. So far so good.

Things get complicated if we go back to the question we started from: which fact makes the proposition that there will be Martian bases in 2070 true? If we apply *prima facie* our theory of truth, we have to say that it is a fact in 2018 that in 2070 there will be bases on Mars. But this is a future

---

[11]As we shall see in Chap. 2 and following, the semantics of future tensed propositions are crucial to understand the issues of foreknowledge and free will.

[12]The philosophical tradition dates back to Aristotle the first formulation of such a view, which is called the *correspondence theory of truth*. Since the concept of correspondence is rather demanding from a theoretical point of view, we will call this view the *classical conception of truth*.

[13]Two seminal papers on the concept of truth-makers are Mulligan et al. (1984) and Fox (1987). A *locus classicus* is Armstrong (2004). An excellent collection is Lowe and Rami (2014). In Sect. 4.5.1 we will thoroughly deal with the issue.

fact already existing, somehow, in 2018. And since it is a fact of the world, it exists not only in 2018 but also in 366 BC as well as in 9866 BC. If it is a fact, it means that the world is made in that way and, consequently, any event in it is unavoidable. Once again: fatalism.

The classic theory on truth, as intended in the theory of truth-making we have briefly sketched, together with the principle of bivalence seem to imply the existence of all the facts: present, past and future.

In the next chapter, we shall peruse many accounts of the metaphysics of time, but we can already catch a glimpse of its relevance in the discussion over fatalism: any modification on the "truth side" will have consequences on the "world side" and vice versa. If we decide, as we soon shall see, to limit the principle of bivalence, then we will have to account for a different metaphysics of time.

1.3 How to Avoid the Battle

There are many ways to confute the argument of logic fatalism. Here we will illustrate the two main strategies[14]: the first attacks the universal validity of the principle of bivalence; the second tries to relativize the principle of immutability of the past.[15] Since such solutions can be—to a certain extent—applied to theological fatalism, we will briefly sketch them out.

First of all, in order to avoid falling into fatalism it is possible to deny that future tensed propositions have a determinate truth value. These propositions *will have* a truth value only when the events they describe *take place* or not. In our case, in 2018 it is semantically indeterminate whether the proposition "in 2070 there will be colonies on Mars" is true or false. It will be determined in 2070. Therefore, ex post we will be able to say that Emma or Thomas was right. But at the very moment

---

[14] Many other views can be interpreted as more or less sophisticated specifications of the two above-mentioned main strategies.
[15] Understanding which strategy Aristotle has really endorsed is a *vexata quaestio*. Standard view is that Aristotle rethought the extension of the principle of bivalence. But there are positions contrary to it. For an overview, Crivelli (2004).

of their prevision nothing in the world can make their propositions true; in particular, what makes their previsions true or false is (also) the free decision of agents who will choose to launch or not to launch a programme of colonization on Mars.

Denying bivalence takes its toll. Firstly, it challenges a sort of realistic intuition according to which states of affairs are determinate and such is the truth value of propositions as well. This holds, regardless of any kind of knowledge of such propositions. Secondly, in the frame of a conception of truth as correspondence, the undeterminatedness of the future tensed propositions has precise metaphysical-like consequences concerning both the ontology of time (i.e. whether future facts do exist) and its topology (i.e. whether the history of the world is linear or branched). In the next chapter, we shall see some possible combinations. Finally, another question is related to the denial of bivalence. If we can admit, relatively speaking, that the truth value of certain future tensed propositions is indeterminate, it still remains *true* that either there will be Martian colonies or there will not be. *Tertium non datur*. In other words, we can maintain that neither Emma nor Thomas is right or wrong; nonetheless, it is true—better, it seems to be *logically true*—that either Emma or Thomas is right and the other is wrong. But this is an evident violation of truth-functionality of disjunction: the truth of the disjunction "In 2070 there will be Martian bases or in 2070 there will not be the Martian bases" does not seem to depend exclusively on the truth value of the disjuncts. For assumption, the disjuncts are indeterminate, whereas the disjunction is true.

A way to counterattack this criticism is to differentiate, in some ways, the idea of truth at stake; one can say that in a possible future the bases on Mars exist, whereas in another possible future they do not. Obviously, agents' free choices will contribute to determining which future will be the actual one. But in each of these possible scenarios the disjunction that there are or are not Martian bases is true.[16] Therefore, whereas the disjuncts are only *locally* true (or false), the disjunction, on the contrary,

---

[16]Again, this passage is guaranteed by the fact that if the proposition p is true, then also the proposition $p \vee \neg p$ is true; analogously, in the scenarios where $\neg p$ is true, the proposition $p \vee \neg p$ is also true.

is always true, whatever future scenario of the world will be. As we will mention in the next chapter, twentieth-century logic has provided a strict model, called supervaluationism, to catch this intuition.

The other strategy consists of undermining the necessity of the past. Someone may try with the following reasoning. Emma is right or wrong when she says that there will be bases on Mars in 2070, depending on what human beings will decide to do in 2070. If human beings decide to launch a programme to colonize Mars in 2070, then Emma would have been right in 2018. But if for some reasons they decide not to realize the colonization programme, then, in 2018, Emma would have been wrong. In short, it seems that the free action of humans in 2070 can *determine* the truth value of the prediction Emma made 52 years before. Some scholars have attacked this solution, because it commits us to a kind of backward causation, that is, a causal relation in which the effect precedes the cause. Michael Dummett gave a famous defence of the possibility of backward agent causation (Dummett 1964)[17] and despite being logically possible, this causation appears to be weird; in fact, some defenders of this solution stressed that it is not the case of a real causal relation but rather of a determination of the past. Others underlined that the kind of influence on the past is only *counterfactual*. It could be said that Emma is right because today it is true that in 2070 there will be colonies on Mars. But if human beings *had decided* otherwise and *had not founded* Martian colonies in 2070, then Emma would have been wrong in 2018. Put in other words, the present truth value of the future proposition "In 2070 there will be colonies on Mars" determines whether Emma is currently right or wrong. But the fact that there will be colonies on Mars in 2070 is absolutely contingent. There will be, but they could have not been. If they were not, if humans had decided not to found them, Emma *would be* wrong today. In general, one may notice here a sort of conceptual trade-off: the more you want to ensure a solid notion of free will, the more effective the causal influence on the past must be, and this brings about all sorts of issues. On the contrary, the less you touch upon the principle

---

[17]And this possibility has been discussed by Freddoso (1983), Mavrodes (1984), Forrest (1985), Talbott (1986) and Reichenbach (1987).

of necessity of the past, the less authentic the agents' possibility of choice becomes.

1.4 From Logic Fatalism to Theological Fatalism

Since the first centuries of the Christian era, the dilemma of logic fatalism has incorporated a theological reasoning. The passage is completely natural: God, who is omniscient, knows everything that happened, happens and will happen. But again, this seems to *fix* the free choices of the agents: if since the dawn of humanity God infallibly has known what Emma would choose in twenty years, how can Emma be free to do otherwise? After all, even from a merely logic point of view, it is easy to notice the structural similarity of the two fatalist arguments. Indeed, the standard definition of omniscience is as follows:

(omn) An entity a is (necessarily) omniscient $=_{def} \Box(\mathbf{B}(a, p) \leftrightarrow p)$

where **B** indicates the belief operator.[18] In other terms, a necessarily believes only and all the true propositions. Therefore, God's knowledge coincides exactly with the truth (God knows all the truths and His knowledge is infallible), so free will seems threatened as much by His knowledge as it was threatened by the fact that what an agent will freely do tomorrow is already *true* today. If God has beliefs concerning what human beings will freely do in the future, and if such beliefs are infallible, then it is already true that human beings will behave in a specific way. From this very truth, the argument in favour of logic fatalism derives that human beings are not free in a *libertarian* sense.

---

[18] Here we assume that divine properties such as omniscience are necessary; the case of a God only contingently omniscient or choosing not to be omniscient is not accounted for. Some scholars proposed similar solutions: see, for instance, Kreiner (1997, ch. 3).

It is now time to present the argument. It is usually formulated by considering three sequential moments of time:

(1) some arbitrary moment in the past; (2) the present; and (3) some arbitrary moment in the future in which a human agent will perform a free act. For simplicity, let us use yesterday, today and tomorrow for these three moments of time.

We will use the clear presentation of Linda Zagzebski in (Zagzebski (1991, ch. 1), Zagzebski (2002, pp. 46–47)): let p be a free action that is meant to be carried out tomorrow.

1. Yesterday, God believed that p. (Divine foreknowledge)
2. If an event e occurred in the past, then it is accidentally necessary that e occurred then. (Necessity of the past)
3. It is now necessary that yesterday God believed p. (1, 2, *modus ponens*)
4. Necessarily, if yesterday God believed p, then p. (Infallibility of divine foreknowledge)
5. If r is accidentally necessary and if $\Box(r \to s)$, then it is accidentally necessary that s. (Principle of transfer of necessity)
6. So it is now necessary that p. (3, 4, 5)
7. If it is now necessary that p, then you cannot do otherwise than p. (Definition of necessary)
8. Therefore, you cannot do otherwise than p. (6, 7, *modus ponens*)
9. If you cannot do otherwise when you do an act, you do not do it freely. (Principle of Alternate Possibilities)
10. Therefore, when you do p, you will not do it freely. (8, 9, *modus ponens*)

Since p is arbitrarily chosen, we have to conclude that human agents are never free. This is exactly the core of the issue we deal with in this book. Let us take a closer look at it. According to premise 1, God has some beliefs about what human agents will do in the future. From the fact that yesterday God believed that a certain agent would behave in a certain way in the future, from the infallibility of such a belief and from the fact that the past is accidentally necessary, the argument infers that today it is accidentally necessary that tomorrow the agent will behave in that way. In this passage, the argument makes use of the logical principle of the transfer of necessity that from $\Box r$ and $\Box(r \rightarrow s)$ derives $\Box s$.[19] Particularly, the argument infers the accidental necessity that the agent will do what God foresees in the future from the accidental necessity of the past divine beliefs about what the agents will do in the future and from the fact that these beliefs are necessarily true. From premises 6. onward, the argument can proceed as that of logical fatalism. In particular, premise 9 makes use of the principle deriving from the libertarian definition of freedom that implies that an agent is free only if she has two alternatives available.

Similar to logical fatalism, the problematic premises are 1., 2., 9., that is, the *temporality of the divine foreknowledge*, the *possibility to change the past* and the *incompatibilist definition of free will*. In fact, premise 1 is more complex than the initial premise of the argument in favour of logical fatalism. This premise involves at least two aspects. First of all, it implies that God has beliefs about what human beings will do in the future. Given that such beliefs are infallible, this premise implies that the future tensed propositions have a truth value and, consequently, provided all the sufficiently plausible assumptions we have mentioned in Sect. 1.2.1, that bivalence holds in the future. On the basis of these assumptions, premise 1, in this aspect, is similar to the first premise of the argument of logical fatalism. But this is not all. The first premise implies that divine beliefs are temporally collocated, that is, they take place in time. We will simply assume here that an event or a state of affairs is temporally collocated if there exists a time t such that that event or state of affairs obtains at t. As we will see, these two aspects, bivalence and the temporal collocation of divine beliefs, may be challenged independently. It is, for instance, possible to state that God knows what human agents will do in the future, but to deny that God's beliefs are temporally collocated.

---

[19] It is a very plausible logical principle. It is particularly easy to understand if we use a possible words semantic where $\Box r$ means that r is true in all possible worlds. If r is true in all possible worlds and it is also true in all possible worlds that $r \rightarrow s$, then it is true in all possible worlds that s, by *modus ponens*. But, in this semantic, the fact that s is true in all possible worlds means that s is necessary.

As we shall see in the following chapters, in our opinion, the dilemma of theological fatalism is more complex than its purely logic counterpart because some solving strategies of the latter are more expensive from a theoretical point of view. However, because of the likeness between the logical and theological arguments, some scholars have denied such complexity. For instance, Warfield (1997) claimed that once logical fatalism is denied, the negation of theological fatalism is a free bonus. Warfield's argument is based on the equivalence between divine knowledge and truth. He maintains that those who deny logical fatalism affirm that the two following propositions are compatible:

(1) Human beings will freely choose to set up colonies on Mars in 2070
(2) It is true in 2018 that human beings will set up colonies on Mars in 2070

Now, those who accept that God is an omniscient being argue that there is an equivalence between the true propositions and God's beliefs. So (2) is necessarily equivalent to (3):

(3) God believes in 2018 that human beings will set up colonies on Mars in 2070

But, Warfield concludes, if two propositions are compatible, then the first proposition will be compatible with any proposition equivalent to the second one. Therefore, if (1) and (2) are compatible, (1) and (3) have to be as well, because (2) and (3) are equivalent.

It is important to point out what Warfield's argument wants to demonstrate. It does not want to prove that God knows the free choices of human beings. Rather, the argument assumes just (3), that is, the equivalence between truth and divine foreknowledge. It aims at demonstrating that, if logical fatalism is believed to be wrong, there is no extra cost, if it is assumed that God foreknows future contingents.

Warfield's argument is undeniably fascinating, but it has many problems.[20] First of all, it assumes that all those who refuse logical fatalism take for granted the compatibility of (1) and (2). But, as we have seen, this is not the case. We have illustrated three possible answers to logical fatalism and only one of them accepts the compatibility of (1) and (2). If the principle of bivalence is denied, then it is also denied that future tensed sentences have a truth value, and then (2) is denied. If the principle of possible alternatives is denied, it is also denied that human beings are free in a libertarian sense, and then (1) is denied in the libertarian sense. Therefore, even those who deny theological fatalism do not necessarily accept the compatibility of (1) and (2). Secondly, we believe that Warfield is undoubtedly right when he claims that those who accept that (1) and (2) are compatible, if they accept (3) too, then they must also claim that (1) and (3) are compatible. However, it is not clear at all that this does not imply further costs if compared to the simple claim that (1) and (2) are compatible. As has been previously stated, if one accepts that (1) and (2) are compatible, they have to claim that there is a sort of backward determination of truth values of future tensed propositions: the future states of affairs determine the truth values of the past sentences that speak of those states of affairs. This weakening of the necessity of the past is of course admissible, but it is a cost that such a solution has to take into consideration. Yet, it is not clear whether the affirmation that God's beliefs are equivalent to the truth of the sentences that speak of future contingents does not represent a further cost. Those who admit this equivalence have to say not only that the truth values of past sentences that speak of future contingents are determined by the future states of affairs but also that God's past beliefs are determined as well. It is not clear, though, whether admitting that God's past beliefs are determined by future states of affairs would represent a major cost. One may think, for instance, that the weakening of the necessity of the past, in the case of truth values, is an acceptable cost, whereas it is not acceptable in the case of divine beliefs. And this could lead one to deny 1., that is human freedom,

---

[20] For two replies to Warfield's argument, see Hasker (1998) and Brueckner (2000). They both differ from the criticism we will illustrate here.

by accepting theological fatalism or divine foreknowledge. Chapter 4 is devoted to this topic.

As for the moment, we can conclude that Warfield's argument demonstrates less than it wants to. Firstly, it does not demonstrate that those who refuse logical fatalism and accept the equivalence between divine beliefs and truths have necessarily to accept divine foreknowledge because there exist solutions to logical fatalism that do not accept the compatibility between (1) and (2). Rather, it demonstrates that those who accept that (1) and (2) are compatible, that is, a certain solution to logical fatalism, and who accepts (3) too, must also accept the compatibility between (1) and (3), human freedom and divine foreknowledge. Secondly, the argument does not demonstrate that accepting the compatibility between (1) and (2) has the same cost as accepting the compatibility between (1) and (3). It follows that the argument for theological fatalism and the solutions that have been given so far deserve a separate investigation and cannot be included in the analysis of the argument for logical fatalism and its solutions.[21]

The book is structured as follows. Chapter 3 is dedicated to what we call "extreme" solutions to the problem, since they radically reshape the concepts at stake. In particular, open theism provides a definition of omniscience which does not imply that God has infallible beliefs about what human beings will do in the future (thus denying the first premise of the theological fatalist argument). On the contrary, the *Calvinist-like* models offer a compatibilist definition of free will and, therefore, they are supposed to avoid the fatalist threat by denying premise 9 of the theological fatalist argument. Chapter 4 is dedicated to the Ockhamist solution, named after William of Ockham. Ockhamism, at least in its contemporary formulation, assumes the existence of a true but not necessary future and admits that there are some facts of the past that can be determined by future events. It therefore denies the necessity of the past, that is, premise 2 of the argument. Chapter 5 investigates a sort of spin-off of Ockhamism, that is, Molinism. The Molinist framework, as we

---

[21] This does not deny the close affinity between the two arguments and that the solutions to logical and theological fatalism have something in common.

shall see, acquires some fundamental traits of Ockhamism, but assumes an even more challenging metaphysics. However, we will show that if one is willing to take such assumptions, it provides an explicative and quite fascinating account.

In both Molinism and Ockhamism, the assumption is that God's knowledge is temporally situated (as it appears in premise 1). Instead, since the first centuries of Christianity (see, for instance, Boethius), another tradition took hold, according to which God's knowledge is out of time or timeless. It does not deny that God has infallible beliefs about the future, but it does deny that they are temporally collocated, that is, it denies the second aspect of premise 1. Chapter 6 has to do with this kind of view; we shall see how to characterize the ideas of eternity and timelessness and how to reconcile God's timelessness with the knowledge of temporal aspects of reality.[22]

Before looking into these solutions, in the next chapter we will introduce some notions of the metaphysics of time and the semantics of future tensed propositions. It is easy to understand, even on the basis of the brief accounts we have provided in this chapter, how crucial these topics can be for the problem we are dealing with. Since one of the solutions of logical fatalism centres on the negation of the bivalence of the future tensed propositions, it is useful to provide a survey of the various possible semantics that can be given to future tensed propositions, in order to evaluate the different options accurately. These options have an impact on the various solutions to theological fatalism, because of the affinity between logical and theological fatalisms. Moreover, as we have seen, necessitism and determinism imply a certain topological structure of time (there is only one possible future), whereas indeterminism believes that the future is open (there are more possible futures). This of course impacts the structure and topology of time, which can be considered linear or branched. Eventually, as we have seen, the correspondentist

---

[22] Of course, there are tons of other problems of the philosophical and theological kind connected to such topics. For instance, the modality of God's knowledge. A frequent criticism claims that the modality by which God knows is not propositional, rather He benefits from a sort of direct intuition (Alston 1986). We are not going to investigate this issue; nonetheless, we think that, with some adjustments and corrections, our analysis can be applied to a conception of that kind.

view of the truth of temporal propositions, according to which every proposition has its own truth-maker, seems to have some implications on the ontology of time, that is, on the existence of future and past events. Do such facts exist in the same way as present facts exist? The various solutions regarding ontology, topology of time and semantics of temporal propositions can be differently interwoven, thus providing a wide range of complex alternatives. It is natural that the various alternatives impact the solutions to theological fatalism. The authors who worked on such solutions are well aware of it. However, we believe that, in general, this is not always the case. The aim of this book is to show how deep the impact of the metaphysics of time and of temporal logic is on the problem of the conciliation of divine foreknowledge with human free will. We shall dedicate the next chapter to these subjects before dealing with the various solutions to the problem. Those who are familiar with such topics can skip it and go directly to Chap. 3.

References

Alston, W.P. 1986. Does god have beliefs? *Religious Studies* 22(3–4): 287–306.
Armstrong, D.M. 2004. *Truth and truthmakers*. Cambridge: Cambridge University Press.
Bernstein, M. 2002. Fatalism. In *The Oxford handbook of free will*, ed. R. Kane, 65–81. Oxford: Oxford University Press.
Brueckner, A. 2000. On an attempt to demonstrate the compatibility of divine foreknowledge and human freedom. *Faith and Philosophy* 17(1): 132–134.
Crivelli, P. 2004. *Aristotle on truth*. Cambridge: Cambridge University Press.
De Laplace, P.S. 1902. *A philosophical essay on probabilities*. London: Wiley.
Dummett, M. 1964. Bringing about the past. *The Philosophical Review* 73(3): 338–359.
Forrest, P. 1985. Backward causation in defence of free will. *Mind* 94(374): 210–217.
Fox, J.F. 1987. Truthmaker. *Australasian Journal of Philosophy* 65(2): 188–207.
Freddoso, A.J. 1983. Accidental necessity and logical determinism. *The Journal of Philosophy* 80(5): 257–278.
Hasker, W. 1998. *God, time, and knowledge*. Ithaca: Cornell University Press.

Kreiner, A. 1997. *Gott im Leid: Zur Stichhaltigkeit der Theodizee-Argumente*. New York: Herder.
Lowe, J.E., and A. Rami. 2014. *Truth and truth-making*. Abingdon: Routledge.
Mavrodes, G.I. 1984. Is the past unpreventable? *Faith and Philosophy* 1(2): 131–146.
Mulligan, K., P. Simons, and B. Smith. 1984. Truth-makers. *Philosophy and Phenomenological Research* 44(3): 287–321.
Øhrstrøm, P., and P. Hasle. 2007. *Temporal logic: From ancient ideas to artificial intelligence*, vol. 57. Berlin: Springer.
Reichenbach, B. 1987. Hasker on omniscience. *Faith and Philosophy* 4(1): 86–92.
Talbott, T.B. 1986. On divine foreknowledge and bringing about the past. *Philosophy and Phenomenological Research* 46(3): 455–469.
Warfield, T.A. 1997. Divine foreknowledge and human freedom are compatible. *Noûs* 31(1): 80–86.
Zagzebski, L.T. 1991. *The dilemma of freedom and foreknowledge*. Oxford: Oxford University Press.
Zagzebski, L. 2002. Omniscience and the arrow of time. *Faith and Philosophy* 19(4): 503–519.

2

Metaphysics and Logic of Time

This chapter is devoted to the analysis of some basic concepts of the metaphysics and logic of time. We will introduce the notions we believe relevant for the discussion about the compatibility between divine omniscience and human freedom. Our working hypothesis is actually stronger: we are convinced that *every* solution to the dilemma crucially depends on the type of metaphysics of time that is assumed and on the logical system that is used to characterize that metaphysics. For this reason, every view that leaves open the ontology of time either implicitly adopts the common sense metaphysics or provides only partial answers. Obviously the material in these pages is not new and the bibliography on these topics is huge. Therefore, we have minimized references to avoid burdening this chapter. We refer the reader to the cited works for further bibliography.

It seems that the question: "what is time?" long plagued Saint Augustine. In one of his most quoted passages, he said that he *intimately* knows what time is, but he cannot give a *conceptual* answer to the question. Since Augustine, metaphysical research has enriched its conceptual framework. In the remainder of this chapter, we will concentrate on three dimensions concerning temporal reality: the *ontology* of time (Sect. 2.1), its *dynamics* (Sect. 2.2) and its *topology* (Sect. 2.5). Two short addenda will be devoted to the question of the persistence of objects through time and to the relationship between the metaphysics of time and the scientific image of the world (Sect. 2.4). The different options regarding the ontology, the dynamics, and the topology of time give rise to various combinations, which have been intensively discussed in literature. We will consider different possibilities, focusing on those themes that are important for our topic.

It might be objected that metaphysical questions—even though legitimate *per se* (an assumption that, however, is not obvious)—are *not* helpful to understand the relationship between God and the world. Our response is based on a simple question: "What does it mean that God is prescient?" The answer seems to be that He knows some propositions regarding the future, such as "Tomorrow Emma will drink a beer". To precisely analyse divine prescience is, therefore, necessary to analyse the truth conditions of these propositions, namely, the conditions that must obtain in order that a proposition such as "Tomorrow Emma will drink a beer" is true. However, it is not possible to do so without questioning the metaphysics of the future. But there are different opinions regarding the identity and the existence of future facts. Metaphysical questions cannot be overlooked and, even when they are explicitly negated, they continue to operate covertly, without any objective control and supervision. Moreover, in line with what we have said in the Preface, it is not possible to reach a high degree of conceptual resolution if we do not use some of the systems of formal logic that philosophical investigation has largely adopted since the first decades of the last century. For this reason, Sect. 2.6 is devoted to the illustration of some systems of temporal logic. As it will be clear, we have paid particular attention to the *semantics* of temporal logic because the meaning of the future operator is strictly linked to the problem of divine prescience.

2.1 Ontology of Time

Metaphysics inquires about the general and basic structures of reality. As a consequence, the metaphysics of time inquires the nature of temporal reality: what is time? Does it consist of instants? Does it make sense to speak of time when nothing exists *in* time? These are typical questions discussed in the metaphysics of time. Here we must make some methodological choices: generally, we will refer to *entities* (or *things*) that exist in time; we will speak about past, present and future facts (and individuals).[1]

Our common sense suggests (or, at least, it seems to suggest) that all that exists is *present*. Hence, the metaphysical view that is called **Presentism**: it assumes that only present things exist, while past and future things do not. We believe that we and the Colosseum exist, while Caesar and the Twin Towers do not exist (any more). In the same way, Martian colonies and the hundredth President of USA do not (yet) exist. Surely, all these things existed or (perhaps) will exist, but they do not exist. Presentism states that there is a very strict connection between existence and being present: existing things are present and present things exist. If what is present changes, what exists also changes. As time passes, new things come into being and others vanish, that is, do not exist anymore. On this matter, we will speak at length when we deal with the dynamics of time.

Presentism has the advantage of being in agreement with common sense, but it also has several drawbacks. Firstly, Presentism does not seem to be sufficiently fine-grained about *non* existence. Intuitively, there is a fundamental difference between Caesar and Mickey Mouse. The former is part of the furniture of the world, whereas the latter is not.[2] According to Presentism, however, both entities do not exist and, therefore, are on the same ontological level.[3] Secondly, we believe in the present truth of sentences such as "Caesar crossed the river Rubicon". However, if Caesar does not exist, it is difficult to see how this sentence can be true because it would concern a non-existent entity: how can we truly predicate something of something that does not exist? The existence of Caesar

---

[1] Actually, it is often held by some scholars that an instant of time is simply the mereological sum of all the things existing at that instant, a sort of giant cosmic slice. If this position is taken for granted, a certain instant will have some temporal properties, such as, for instance, being present, because the things that constitute it are present.
[2] Or better: Mickey Mouse is a fictional entity whose "existence" depends on the intellectual works in which his adventures are described.
[3] Clearly, the presentist has some resources to evade this objection: she can say that Caesar had the property of being present, whereas Mickey Mouse has never instantiated this property.

seems to be a necessary condition of the possession of some properties, including that of having crossed the Rubicon.[4] A further problem has to do with transtemporal relationships. For instance, the sentence "Obama is taller than Caesar" seems to have a truth value: either it is true or it is false, depending on the heights of Obama and Caesar. However, if Caesar does not exist, one of the relata of the relationship does not exist and, therefore, the sentence does not seem to have a truth value.[5]

Presentism has a very sober ontology, allowing only what is present as existing. **Eternalism** is at the other end of the spectrum: according to this ontology, past, present and future things exist in the same way. This might sound odd since we cannot meet Caesar or visit a Martian colony today. However, Eternalism is a very strong theory, which is able to easily solve the objections that have been advanced against Presentism: there is a fundamental difference between Caesar and Mickey Mouse because Caesar exists at a certain temporal collocation whereas Mickey Mouse does not. Moreover, "Caesar crossed the river Rubicon" is true now because Caesar exists (in an absolute sense) and because he has the property of having crossed the Rubicon at a time previous to the present. Finally, since Caesar exists as Obama does, a sentence such as "Obama is taller than Caesar" has a truth value.

On the eternalist view, temporal reality is similar to a block extruded in four dimensions.[6] Caesar and Obama are part of this block, even though they are "distant" with respect to the temporal coordinate, in the same way that Italy and Australia are both part of the Earth's surface in spite of the spatial distance separating them. Obviously, Eternalism has to deal with the common sense intuition that only present entities exist whereas past and future entities do not. Eternalists usually respond that common sense confuses two distinct concepts: that of being present and that of

---

[4]This problem is called the *Grounding Problem* in the literature on these topics and will be extensively discussed in Sect. 4.5.1.

[5]We do not claim that these are knock-down arguments against Presentism. Presentists can try to resist these arguments, and answers abound in literature (see, for instance, Bourne 2006). Our aim is just to clarify some of the reasons why theories alternative to Presentism have been embraced.

[6]For this reason, Eternalism is sometimes called four-dimensionalism.

being existent. Many entities exist but are not present, and Caesar is one of them.

Eternalism has a rich ontology since it admits more entities than Presentism.[7] A position *intermediate* between Presentism and Eternalism is based on the intuition that past and future are not on par. The past seems to be something already existing and determinate, since there was a time at which the past has been present. On the contrary, the future is "yet to be made" and, thus, does not exist. This position is called the **Growing Block view**. Since more and more entities pass from the present to the past, this position claims that the catalogue of the universe becomes longer and longer: more and more things exist.

This view accounts for the truth-makers of sentences such as "Caesar crossed the river Rubicon" or "Obama is taller than Caesar" because both Obama and Caesar are considered existent, although at different times. However, what about sentences such as "Humans will land on Mars in 2040" or "Obama is taller than the first man who will land on Mars"? In general, the basic idea of the Growing Block view is that the propositions about the future have no truth-maker because the future is "empty". Therefore, these propositions lack truth value. In fact, the Growing Block theorist can say that at least *some* of the propositions about the future are true if it is assumed that the present state of the world determines, at least in part, the future state of the world and, thus, it makes true today some propositions about tomorrow. If this view is adopted, the future does not exist yet, but it is already partially determinate and, consequently, some sentences about the future are already true or false. Even if this position is consistent, it would be odd for the Growing Block theorist to say that the future is completely determined by the present state of the world. Indeed, the basic intuition of this view is the difference between the past, which seems to be already written and determinate, and the future, which seems, at least in part, open and indeterminate.

Finally, the position opposite to the Growing Block view is also possible, even if it is minority: according to this position, often called the

---

[7] Eternalists usually reject this criticism, stating that their theory does not give rise to an ontological inflation. By contrast, presentists must admit temporal dynamics, and this is metaphysically more expensive, at least, in the eyes of eternalists. On this, see the next section.

Shrinking Block view,[8] the past does not exist, whereas the future and the present do. As things enter the past, they vanish. The intuition at the base of this position is perhaps the common sense idea that a baby "has still much time", while elderly people do not have "much time ahead". The Shrinking Block view is not committed to a particular topology of time, but, as we will see in Sect. 2.5, there is a particular version of this view that combines the idea that the future erodes as time passes with a branching structure of time.

The ontology of time is strictly connected with the question of the dynamics of time, that is, of the flow of time. This is the topic of the next section.

2.2 Dynamics of Time: A- and B-Theory

Let us start again from a common sense intuition: time goes by. We have the impression that things flow from the present to the past and from the future to the present. As we will see shortly, some scholars believe that the *dynamic* aspect of time is a real property; by contrast, other scholars believe that the flow of time is a mere illusion. To characterize these two positions, it is useful to distinguish between *tensed* properties (or aspects) and *tenseless* properties (or aspects). Tensed properties are features that change through time; on the contrary, tenseless properties are constant through time. For instance, the property of being future is clearly tensed. Emma does not yet have children, but she could. Therefore, being a mother is a property that Emma will have in a (possible) future. Obviously, the fact that Emma has children will not always remain future: as time flows, this fact will "come closer" to the border of the present until Emma gives birth to a child (under the assumption that this is the true future). After that, the event—the birth of the child—will slip into the past and, therefore, will acquire another temporal property, that is, being past. By contrast, if we take into consideration the fact that Emma gives birth to a baby on 4 May 2038, we can see that it is not characterized by

---

[8] See Casati and Torrengo (2011).

properties that change through time. If that fact is actual, that is, if the proposition describing it is true, then it is true at every time.[9]

It is difficult to overestimate the importance of McTaggart (1908) for the contemporary philosophy of time. McTaggart introduces an important distinction, which has been widely adopted. The conceptions of time, according to which the flow of time and its dynamics are objective features of reality, are called A-theories. In these views, temporal entities are basically characterized by tensed properties, such as being past, present or future. These proprieties are also called A-properties. However, McTaggart believes that the A-series (i.e. the sequence past, present, future) is not the sole aspect of temporal reality. Temporal instants, or alternatively temporal facts, are ordered on the basis of the relationships of before-after and simultaneity: we can say that the birth of Emma's first child precedes human colonization of Mars; analogously, Napoleon's death follows Caesar's death. These relations are tenseless proprieties of things, which do not change through time and are called B-relations by McTaggart. The theories that assume that B-relations are ontologically fundamental are B-theories. In a nutshell: on A-views, temporal dynamics is an irreducible aspect of reality; by contrast, B-views assume that reality is static and that the flow of time is illusory.

Although McTaggart distinguished A- and B-properties, his aim was different. He wished to demonstrate that time is unreal, in line with his Idealism. His argument has two steps: firstly, he shows that B-relations are not sufficient for characterizing the experience of time; secondly, he demonstrates that the A-series is contradictory. It follows that time is not real. There is a dose of philosophical irony in the reception of McTaggart's paper: almost no one accepts the whole argument of the British philosopher, and scholars are divided into those who consider the first part valid (and, thus, advocate an A-theory of time) and those who are convinced by the second part (and, thus, advocate a B-theory of time).

McTaggart's argument proceeds as follows. B-relations are insufficient to capture the experience of time because the experience of becoming

---

[9]Some scholars (for instance, see Torrengo 2011) consider the distinction between tensed and tenseless properties as an exclusively semantic matter. We will deal with semantic questions if they are relevant for our aims.

and change cannot be accounted for solely in terms of B-relations. The A-series is ineliminable. However, McTaggart continues, a single event cannot possess the properties of being past, present and future because they are contradictory: if, for instance, something is present, it cannot be past or future. The natural answer to this argument is that a single event is not past, present and future at the same time, but at different times. But McTaggart rejects this response because it calls into question a further temporal dimension, different from that of the A-series, in order to account for becoming. This further temporal dimension (which today we would call hyper-time) must possess the same properties as the A-series (being past, present and future). But, then, the same argument can be advanced again: a third temporal dimension is needed to account for the flow of hyper-time, and so on.

An excellent way to clarify this not so straightforward argument is Fine's construal (Fine 2005, 2006). According to Fine, McTaggart's argument is based on four premises, the aim of the argument being to show that they lead to a contradiction:

Realism Reality is constituted (at least in part) by tensed facts.
Neutrality No time is privileged; the tensed facts that constitute reality are not oriented towards one time as opposed to another.
Absolutism The constitution of reality is an absolute matter, that is, not relative to a time or other form of temporal standpoint.
Coherence Reality is not contradictory; it is not constituted by facts with incompatible content.

These four premises lead to a contradiction. It is easy to see why. Suppose that Emma is standing; then, Emma sits down. Then, both the tensed fact that Emma is standing now and the tensed fact that Emma is sitting now are part of reality, if we accept Realism. If we also accept Neutrality and Absolutism, these two tensed facts are absolutely part of Reality, not relatively to a certain instant. By Neutrality, there is no absolute present, namely, a time with regard to to which all past facts are past, all present facts are present and all future facts are future. By Absolutism, there is only one reality, and, therefore, we cannot relativize the two tensed facts to two different realities. Therefore, both "Emma is standing now" and "Emma is sitting now" are facts that constitute reality in an absolute way, and this contradicts Coherence.

The standard answer of the realist about tensed facts is to reject Neutrality: the present is a privileged time over the others (classical A-theory) and one of the tensed facts obtains at the present time, while the other does not. The problem of this response is that every time becomes present sooner or later, and from this point of view, none is privileged. If one retorts that the instants are not privileged at the same time, but one by one, then McTaggart answers that this rebuttal presupposes the existence of a hyper-time for which the same problem arises again.[10]

So, there are reasons to reject such an intuitive theory such as A-theory. Philosophers who do so assume that temporal dynamics is an illusion (denying Realism) and embrace the idea that there are no objective past, present and future: these proprieties are always relativized to an instant of time. In other words, *every* time is present relatively to itself, and in relation to it every following time is future, and every preceding time is past. No time is, therefore, present at the expense of other times; the unique objective relations are those of temporal priority and succession. On this view, called B-theory, it is still possible to speak about past, present and future. However, the past of every time t is what obtains prior to t, which we assume as present; the future is treated analogously. There is no objective fact that can discriminate the true present. The feeling of living in the "true" present is a cognitive illusion: the inhabitants of every time t consider t present. And there is no *fact of the matter* that could tell us who is right.

It is usually held that in B-theory, time is very similar to space. There is no spatial point that is privileged with respect to the others. For every person, the spatial point at which she is located is "here", but there is no privileged "here". In the same way, since we are located at a certain point t of the temporal series, t is "now" for us, but there is no privileged "now".

---

[10]Again, we do not mean that this argument cannot be overcome and that the realist about tensed facts has no response. We want just to explain which reasons can lead one to accept the B-theory, which is in sharp contrast with common sense.

If another person is located at another time, that point is "now" for her; "now" and "here" are pure indexical terms.

B-theorists deny Realism. However, there are other ways to face McTaggart's argument. As we have seen, classical A-theorists deny Neutrality: the present is a privileged time with respect to the others. But it is possible to react in other ways, denying the other premises of the argument: Absolutism or Coherence. These non-standard tensed theories have been explored by Fine (2005, 2006). If Absolutism is denied, then there is not a unique reality, but as many realities as the instants of time. Fine calls this theory *external relativism*. On this view, if we assume the point of view of the instant t, reality is constituted just by the tensed facts relative to t. In particular, the facts that obtain at t are present, the facts previous to t are past, and the facts following t are future. There are no other facts, in particular the tensed facts relative to another time t'. However, if the point of view of time t' is assumed, other tensed facts are real, those relative to t', whereas the facts relative to t do not exist. There is not a unique reality that can accommodate the tensed facts relative to both instants of time. However, there is no reason to deny Coherence within this view because every reality is coherent in itself.

Instead, if Coherence is negated and Absolutism is maintained, then only one reality exists, which contains every tensed fact, but this reality is not coherent. In particular, reality is constituted by fragments not coherent with each other. For this reason, this view is called by Fine **Fragmentalism**. According to Fragmentalism, both the fact that Emma is sitting now and the fact that Emma is standing now are part of the reality, thus making the reality incoherent. However, there are fragments of reality coherent in themselves. For instance, there is a fragment centred around time t, in which the facts that obtain at t are present, the facts previous to t are past and the facts following t are future. This fragment is coherent in itself because it contains, for instance, the tensed fact that Emma is standing now and the tensed fact that Emma will sit (in the future). However, there is another fragment of reality centred around t' in which the facts that obtain at t' are present, the facts previous to t' are past and the facts following t' are future. This fragment is also coherent in itself because it contains, for instance, the tensed fact that Emma was standing (in the past) and the tensed fact that Emma is sitting now. It is clear that the two fragments are incoherent with each other because an overall description should include both the fact that Emma is standing now and the fact that Emma is sitting now. Therefore, the reality *as a whole* is incoherent.

Fragmentalism and external relativism are different theories because, according to Fragmentalism, two tensed facts, such as Emma is sitting and Emma is standing, are part of the same incoherent reality. On the contrary, according to external relativism, they are part of different realities. On Fragmentalism, reality is unique but structurally fragmented. On external relativism, there are as many realities as instants of time. It is not our aim here to follow the consequences of these theories: external relativism and Fragmentalism are minority theories because they reject very plausible principles, such as the coherence and unicity of reality. However, we have given some space to these theories because, as we will see in Sect. 6.5, given a certain conception of God and of His knowledge, non-standard A-theories seem to be the only way to conciliate divine omniscience and worldly tensed facts.

2.3 Dynamics and Ontology

Let us see now the relationships between the ontologies of time analysed in Sect. 2.1 and the A- and B-theories. As will be evident shortly, not every combination is possible: some ontologies are "closer" to either a dynamic conception of time (A-theory) or a static one (B-theory).

The metaphysics that negate the existence of at least some temporal facts (Presentism, Growing Block, Shrinking Block) seem to be in agreement with a dynamic conception of time. In the case of Presentism, for instance, it is implicit in formulation of the theory that the present changes: things that were future are now present and will be past. An analogous remark applies to the Growing Block theory (and to its Shrinking counterpart): according to this view, as time flows, more and more facts are stored in the big repository of the past. All these views reject Neutrality because the present is seen as a privileged time and the dynamics of time is characterized on the basis of the change of the property of being present.

Those who are convinced by McTaggart's arguments on the contradictory nature (or at least on the conceptual instability) of the A-series and who are sympathetic to the B-theory of time consider Eternalism the most natural choice. The combination of Eternalism and B-theory is the Block Universe view. On this view, temporal reality is a four-dimensionalist block of facts,[11] in which no time is privileged. The Block Universe view certainly has counterintuitive aspects: it is, for instance, true that Caesar exists (at t) and is murdered. From our perspective of twenty-first century, we can refer to that event as a past event (and indeed we use the past tense to describe it), but, in fact, there are no tensed properties, such as being past, that characterize that fact. We can only say, for instance, that the assassination of Caesar temporally *precedes* the event of writing these words. The theoretical benefits of the Block Universe view are of two types: conceptual economy and, according to some scholars, compatibility with the scientific image of the world, that is, with Special Relativity.[12]

Eternalism is, however, also compatible with a dynamic conception of time: it is possible to combine the intuition according to which past, present and future exist with the idea that there is a privileged time—the present—and that this feature of the world is dynamic. This combination of theories takes its name from a fortunate metaphor by Broad:

> We are naturally tempted to regard the history of the world as existing eternally in a certain order of events. Along this, and in a fixed direction, we imagine the characteristic of presentness as moving, somewhat like the spot of light from a policeman's bull's-eye traversing the fronts of the houses in a street. What is illuminated is the present, what has been illuminated is the past, and what has not yet been illuminated is the future. (Broad 2014, p. 59)

---

[11] On this, see Sect. 2.4 on the persistence of objects through time.
[12] On this, see Sect. 2.4 again.

Broad's metaphor is communicatively incisive.[13] All the facts exist—as the houses of the district—but only a bunch of these facts are illuminated by the light of the present. This means that the property of being present is gradually instantiated by different facts. Past facts do not vanish—as it is maintained by Presentism—but they are not illuminated by the present any more and, thus, they are no longer present. Similarly, the future tenselessly exists, but it does not have yet the property of being present. On the basis of Broad's metaphor, this combination is called Moving Spotlight Theory (MST, for short): it is a rich theory from the ontological point of view because it assumes both the whole temporal manifold of Eternalism and the dynamical property of being present. Clearly, this richness is justified only if MST is able to account for our intuitions better than rival theories. Some scholars have argued for this thesis: for instance, Cameron has defended a form of MST in Cameron (2015); others are more sceptical. Certainly, to argue in favour of MST it is necessary to drop the fortunate metaphor and to offer a *theory*.[14]

2.4 Intermezzo: Persistence and Scientific Image of the World

Before tackling the last dimension of temporal reality, the *topology* of time, it is worth saying a few words on two philosophical questions strictly linked to the metaphysics of time: the persistence of objects and the relationship between metaphysical and scientific images of the world. It is clear that these are huge questions to which we can devote just brief hints here.

Suppose that Emma has a beautiful apple in front of her. The apple is on the table, ready to be eaten. After a minute, Emma's apple is still there. How can we know that the apple that is in front of Emma *now* is the *same* apple that was in front of her a minute ago? What makes it

---

[13] Actually, however, Broad did not defend this theory; rather, he was an advocate of the Growing Block view.
[14] On this, see De Florio, Frigerio, Giordani (forthcoming).

the same object? These are typical philosophical questions, which sound bizarre to common sense. However, we can immediately turn to more intriguing questions. Let us take into consideration a longer interval of time, for instance some days: the apple possesses some properties at t_0, for instance it is green and unripe, whereas at t_1, it is red and ripe. How can the same object possess incompatible properties, such as being unripe and ripe? How can we explain the apple's becoming?

In general, there are two different families of answers to the problem of the *persistence* of objects through time. According to some scholars, objects persist through time because they progressively occupy different temporal positions: the apple is wholly present at time t_0 (where it has some attributes) and wholly present at time t_1 (where it has other attributes). This view is called three-dimensionalism, or *endurantism*, and it is clearly the closest to common sense. It naturally combines with dynamic theories of time; presentists, for instance, will find it natural to think that the content of the present changes and includes the green and unripe apple first and then the red and ripe apple.

According to other scholars, objects persist through time exactly as they extend into space. The apple extends into space in virtue of its spatial parts (the core, the pulp, the peel, etc.); analogously, the apple has *temporal parts*, by which it extends into the four-dimensional block. This position is unsurprisingly called four-dimensionalism or *perdurantism* and it is equally unsurprisingly accepted by many B-theorists. It is famously pictured by the image of four-dimensional worms (see Quine 1981). Think about the apple: it has four dimensions (one temporal and three spatial): some temporal parts instantiate some properties (such as being green), other parts instantiate other properties (such as being red). Likewise, different spatial parts instantiate different properties: for instance, the apple is tender here, but hard there.

Theories of persistence give us the opportunity to clarify the notion of becoming within the Block Universe view in more detail. We have said that on this combination of B-theory and Eternalism there is no flow of time and the world is static. However, Block Universe theorists have a precise account of becoming of objects. Let us take into consideration Emma's apple again: according to four-dimensionalists, the apple is a worm in four dimensions. As we have said, the apple is green and unripe first and then it is red and ripe. On the four-dimensionalist view, this is explained by postulating a certain *temporal region* of the apple that is green and unripe and another temporal region that is red and ripe. In the same way, an iron bar can be hot at one end and cold at the other end. We experience only some "slices" of the space-time manifold; thereby we have the impression of a qualitative change of the *whole* apple, whereas the "becoming" of the apple should be interpreted just as the possession of different properties at different temporal parts.

It is not our aim in this book to discuss the pros and cons of every position on persistence[15]; as in the case of the ontology and the dynamics of time, many combinations among endurantism, perdurantism and the different metaphysics of time are possible. Since this book especially concerns God, we just briefly mention the question of God's persistence through time. This problem regards only the positions according to which God is in time.[16] Endurantists can state that God wholly exists at every instant just as Emma's apple. Perdurantists, instead, should say that God is a four-dimensional entity, which has temporal parts. But this seems to be contrary to a tenet of classical theism, that is, the absolute simplicity of God: He has no part and no internal structure. Some scholars[17] have advanced the idea that God is an *extended simple*, namely, an entity extended in time but devoid of parts. It is difficult to image such an entity and one might wonder if they are trying to explain something mysterious by means of something more mysterious.

Another bunch of questions regards the relationships between metaphysical and scientific images of the world. It is philosophical folklore to say that the Theory of Special Relativity entails a substantial revision of our metaphysics of time. Some authors have even stated that, in light of Einstein's work, the tensed conception of time must be abandoned and that the Block Universe view is the only one in line with our scientific results. Perhaps the first philosophical argument along these lines is that

---

[15] For an introduction to this topic, see: Lowe (2002), Haslanger (2003), Loux and Crisp (2017).
[16] Chapters 4 and 5 are focused on these positions.
[17] Pasnau (2011, pp. 11–28).

of Putnam (1967). The idea, in a nutshell, is the following: the Theory of Special Relativity entails that the concept of simultaneity is relative to each inertial frame. Therefore, the frame A can be simultaneous with the frame B and B simultaneous with C without A being simultaneous with C. In other words, depending on the inertial state of the frame taken into consideration, we can have frames which are simultaneous with the future regions of the cone-light of another event. If simultaneity is relative, a fundamental tenet of A-theory—the idea that being present is a genuine property objectively possessed by some entities—is meaningless.

Actually, things are much more complex than this, as it is easy to suppose. On the market there are two big families of argumentative strategies available to those who wish to maintain the A-theory in face of the Theory of Relativity. One can assume that the physical description of the world does not grasp everything: in particular, there are metaphysical properties—such as being present—that cannot be detected by our best empirical science (for this strategy see, for instance, Bourne (2006) and Orilia (2012)). Alternatively, one can take more seriously the interplay between science and metaphysics and can try to confer meaning to the notion of metaphysical present within a relativistic context (see Gilmore et al. (2016) for an excellent survey of these attempts). In the following, we do not deal with compatibility of the various metaphysics of time with the Theory of Relativity and its interpretations. It suffices here to have noted that there are influential attempts to make the results of empirical science compatible with tensed theories of time.[18]

2.5 Topology of Time: Closed and Open Universe

The third dimension along which theories of time can differ is the *topology* of time, in particular its linearity or branching. According to the first conception, time can be represented as a line, namely, as a sequence of

---

[18] See Sect. 6.4.3 for the use of some concepts borrowed from the Theory of Relativity in the discussion of God's timelessness.

instants such that, for every couple of instants t_1 and t_2, it is always true that $t_1 < t_2 \vee t_1 = t_2 \vee t_1 > t_2$, where $<$ indicates the relation of temporal precedence. By contrast, the branching view considers time as a tree with a trunk from which some branches radiate; in turn, branches can split into other branches. It is plain that in the branching view no total order among all the instants can be established: only some subsets of instants can be totally ordered (on this, see below). According to the linear conception of time, one of the points on the line is the present, all that precedes is the past, all that follows is the future. However, there are reasons to think that a branching conception of time is closer to some common sense intuitions. As we have noted in Chap. 1, we tend to think of the past as closed and the future as open. We have the feeling that we can determine at least some aspects of our future: for instance, today we could keep working, or take a pause and go for a walk in the park. Our idea of freedom seems to entail that different possibilities are open in front of us and we can choose one or the other. In a slightly more technical way, we can say that there are different possible histories for which we can opt. Moreover, if we decide to walk in the park, we have to take further decisions: we can choose to sit down on a bench and watch the passers-by or go jogging or buy an ice cream. Every decision corresponds to a node of the tree from which two or more histories branch off. These histories represent the options among which we can choose. The future is, then, a complex structure of possibilities stemming from previous stages of the world.

One of the most important features of the temporal tree is that branching is usually oriented towards the future: in standard ontologies there are no converging branches. Many courses of future events can start from a certain instant—which can be seen as a momentary stage of the evolution of the world—but two different courses of events cannot arrive at the same moment.

The different conceptions regarding the topology of time can be interwoven with ontological and dynamic views in different ways. For instance, we can combine a closed topology of time with dynamic theories such as Presentism as well as Growing and Shrinking Block views. For example, take Presentism, according to which only what is present exists.

Future things do not exist, but we can suppose anyway that it is *already* established what will exist: the progression of the world, that is, what will be present and will exist is fixed in a deterministic way by the present state of the world and by the laws that govern it. There is just a future history of the world. Similar considerations apply to the Growing and Shrinking Block views. If a linear topology of time is taken on board, the anti-realist positions about the future, that is the positions according to which the future does not exist yet (Presentism and Growing Block view), have a very natural solution to the problem of the truth of future tensed sentences. We will return to this issue in more depth; here it suffices to observe that the question of the truth of future tensed sentences is connected in these frameworks to the non-existence of truth-makers for these truths: there is not yet a child of Emma's who could make the future tensed sentence "Emma's child is blonde" true. However, in a determinist world, the present state of the world and the laws determine a unique future and this makes true the future tensed statement about the hair of Emma's (future) child. Of course, determinism or more generally necessitism[19] can be combined also with Eternalism—and this is a very natural interpretation of the Block Universe view—and with the MST: the light of the present gradually illuminates different instants, but it is completely determined which instant will follow the present one.

Those convinced by the openness of the future also have many metaphysical options at their disposal. Presentism and Growing Block view are compatible with an open future and, therefore, with a branching topology. In fact, the openness and indeterminateness of the future are probably at the root of the intuitions grounding these metaphysics of time, so that the combinations of a dynamic theory of time with a branching future is very natural. However, the Shrinking Block view, or at least a particular version of it, is also compatible with an open conception of the future, as claimed by McCall et al. (1994). According to McCall, both the trunk and the branches of the tree represent real facts. The different branches are not mere representations of how the future could be, but sequences of real events, alternative to each other. As time goes

---

[19] For the distinction between determinism and necessitism, cf. Sect. 1.1.

by, the world "takes" one of the future branches. According to McCall, the branches that are not chosen are pruned from the tree, that is, they cease to exist. By going by, time continuously thins out the tree, cutting the branches that do not become present. This is an unorthodox version of the Shrinking Block view: firstly, not the whole future is eroded by the passage of time, but only the branches that do not become present; secondly, the branch that becomes present is not cut and, therefore, the past exists. However, McCall's theory can be considered as a form of Shrinking Block view because the passage of time erodes future things, pruning the tree: the flow of time determines the reduction of existing things. We will refer to this version of the Shrinking Block view in the following.

One may wonder whether the branching structure of time can also be accepted by eternalists, who believe that the whole temporal series of facts exist at once. Here things become more complicated and we must be careful. The advocates of a dynamic version of Eternalism, namely, the MST theorists, can embrace the branching future and say that the light of the present will illuminate one of the histories stemming from the present. This idea is similar to some extent to McCall theory, which we have described in the last paragraph. However, in branching MST the histories that are not illuminated by the light are not annihilated, but remain in a sort of metaphysical limbo of discarded possibilities. The advocate of this theory must then admit *three* modalities of existence: the present time (namely, what is illuminated by the light, according to the metaphor); the future possible histories that could be illuminated; and the lost possibilities, that is, the histories that were possible in the past and that now are no longer possible. It is difficult to build a sufficiently structured picture to accommodate this ontological richness, but it is necessary if one wishes to combine dynamic Eternalism and branching.

But what happens if we want to be eternalist, to adopt a static theory of time, and to assume a branching view? Is this combination possible? First of all, let us notice that this set of assumptions can be theoretically attractive; it combines the ontological simplicity of the Block Universe, a standard interpretation of the Theory of Special Relativity, and the intuition that the future is open and that we can determine at least in part our future history. However, this branching static Eternalism incurs difficult issues. Let us assume that at time t_0 Emma is deciding whether to go to the party (at time t_1) or to stay at home to read a novel (at time t_2). The eternalists might assume that all these instants, that is t_0, t_1, and t_2, exist on par. Indeed, there are two Emmas, the Emma who goes to the party and the Emma who stays at home. This seems a metaphysical oddity. Notice that MST can differentiate between the two Emmas: for instance, the Emma who decides to go to the party will be illuminated by the present light, while the Emma who stays at home will not and will remain a mere possibility. However, for the branching Block Universe view (a static view), things are more complicated because, in this case, we cannot differentiate between the present and non-present entities because the present is a mere indexical property. For the Emma who goes to party, t_1 is the present, for the Emma who stays at home, t_2 is the present. Therefore, this position duplicates Emma. Even worse: *before* t_0 there is only one Emma; then, a sort of metaphysical *mitosis* occurs.

One might formulate a possible answer to this problem on the basis of David Lewis' modal metaphysics (see Lewis 1986). As is well known, all possible worlds exist on par, according to Lewis. Then, Emma has counterparts, that is, individuals similar to Emma who live in other possible worlds. The fact that, *for us*, our world is actual is a mere indexical fact. For the inhabitants of another possible world, their world is actual and we are possible counterparts. The branching Block Universe might be interpreted on the basis of Lewis' modal metaphysics. A solution that escapes the metaphysical mitosis is to consider two counterparts of Emma, let us call them Emma$_1$ and Emma$_2$. Emma$_1$ goes to the party and Emma$_2$ stays at home. Since Emma$_1$ and Emma$_2$ are very similar before t_0, we can consider them identical. Hence, the *illusion* of branching. The world is constituted by many closed temporal lines. Emma$_1$ is eternally determined to go to the party and Emma$_2$ is eternally determined to stay at home. This position is certainly coherent, but it throws the baby out with the bath water: to solve the problem of the ontology of the future possible histories, it nullifies them.

Not everything is lost for the branching Block Universe theorist. She has a much more promising possibility: she can state that there is only *one* four-dimensional history of the world, but that the different stages of this history do not univocally determine the following stages. Only the fact that Emma is at the party obtains, and it obtains tenselessly. The fact that Emma is at home does not obtain. However, there is a stage of the world at which Emma has not decided yet what to do—a stage that exists tenselessly too—and this stage does not determine whether Emma will go to the party or will read at home. Consequently, there is a possible history of the world in which Emma reads a novel at home. This history is a mere possibility because it did not occur. Actually, it will never occur because there is no dynamics in this view. However, it is a contingent fact that Emma is at the party: she is a free agent and she could have chosen differently. As a matter of fact, she decides not to stay at home, but this decision is not necessitated. To better understand this view, think about the past. We believe that there is only one actual past history, but we also believe that the past might have been different, so that there are many possible histories arising from past instants that contain facts different from the actual facts. These are histories that could have occurred, but that, as a matter of fact, did not occur. The branching Block Universe theorist regards the *whole* history of the world as we regard the past. This view escapes metaphysical mitosis—just one Emma exists—but, at the same time, it does not renounce indeterminism because Emma is free to do otherwise. As we will see in Sect. 4.5.3, this kind of metaphysics fits very well with one of the solutions to the problem of divine prescience, Ockhamism.

This concludes our overview about the metaphysics of time. In the following, however, we will return to the different kinds of metaphysical views in more detail when it is necessary.

2.6 Temporal Logic

In this section, we define some notions of temporal logic that will be used in this book. Some amendments will be made in the course of our analysis in order to account for the specificity of the various solutions to the dilemma of divine foreknowledge and human freedom. The logic system we present here is a classical system of propositional modal logic having two temporal operators. Our alphabet is the following:

- Propositional letters: $p, q, r, \ldots$
- Usual basic logical connectives: $\neg, \wedge$ and those definable on the basis of the basic ones.
- Two temporal operators: **P, F**

As usual, the set of formulas is defined by induction:

$$\varphi, \psi := p \mid \neg \varphi \mid \varphi \wedge \psi \mid \mathbf{P}\varphi \mid \mathbf{F}\varphi \mid$$

The intuitive meaning of $\mathbf{P}\varphi$ and $\mathbf{F}\varphi$ is respectively: it was the case that φ and it will be the case that φ. On the basis of these two operators, we can define at least two other operators: **H** (defined as $\neg\mathbf{P}\neg$), which we can translate as: it has always been true that ...and **G** (defined as $\neg\mathbf{F}\neg$), which we can translate as: it will always be true that ...It is possible to reiterate the operators to translate some other verb tenses of natural languages (for instance, $\mathbf{FP}\varphi$ corresponds to: φ will have been the case; $\mathbf{PF}\varphi$ corresponds to: φ was going to be the case or would be the case).

Temporal structures are usually a couple $< T, <>$, where T is a set of instants $(t_1, t_2, t_3, \ldots)$ and $<$ is a relation among instants. Intuitively, $t_1 < t_2$ means that t_1 precedes t_2 in the temporal series. The properties of $<$ have been intensively studied: it is usually assumed that this relation is, at least, transitive, irreflexive and asymmetric:

transitivity : $\forall t, t', t''(t < t' \wedge t' < t'' \rightarrow t < t'')$
irreflexivity : $\forall t, \neg(t < t)$
asymmetry : $\forall t, t'(t < t' \rightarrow \neg(t' < t))$

In the following four subsections, four different temporal semantics will be introduced. The first one models a universe with a closed future (Sect. 2.6.1). The last three have an open future structure, but give different truth conditions to the formulas containing a future operator: the Ockhamist, the Peircean and the Thin Red Line semantics will be examined in Sects. 2.6.2, 2.6.3, and 2.6.4, respectively.

2.6.1 Linear Time

The relation < orders the instants of time. However, as we have seen in Sect. 2.5, time can have at least two different structures: closed and open future. We can model these two structures by postulating further conditions on the relation < among the instants of time. Let us start with the simplest structure, the closed future. In this case, it is necessary to place the following condition on <:

closed future $\quad \forall t, t', t''((t'' < t \wedge t'' < t') \to (t < t' \vee t = t' \vee t' < t))$

In other terms, given two instants, either the first precedes the second, or the second precedes the first, or the two instants coincide. If we place this condition, time is linear and it has no branching.

We can now define a model of temporal logic that corresponds to the closed future. A model of temporal logic is a triple $< T, <, V >$, where the first two elements constitute the temporal structure and V is an evaluation that assigns truth values to propositional letters with respect to the various moments of time: a little more formally, V assigns to every $p \in PROP$ a set of time instants $V(p) \subseteq T$ at which p is true. In the closed future model, truth clauses containing temporal operators are simple and intuitive: a formula such as $\mathbf{P}\varphi$ is true iff φ is true at at least an instant preceding the instant of evaluation. For example, a proposition such as:

1. Emma drank a beer

is true at a certain instant iff at at least one time previous to that instant the proposition

2. Emma drinks a beer

is true. Symmetrically, the formula $\mathbf{F}\varphi$ is true iff φ is true at an instant subsequent to that of evaluation: More formally:

$$\begin{aligned}
\mathcal{M}, t \vDash p & \Leftrightarrow t \in V(p), \text{for } p \in PROP \\
\mathcal{M}, t \vDash \neg\varphi & \Leftrightarrow \mathcal{M}, t \nvDash \varphi \\
\mathcal{M}, t \vDash \varphi \wedge \psi & \Leftrightarrow \mathcal{M}, t \vDash \varphi \text{ and } \mathcal{M}, t \vDash \psi \\
\mathcal{M}, t \vDash \mathbf{P}\varphi & \Leftrightarrow \exists t' < t, \mathcal{M}, t' \vDash \varphi \\
\mathcal{M}, t \vDash \mathbf{F}\varphi & \Leftrightarrow \exists t' > t, \mathcal{M}, t' \vDash \varphi \\
\mathcal{M}, t \vDash \mathbf{H}\varphi & \Leftrightarrow \forall t' < t, \mathcal{M}, t' \vDash \varphi \\
\mathcal{M}, t \vDash \mathbf{G}\varphi & \Leftrightarrow \forall t' > t, \mathcal{M}, t' \vDash \varphi
\end{aligned}$$

2.6.2 Branching Time

Things become more complicated in branching models. In this case, the **closed future** axiom must be negated:

open future $\quad \forall t, t', t''((t'' < t \wedge t'' < t') \nrightarrow (t < t' \vee t = t' \vee t' < t))$

Open future denies that the instants subsequent to a given instant are *always* ordered by the relation $<$. Of course, one can deny the linearity of the future, but not that of the past: $\forall t, t', t''((t < t'' \wedge t' < t'') \rightarrow (t < t' \vee t = t' \vee t' < t))$. These conditions account for our intuition that the future is open, thereby having a branching structure, but the past is linear and closed. Moreover, if we want a universe composed by just one tree (**open future** does not exclude multiple trees), we need to add the following condition:

historical connectedness $\quad \forall t, t' \exists t''(t'' < t \wedge t'' < t')$

In words: given two instants t and t', there is always a third instant that precedes the other two. The conditions concerning the formulas without temporal operators and with past operators are identical to the previous ones, regarding the closed universe. This is not a surprise since the past is linear in the future branching model:

$$M, t \vDash p \Leftrightarrow t \in V(p), \text{for } p \in PROP$$
$$M, t \vDash \neg \varphi \Leftrightarrow M, t \nvDash \varphi$$
$$M, t \vDash \varphi \wedge \psi \Leftrightarrow M, t \vDash \varphi \text{ and } M, t \vDash \psi$$
$$M, t \vDash \mathbf{P}\varphi \Leftrightarrow \exists t' < t, M, t' \vDash \varphi$$
$$M, t \vDash \mathbf{H}\varphi \Leftrightarrow \forall t' < t, M, t' \vDash \varphi$$

Since **open future** and **historical connectedness** ensure that past moments are linearly ordered, it still holds that $\mathbf{P}\varphi$ is true iff there is an instant previous to the instant of evaluation at which φ is true and that $\mathbf{H}\varphi$ is true iff φ is true at every instant previous to the instant of evaluation. However, for the future we cannot propose again the following clause:

$$M, t \vDash \mathbf{F}\varphi \Leftrightarrow \exists t' > t, M, t' \vDash \varphi$$

Suppose that two different branches stem from the moment of evaluation t and that in one of these branches there is an instant subsequent to t at which φ is true, while in the other branch there is an instant subsequent to t at which $\neg\varphi$ is true. The clause says that $\mathbf{F}\varphi$ is true iff there is an instant subsequent to that of evaluation at which φ is true. In fact, such an instant exists in the hypothesized scenario because φ is true at an instant subsequent to t in one of the branches departing from t. So, $\mathbf{F}\varphi$ would be true in this scenario. However, this is counterintuitive because, in every situation in which there is a future history in which φ is true, $\mathbf{F}\varphi$ would be also true. Every sentence describing a future contingent would turn true. For instance, if "Emma will drink a beer" is a future contingent, it would be true because there is a history in which Emma drinks a beer (as well as a history in which Emma does not drink a beer). This is implausible and similar remarks apply to the dual of $\mathbf{F}$, $\mathbf{G}$.

We have to provide a more plausible clause for future contingent sentences. A very simple solution is to relativize our evaluations not only to instants but also to histories. As we have seen, a history is a possible course of events of the world: from the logical point of view, it is a *maximal subset of instants*. This means that a history cannot be extended in any way.

In such a solution, our evaluations are indexed not only to an instant t, but also to a history h, in particular to couples t/h, where t/h means that $t \in h$. The clauses are, then, the following:

$$M, t/h \vDash \mathbf{F}\varphi \Leftrightarrow \exists t' > t \wedge t' \in h, M, t'/h \vDash \varphi$$
$$M, t/h \vDash \mathbf{G}\varphi \Leftrightarrow \forall t' > t \wedge t' \in h, M, t'/h \vDash \varphi$$

A formula such as $\mathbf{F}\varphi$ is true with respect to a model M and to a couple instant-history t/h iff in the history h there exists an instant t', subsequent to the instant t, at which φ is true. The clause for $\mathbf{G}\varphi$ is analogous. This solution is called **Ockhamism**.[20] Let us consider again the scenario described above: Emma is free to drink a beer tomorrow. Therefore, there exists a history in which Emma drinks a beer and a history in which Emma does not drink it. Which is the truth value of the sentence "Emma will drink a beer tomorrow", when uttered today? The Ockhamist responds that this sentence is true in the history in which Emma drinks a beer and false in the history in which Emma does not drink it.

Different arguments speak in favour of Ockhamism. Firstly, it keeps together two different ideas that are in tension with each other: the idea that the future is open and the idea that future tensed sentences have a truth value. As we have seen in Chap. 1, the Aristotelian problem of future contingents arises from this conceptual tension. Ockhamist evaluations are relativized to histories and, therefore, they are similar to those concerning a closed universe. The formulas containing the future operator are true depending on the history to which they are indexed and, in particular, if in that history there is a moment subsequent to that of evaluation at which the formula in the scope of the future operator is true. The same argument holds symmetrically for past formulas. Secondly, Ockhamism preserves the validity of intuitive logical principles such as the law of excluded middle: $\mathbf{F}\varphi \vee \neg \mathbf{F}\varphi$ is valid in the Ockhamist system

---

[20] As we will see in the chapter on Ockhamism, this term is ambiguous and has many different uses in literature. On the one hand, it indicates the particular semantics about future sentences we have illustrated here. On the other hand, "Ockhamism" is used to designate a particular solution to the problem of divine prescience and human freedom. In addition, the use of this term raises a historical-exegetical question: how much of the contemporary Ockhamism has actually been stated by the historical Ockham?

because, in every history, there is or there is not a moment following that of evaluation at which φ is true.

However, there are also reasons that militate against Ockhamism. The main problem is that Ockhamism is not able to account for the meaning that is usually assigned to future tense. Suppose, for instance, to ask Thomas whether he will leave or stay at home tomorrow. Suppose that Thomas answers as follows: "In the future history in which I leave, it is true that I leave; in the future history in which I stay at home, it is true that I stay at home". This answer is bizarre and, probably, we would reject it: when we wonder about the truth of a future tensed sentence, we would like to know the truth value of that sentence *tout court* and not relative to a history.

2.6.3 Peircean Semantics

An intuition that is an alternative to Ockhamism is that $\mathbf{F}\varphi$ is true if φ is true in every possible future. For instance, "Emma will drink a beer tomorrow" is true iff Emma drinks a beer in every history that passes through the instant of evaluation. If in some of the alternatives it is true that Emma drinks a beer and in others it is false that she drinks it, then the sentence "Emma will drink a beer tomorrow" is false. This solution, which makes all future contingents false, is called **Peircean**.[21]

To sketch Peircean semantics we need a further concept. $\mathcal{H}_t = \{h | t \in h\}$ indicates the set of histories that have t among their instants, that is, the set of histories that pass through t. The clause for the future formulas in Peircean semantics is then:

$$\mathcal{M}, t \models^{\mathbf{PRC}} \mathbf{F}\varphi \Leftrightarrow \forall h \in \mathcal{H}_t \exists t' > t, \mathcal{M}, t' \models^{\mathbf{PRC}} \varphi$$

false otherwise.[22] The Peircean conditions for $\mathbf{G}\varphi$ are similar.

---

[21] As in the case of Ockhamism, the reference to Peirce should not be taken literally. On the connections between Peircean semantics and the conception historically stated by Peirce, see Øhrstrøm and Hasle (2007).

[22] The superscript **PRC** indicates that the semantics under concern is Peircean.

Notice that this semantics does not relativize the evaluation to couples of an instant and a history, but simply to instants. This permits to escape from the counterintuitive consequences of Ockhamism mentioned in the previous section. Moreover, the idea that a statement concerning the future is true iff its content is true in every future history seems plausible: if Emma drinks a beer in some histories and does not drink it in other histories, we are not allowed to say that it is true that Emma will drink a beer. So, this statement is false. However, Peircean semantics runs into some problems. Firstly, it gives counterintuitive results when the future operator **F** interacts with negation. In fact, **F** is similar to a universal quantifier on histories, and thus we have to consider two possible scopes for the negation: $\neg \mathbf{F}\varphi$ and $\mathbf{F}\neg\varphi$. In Peircean semantics, the first formula says that it is not true in every history passing through the instant of evaluation that φ will obtain; by contrast, the second formula says that, in every history passing through the instant of evaluation, $\neg\varphi$ will occur. From the logical point of view, these two formulas are not equivalent. However, our negative future tensed sentences are not so ambiguous. Consider, for example:

3. Emma will not drink a beer tomorrow

This sentence does not sound ambiguous between two different meanings.

Secondly, we can state two laws of excluded middle:

4. $\mathbf{F}\varphi \vee \neg\mathbf{F}\varphi$
5. $\mathbf{F}\varphi \vee \mathbf{F}\neg\varphi$

The first principle is valid in Peircean semantics: either in every future history it is true that φ or not in every future history it is true that φ. The second principle, however, is not valid. Suppose that in some future histories it is true that φ, whereas in others it is not true that φ. In this case, $\mathbf{F}\varphi$ is false because not in every history it is true that φ, but also

$\mathbf{F}\neg\varphi$ is false because not in every future history it is true that $\neg\varphi$. The disjunction is, then, false. But a sentence such as:

6. Emma will drink or will not drink a beer tomorrow

sounds tautological and does not seem to have a true and a false reading. It is true, full stop. Peirceans might respond that, for some reasons, negation always takes large scope with respect to the future operator. However, assuming this thesis has problematic consequences on the interpretation of negative sentences:

7. Emma will not drink a beer tomorrow

would be true if, in at least one future history, Emma does not drink a beer tomorrow. So, this sentence would be true even if in many future histories Emma drinks a beer tomorrow. But it is odd to affirm that it is true that Emma will not drink a beer when the possibility that she will drink is open. Within the Peircean semantics, the most plausible interpretation is the narrow scope reading of the negation: in every future history Emma does not drink a beer tomorrow. But, as we have seen, in this case, the law of excluded middle is not valid.

Another problem for the Peircean semantics is the failure to distinguish between necessity and truth of the future. Let us consider these sentences:

8. Emma will drink a beer tomorrow
9. Emma will necessarily drink a beer tomorrow

As we have seen, the first sentence is true iff in every history Emma drinks a beer tomorrow. Now, it seems that Peirceans must assign the same truth conditions to the second sentence: it seems to say that in every possible history Emma drinks a beer tomorrow. However, these two sentences have different meanings. This criticism can be expressed in the following way: Peircean semantics collapses the concept of future into that of future *inevitability*. Other semantics, as we will see shortly, are able to keep these concepts apart.

Finally, Peircean semantics states that all future contingents are false. Therefore, it is false that Emma will drink a beer tomorrow because there are histories in which Emma does not drink a beer. Emma might have not even decided whether to drink a beer or not and can even have no idea about what to do, but according to Peirceans it is false that she will drink a beer. Instead, it seems more appropriate to say that it is neither true nor false that she will drink a beer because it is indeterminate whether she will drink it.

The *supervaluationist model* has been developed to fix some of the problems of the Peircean model (see Thomason 1970). The basic idea is to export the supervaluationist solutions to the issue of vague predicates to the semantics of future contingents. There are cases that are clearly part of the extension of a vague predicate (such as "bald") and there are cases that are clearly not part of the predicate. However, there are also "border" cases. Analogously, there are cases of true future tensed propositions and cases of false future tensed propositions. But there are also middle cases: future tensed propositions that are neither true nor false. If Emma has not yet decided whether to drink a beer or not, it is neither true nor false that she will have a beer. This sentence has no truth value and it will acquire a truth value only after Emma's action. If there are two future histories in which contradictory formulas are true, then those formulas have an indeterminate truth value at the present.

The formal apparatus of the supervaluationist model brings about two new ingredients with respect to Peircean semantics. Firstly, in addition to the concept of the truth in a history, it introduces that of *supertruth*, that is, what is true in every history. Analogously, in the case of vague predicates, we can distinguish between what is true with respect to a precisification and what is true with respect to every precisification. A formula is true with respect to a history as in Ockhamist semantics, but it is supertrue or superfalse with respect to every history. To calculate the supertruth of a formula, we must first calculate its truth value in each history. Secondly, supervaluationism allows truth value gaps: a formula is supertrue if it is true in every history, and superfalse if it is false in every history, but it is neither supertrue nor superfalse if it is true in some histories and false in others. The truth conditions of the future operator are the following:

$$\mathcal{M}, t \models^{SEV} \mathbf{F}\varphi \Leftrightarrow \forall h \in \mathcal{H}_t \exists t' > t, \mathcal{M}, t' \models^{SEV} \varphi$$
$$\mathcal{M}, t \not\models^{SEV} \mathbf{F}\varphi \Leftrightarrow \forall h \in \mathcal{H}_t \exists t' > t, \mathcal{M}, t' \not\models^{SEV} \varphi$$

indeterminate otherwise.[23] Truth conditions for $\mathbf{G}\varphi$ are similar.

Hence, "Emma will drink a beer tomorrow" is supertrue if Emma drinks a beer in every future history, superfalse if she does not drink it in every future history, and neither supertrue nor superfalse if there is at least one future history in which she drinks a beer and at least one future history in which she does not. If Emma is free in a libertarian sense and she can do otherwise, then it is really indeterminate whether she will drink a beer or not.

Supervaluationist semantics solves at least some of the problems of Peircean semantics. Firstly, all future contingents are judged as neither true nor false and this seems more adequate than judging them simply false. Secondly, this semantics accounts for the law of excluded middle. Consider these formulas:

4. $\mathbf{F}\varphi \vee \neg \mathbf{F}\varphi$
5. $\mathbf{F}\varphi \vee \mathbf{F}\neg\varphi$

To evaluate them, we have to determine their truth values in every history that passes through the moment of evaluation. Both formulas are true in every history. Consequently, both of them are supertrue. The law of excluded middle is vindicated, just as the intuition that "Emma will drink or will not drink a beer tomorrow" is true even though Emma has not yet decided to drink it.

However, supervaluationist semantics does not remove some problems of Peircean semantics and adds a new one. Firstly, supervaluationists distinguish between $\neg \mathbf{F}\varphi$ and $\mathbf{F}\neg\varphi$. However, we have seen that this distinction has no role in the evaluation of our natural language sentences.

---

[23] Here we are sloppy about symbols. As a matter of fact, the symbol $\models$ represents "supertrue"; therefore, we should introduce another symbol for "superflase" with their respective negations. However, in the interest of a lighter formlization, we skip this point.

Secondly, just as Peirceanism, supervaluationist semantics does not distinguish between truth and necessity of the future. Two sentences such as

8. Emma will drink a beer tomorrow
9. Emma will necessarily drink a beer tomorrow

are true if Emma drinks a beer tomorrow in every history.

As said above, the supervaluationist has a further problem. Suppose that Emma is free to drink a beer tomorrow. As there are histories in which Emma drinks a beer and histories in which she does not drink it, both $\mathbf{F}\varphi$ and $\mathbf{F}\neg\varphi$ are neither true nor false. However, the formula $\mathbf{F}\varphi \vee \mathbf{F}\neg\varphi$ is (super)true. This is peculiar because the disjunction of two indeterminate formulas should be indeterminate in turn. Supervaluationists must accept a not fully truth-conditional interpretation of disjunction. Yet, supervaluationism accounts for a strong intuition: if Emma is free, we feel that the sentences "Emma will drink a beer tomorrow" and "Emma will not drink a beer tomorrow" are devoid of truth value, but we are resolute to consider the disjunction "Tomorrow Emma will or will not drink a beer" true, even if Emma has not decided yet what to do.

2.6.4 Thin Red Line Model

Let us present another model based on completely different intuitions: the Thin Red Line model. The intuition that grounds this model is the following: although Emma is free to perform an action or not, she will drink a beer tomorrow or not. As a consequence, Emma will make one of the future histories true. Therefore, there is a future history that Emma will make true and this history is, so to say, marked with respect to the others because it is the actual history of the world. Metaphorically, it is thought of as marked in red and, thus, as distinct from the others.[24] The future tensed sentences are true if they are true with respect to this marked

---

[24] The origin of this metaphor is intriguing: it was introduced by Belnap and Green (1994) and stems from the idea according to which the British Empire was held by a "thin red line" of soldiers all over the world.

history, the Thin Red Line (**TRL** for short). We can write the following truth conditions:

$$\mathcal{M}, t \models^{\text{TRL}} \mathbf{F}\varphi \Leftrightarrow \exists t' > t \wedge t' \in \text{TRL}, \mathcal{M}, t' \models^{\text{TRL}} \varphi$$
$$\mathcal{M}, t \models^{\text{TRL}} \mathbf{G}\varphi \Leftrightarrow \forall t' > t \wedge t' \in \text{TRL}, \mathcal{M}, t' \models^{\text{TRL}} \varphi$$

To evaluate the future tensed sentences, we have to consider what happens in the marked history. Since the **TRL** is a totally ordered set of events, the Thin Red Line theory can account for the law of excluded middle and preserve bivalence. Furthermore, this view is able to discriminate between the truth of the future tensed sentences and their necessity: "Emma will drink a beer" is true if in the **TRL** Emma will drink a beer, while "Necessarily, Emma will drink a beer" is true if Emma drinks a beer in every future history. If the first sentence is true, then Emma is free because there are future histories in which she does not drink a beer and that she could have chosen. If the second sentence is true, Emma is not free because she has no choice.

Two remarks about this semantics are in order. Firstly, the fact that Emma will choose in some ways is an entirely contingent fact: she could have chosen otherwise. It is important to point out this aspect because this feature distinguishes this view from the closed future model. The **TRL** model aims at preserving indeterminism and freedom of agents. The present state of the world and the laws do not univocally determine the future, but leave many possible alternatives open. However, one of these alternatives is the alternative that will contingently occur because it will be contingently chosen by Emma. Secondly, the fact that the truth of future tensed sentences depends on what happens in the **TRL** does not mean that we can know their truth value. The future can be epistemologically indeterminate although the truth value of future tensed sentences is logically determined.

The **TRL** view has been criticized on many grounds. One kind of objection concerns the compatibility of the **TRL** with a genuinely indeterministic conception of the world and with a strong conception of freedom. As said above, the advocates of this view believe that **TRL** semantics is fully compatible with indeterminism, but questions have arisen about this point. For example, one might object that the **TRL**-

theorist sees the future in the same way as we see the past: when we look at the past, we can identify some alternative histories that could have been actualized; the real history of the world is different from these since it is what has actually been chosen. Can we also reason in the same vein about the future? One could say no, and in this can be found the asymmetry between the past and the future: presently, there is not a true future history because the agent has not yet chosen any alternatives. Surely, tomorrow we will be able to say that between two histories h_1 and h_2, h_1, say, has been actualized. However, today we cannot say anything of the kind because h_1 and h_2 are on a par. There is an advancing of the world just because that which was open and indeterminate before becomes closed and determinate. But if the future is really undetermined, there is no real history of the world until it happens: the fact that we will be able to say tomorrow that, for instance, h_1 is the real history of the world does not mean that, today, h_1 is already the real history of the world. Emma's choice consists in privileging what was not privileged before: hence, if we seriously consider the idea that the world is undetermined, then it seems that we must allow that there is no privileged history. Philosophers do not agree on this point. Some (for instance Belnap and Green (1994), MacFarlane (2003)) maintain that the TRL-view is incompatible with indeterminism; others (for instance, Øhrstrøm (2009), Rosenkranz (2012)) believe that the TRL view can be defended against the charge of being incompatible with Libertarianism.

Another set of objections against the TRL view is of logical kind. They were advanced by Belnap and Green (1994) and Belnap et al. (2001). Basically, they point out that the TRL view can give no truth value to future tensed sentences when evaluated at a point external to the TRL. However, some well-formed sentences seem to require an evaluation of future tensed sentences at points of the tree that are not part of the TRL. To see this, let us consider the following example: suppose that Mary has invited Emma to a party. Emma must decide whether to accept the invitation or stay home and read a novel. Suppose Emma decides to dedicate herself to reading in the TRL. What would Emma have done if she had gone to the party? She would have had to decide whether to drink

2 Metaphysics and Logic of Time 61

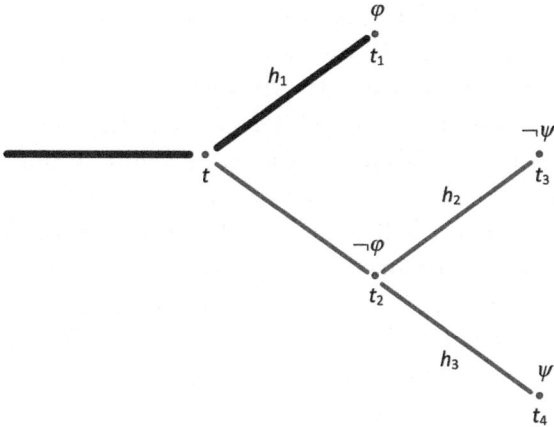

Fig. 2.1 Emma's case

a beer. What would she have decided to do? The situation is depicted in Fig. 2.1.

The moment t is the moment at which Emma decides to stay at home and read a novel (φ) or to go to the party ($\neg\varphi$). As Emma will choose to read a novel, the history h_1 is marked. However, if Emma had gone to the party, she would have had to decide whether to drink a beer (ψ) or not ($\neg\psi$), that is, to make h_3 or h_2 true. What would she have done in such a circumstance? According to Belnap and Green (1994), the **TRL** theory should account not only for sentences such as

10. Emma will read a novel, and she will not go to the party

but also for sentences such as

11. Emma will read a novel and will not go to the party, but, if she had gone to the party, she would have drunk a beer.

For every bifurcation of the tree, regardless of whether it belongs to the actual history of the world, it is necessary to assign a truth value to the proposition that describes what an agent will do in that circumstance.

Among advocates of **TRL**, one of the main aims is to preserve bivalence. However, bivalence must be preserved not only for sentences such as (10) but also for sentences such as (11). Øhrstrøm (2009) presents a model that solves this problem. In a nutshell, Øhrstrøm's idea is not to consider the **TRL** semantically as a history of the world but as a function (indicated here in lower case, **trl**) that takes times and yields histories. For every instant, **trl** defines the **TRL** relative to that instant. Local **TRL**s enable us to solve cases such as Emma's and respond to Belnap and Green's criticism of the concept of **TRL**. It is worth noting that in this model, there is no unique marked history (the **TRL**) but a function defined on elements of the structure. We call this model **TRL+**. According to **TRL+**, the clauses for the future are:

$$\mathcal{M}, t \vDash^{TRL+} \mathbf{F}\varphi \Leftrightarrow \exists t' > t \wedge t' \in \mathsf{trl}(t), \mathcal{M}, t' \vDash^{TRL+} \varphi$$
$$\mathcal{M}, t \vDash^{TRL+} \mathbf{G}\varphi \Leftrightarrow \forall t' > t \wedge t' \in \mathsf{trl}(t), \mathcal{M}, t' \vDash^{TRL+} \varphi$$

For every point of evaluation t, a future tensed sentence $\mathbf{F}\varphi$ is true iff there exists a moment subsequent to t belonging to the **TRL** relative to t, at which φ is true. The function **trl** must satisfy at least the following principle:

Domain of *trl*   The instant at which the function is defined must be a member of the local **TRL**: $t \in \mathsf{trl}(t)$.

This principle is wholly reasonable: every instant t must belong to the **TRL** relative to that instant.

However, Belnap and Green (1994) show that some very plausible principles are falsified in **TRL+**. Consider:

12. $\mathbf{FF}\varphi \to \mathbf{F}\varphi$
13. $\mathbf{F}\varphi \to \mathbf{FF}\varphi$

Let us see why these principle are invalid in **TRL+**. $\mathbf{FF}\varphi$ is true in **TRL+** at an instant of evaluation t iff there is an instant t' subsequent to t belonging to $\mathsf{trl}(t)$ at which $\mathbf{F}\varphi$ is true. In turn, $\mathbf{F}\varphi$ is true at t' iff there is an instant t'' subsequent to t' belonging to $\mathsf{trl}(t')$ at which φ is true.

But trl(t) = trl(t') is not guaranteed. The local **TRL**s relative to the two moments might be different. Then, φ might be true in a history different from trl(t) making **F**φ false, as this formula is evaluated with respect to trl(t). However, these principles are plausible. If tomorrow it will be true that the day after tomorrow Emma will drink a beer, then it should also be true today that Emma will drink a beer the day after tomorrow. In other words, if in the future a certain future tensed proposition will be true, then that proposition should already be true today. One possible way to overcome this problem is to postulate that trl(t) = trl(t'). This can be done adding the following condition on trl:

Identity of *trl* $\quad t < t' \wedge t' \in \text{trl}(t) \to \text{trl}(t) = \text{trl}(t')$

In other terms, if an instant t' belongs to the future part of the **TRL** relative to t, then the **TRL** relative to t' must be identical to that relative to t. This condition validates the principles **FF**$\varphi \to$ **F**φ and **F**$\varphi \to$ **FF**φ.

However, **TRL+** has a further problem, pointed out by Belnap. Another plausible principle is not valid in this system:

14. $\varphi \to$ **HF**φ

In words: if φ is true, then **F**φ has always been true. If Emma drinks a beer today, then it was true yesterday that Emma would drink a beer. In the same way, it has been true at every moment of the past that she would drink a beer. It is easy to see why this principle is invalid in **TRL+**. Suppose that φ is true at the instant t and that $t \in h$. Then, the principle would be valid if **F**φ is true at every moment t' previous to t. However, it might be true that trl(t') $\neq h$ at some of the moments t' previous to t. In fact, the **TRL** relative to some of the moments of the past of t might be different from the history h to which t belongs. But the formula **F**φ will be evaluated on trl(t') and in this history φ might not be true in the **TRL** of t'.

One can react to this problem in different ways. Firstly, one might simply deny the plausibility of the principle. A second proposal by Braüner et al. (2000) is based on a profound redefinition of the model **TRL+**. A third possibility is by Malpass and Wawer (2012), who propose to adopt the clause for the future of the **TRL** semantics when the instant of evaluation belongs to the **TRL** and, instead, to adopt the supervaluationist clause for the future when the instant of evaluation is external to the **TRL**. Finally, Wawer (2014) attempts to rephrase the formulas evaluated at moments not belonging to the **TRL** as modalized formulas evaluated at moments belonging to the **TRL**. These last two solutions reject the relativization of the **TRL** to times and keep the original idea of a unique **TRL**.

As we will see in the chapter on Molinism, Molinists need the model **TRL+** for supporting their solution to the dilemma of divine foreknowledge and human freedom. Therefore, the validity of the principle $\varphi \rightarrow \mathbf{HF}\varphi$ is a problem for Molinists. Restall (2011) proposes to abandon Molinism precisely because Molinism need **TRL+** and **TRL+** does not validate this principle. Molinists should respond to Restall's criticism about $\varphi \rightarrow \mathbf{HF}\varphi$, but they cannot adopt the solutions of Braüner, Malpass and Wawer and Wawer because they entail a redefinition of **TRL+**, which is essential to the Molinist solution. Certainly, Molinists might line up behind those who do not believe that the principle is so intuitive. Alternatively, they might search for a solution within **TRL+** and show that some versions of this model validate the principle. In this book, we will not deal with the possible Molinist solutions to Restall's objection,[25] but in Sect. 6.5.1 we will propose a perspectival semantics that validates the principle $\varphi \rightarrow \mathbf{HF}\varphi$. This concludes our analysis of the semantic models for future tense. There are other possible solutions, but some of them will be treated in the remainder of this book.

The choice of the temporal logic to adopt is partly independent of the various metaphysics of time we have examined in the preceding sections. For instance, a closed future logic can be adopted by presentists, Growing Block theorists, MST theorists, and eternalists, if they are determinist or necessitist. As we have seen, the ontological differences are significant: for presentists and Growing Block theorists, the future stages of the world

---

[25] In De Florio and Frigerio (2019) we have offered a semantics for **TRL+** that is satisfactory for Molinists and that validates the principle $\varphi \rightarrow \mathbf{HF}\varphi$. Therefore, this semantics can overcome Restall's objection.

do not exist—only representations of these stages exist at the present. Conversely, the future stages exist for MST theorists and eternalists. However, as for the truth conditions of future tensed sentences, the clauses of the closed future can be adopted by all of them if they are determinist because they see the future as an ordered series of instants.

Things are much more complex for the open universe. Generally, Peircean semantics seems the natural solution for the indeterminists who believe that the future does not exist (presentists and Growing Block theorists) and for those who believe that there are many future branches having equal ontological dignity (eternalists who believe that all the future branches exist and Shrinking Block theorists who adopt McCall's version of this view). Indeed, on these views, either the future branches are mere representations or they exist in the same way and none of them is marked with respect to the others. On the other hand, the **TRL** semantics seems natural for those who believe that a branch is privileged with respect to the others, namely, for eternalists who accept indeterminism and who believe that just one branch exists, whereas the others are only representations of how the world could have been. However, it is an open question whether the former are *forced* to accept Peircean semantics and the latter are *forced* to adopt the **TRL** semantics. Here we will not investigate this problem, but in Sect. 4.5.4 we will show that the **TRL** semantics is not available for presentists and Growing Block theorists, for McCall's version of the Shrinking Block view and for the MST theorists. Only eternalists who accept indeterminism and who believe that just one branch exists can embrace the **TRL** semantics.

We now have sufficient tools of metaphysics and temporal logic to analyse the different solutions that have been proposed to the problem of the compatibility between divine prescience and human freedom. These tools will allow us to formulate precisely the different solutions and to evaluate the costs and the benefits of each of them. We will start with "extreme solutions", namely, with the solutions that tend to negate one of the horns of the dilemma: either divine prescience or human freedom.

References

Belnap, N., and M. Green. 1994. Indeterminism and the thin red line. *Philosophical Perspectives* 8: 365–388.

Belnap, N.D., M. Perloff, M. Xu, et al. 2001. *Facing the future: agents and choices in our indeterminist world*. Oxford: Oxford University Press.

Bourne, C. 2006. *A future for presentism*. Oxford: Oxford University Press.

Braüner, T., P. Hasle, and P. Øhstrøm. 2000. Determinism and the origins of temporal logic. In *Advances in temporal logic*, ed. H. Barringer, M. Fisher, D. Gabbay, and G. Gough, 185–206. Berlin: Springer.

Broad, C.D. 2014. *Scientific thought: A philosophical analysis of some of its fundamental concepts*. Abingdon: Routledge.

Cameron, R.P. 2015. *The moving spotlight: An essay on time and ontology*. Oxford: OUP Oxford.

Casati, R., and G. Torrengo. 2011. The not so incredible shrinking future. *Analysis* 71(2): 240–244.

De Florio, C., and A. Frigerio. 2019. Molinism and thin red line. *Journal of Logic, Language and Information*. https://doi.org/10.1007/s10849-019-09304-4.

De Florio, C., A. Frigerio, and A. Giordani. forthcoming. A logical framework for the spotlight theory of time. In *Logic and philosophy of time. Themes from prior II volume*, ed. P. Hasle, O. Blackburn, and P. Øhrstrøm. Aalborg: Aalborg University Press.

Fine, K. 2005. Tense and reality. In *Modality and tense: Philosophical papers*, ed. K. Fine, 261–320. Oxford: Oxford University Press.

Fine, K. 2006. The reality of tense. *Synthese* 150(3): 399–414.

Gilmore, C., D. Costa, and C. Calosi. 2016. Relativity and three four-dimensionalisms. *Philosophy Compass* 11(2): 102–120.

Haslanger, S. 2003. Persistence through time. In *The Oxford handbook of metaphysics*, ed. M.J. Loux, and D.W. Zimmerman, 315–354. Oxford: Oxford University Press.

Lewis, D. 1986. *On the plurality of worlds*. Oxford: Blackwell Publisher.

Loux, M.J., and T.M. Crisp. 2017. *Metaphysics: A contemporary introduction*. Abingdon: Routledge.

Lowe, J.E. 2002. *A survey of metaphysics*, vol. 15. Oxford: Oxford University Press.

MacFarlane, J. 2003. Future contingents and relative truth. *The Philosophical Quarterly* 53(212): 321–336.

Malpass, A., and J. Wawer. 2012. A future for the thin red line. *Synthese* 188(1): 117–142.

McCall, S. et al. 1994. *A model of the universe: Space-time, probability, and decision*. Oxford: Oxford University Press.

McTaggart, E.J. 1908. The unreality of time. *Mind* 17(68): 457–474.

Øhrstrøm, P. 2009. In defence of the thin red line: A case for Ockhamism. *Humana. mente* 8: 17–32.

Øhrstrøm, P., and P. Hasle. 2007. *Temporal logic: from ancient ideas to artificial intelligence*, vol. 57. Berlin: Springer.

Orilia, F. 2012. *Filosofia del tempo: Il dibattito contemporaneo*. Rome: Carocci.

Pasnau, R. 2011. On existing all at once. In *God, eternity, and time*, ed. C. Tapp, and E. Runggaldier, 11–28. Farnham: Ashgate Publishing.

Putnam, H. 1967. Time and physical geometry. *The Journal of Philosophy* 64(8): 240–247.

Quine, W.V.O. 1981. *Theories and things*. Cambridge: Harvard University Press.

Restall, G. 2011. Molinism and thin red line. In *Molinism: The contemporary debate*, ed. K. Perszyk, 227–238. Oxford: Oxford University Press.

Rosenkranz, S. 2012. In defence of ockhamism. *Philosophia* 40(3): 617–631.

Thomason, R.H. 1970. Indeterminist time and truth-value gaps. *Theoria* 36(3): 264–281.

Torrengo, G. 2011. *I viaggi nel tempo. Una guida filosofica*. Laterza.

Wawer, J. 2014. The truth about the future. *Erkenntnis* 79(3): 365–401.

3

Extreme Measures

In this chapter, we will analyse those views that we call *extreme measures* for the solution of the foreknowledge dilemma. They are extreme measures since they construe in a radical way the horns of the dilemma (either divine foreknowledge or human free will). Thus, the strategy of the advocates of the extreme measures is to redefine, on the one hand, divine omniscience in order to make it compatible with the divine ignorance of the outcomes of the future human actions and, on the other hand, human freedom in order to make it compatible with the principle according to which human beings cannot choose otherwise than they actually choose.

Given these hermeneutical manoeuvres, the views at issue are able to secure compatibility between divine omniscience and human freedom. There are, however, other troubles with these strategies; they are, so to speak, *external* questions: such views seem incompatible with what Scripture and Tradition affirm.[1] The Bible, at least in some passages, seems to endorse the Father's and Jesus' full foreknowledge of the outcomes

---

[1] In this chapter, we will mainly refer to Jewish and Christian Traditions. We believe, nevertheless, that many of the proposed analyses could be exported also to the Islamic Tradition, covering, then, the whole spectrum of monotheisms.

of human actions; on the other hand, the Bible implicitly assumes a libertarian conception of free will, according to which human beings have at least two alternatives to choose from. The Tradition of the Fathers of the Church, with some exceptions, assumed these two principles.

Since the difficulties of these views are largely theological, rather than philosophical, we do not dwell on details. The aim of this chapter is, on the contrary, to present the general conceptual framework of these positions, to show their philosophical advantages and to mention the theological difficulties they must deal with. In Sect. 3.1, we will focus on the attempt to redefine the concept of omniscience, while in Sect. 3.2, the redefinition of the concept of freedom is taken into account.

3.1 Open Theism

Let us briefly recap the argument that aims to show the incompatibility between divine foreknowledge and human freedom. Where p is an action performed by the agent a:

1. Yesterday God believed that p. (Divine foreknowledge)
2. If an event e occurred in the past, then it is accidentally necessary that e occurred then. (Necessity of the past)
3. It is now necessary that yesterday God believed p. (1, 2, *modus ponens*)
4. Necessarily, if yesterday God believed p, then p. (Infallibility of divine foreknowledge)
5. If r is accidentally necessary and if $\Box(r \rightarrow s)$, then it is accidentally necessary that s. (Principle of transfer of necessity)
6. So it is now necessary that p. (3, 4, 5)
7. If it is now necessary that p, then you cannot do otherwise than p. (Definition of necessary)
8. Therefore, you cannot do otherwise than p. (6, 7, *modus ponens*)
9. If you cannot do otherwise when you do an act, you do not do it freely. (Principle of Alternate Possibilities)
10. Therefore, when you do p, you will not do it freely. (8, 9, *modus ponens*)

One of the simplest ways to attack the argument is to deny premise 1: God does not foresee what the agent is going to do tomorrow. This is the solution to the dilemma proposed by so-called *Open Theism*, a current of thought that, among other things, aims to redefine the concept of divine omniscience.[2] Obviously, when the first premise is denied, the conclusion does not follow and free will is safe. Actually, open theists are convinced proponents of human freedom in a strong sense, that is, as the possibility of doing otherwise.

On open theists' agenda, God's ignorance of the free human choices is inscribed in a more general operation of rethinking God's concept. In the next subsection, we will briefly sketch this new idea of God. Let us consider, however, that open theists claim that their concept is new only with respect to the concept of God of classical theism; on the contrary, they argue that their God is closer to the Biblical God. In Sect. 3.1.2, we will take into account the different senses in which the future can be open, whereas in Sect. 3.1.3 we will see to which of these senses the open theist is committed. Section 3.1.4 focuses on the theological difficulties of Open Theism, while Sect. 3.1.5 contains some concluding words on this extreme solution.

3.1.1 A Different Concept of God

Open Theism is advocated both by philosophers (David Basinger, William Hasker, Richard Swinburne, Alan Rhoda) and by theologians (Gregory Boyd, Richard Rice, John Sanders, Clark Pinnock) belonging to different religious denominations, even though the Reformed are prevalent, whose reflection can be included within the analytical philosophy of religion. Open theists believe that the concept of God

---

[2] As we previously said, and as we will see in the following, one can deny the first premise by stating that God does not know in time: therefore, it is not correct to say that *yesterday* God believed that p (see Chap. 6). The negation of the open theist is more radical since it redefines the very idea of foreknowledge.

of the theistic tradition is, actually, a synthesis between the God of the Bible and Greek philosophy. So Sanders sums up:

> The early church fathers lived in the intellectual atmosphere where Greek philosophy (especially middle Platonism) dominated [...] Moreover, they saw a need to proclaim that the Father of Jesus was the universal God and not merely the ethnic God of the Jews. Hence, they sought to demonstrate that the Christian God was the author of all creation according to the idea of the universal God articulated by the philosophers.
>
> In seeking to accomplish these objectives the early fathers did not sell out to Hellenism, but they did, on certain key points, use it both to defend and to explain the Christian concept of God to their contemporaries. (Sanders 1994, pp. 59–60)

Greek Neoplatonist philosophy—which influenced the Fathers of the Church and many medieval thinkers, at least until the rediscovery of Aristotle's works of Physics and Metaphysics—believed that change is a sign of imperfection; a perfect being, consequently, is essentially immutable. That leads Plato to conceive the divine as totally impassible and structurally separated (transcendent) from the contingent features of the world. If God were capable of emotion, He would change and, therefore, He would lose His perfection. If God loved, He would be imperfect since, according to the platonic analysis of love, the lover needs the beloved. Actually, even the rediscovery of Aristotle's works did not substantially change this conception of the divine. According to Aristotle, God is an immutable being who thinks of Himself (since He can think only perfect things and He is the most perfect thing of all), totally disinterested in contingent facts of the world and in no way affected by them. He moves the Universe but only as final cause and not as an agent who intervenes upon it.

The Bible provides a completely different view of God: He is emotionally involved in human history and He acts on it, to such an extent that He incarnated in a human being. The Fathers of the Church and the Christian medieval philosophers tried to work out a synthesis between these two—somehow opposed—views of the divine:

> [...] their [of the early fathers] understanding of God is a mix of Greek metaphysics and biblical faith. They wrestled with how to explain the Christian God as the universal God of philosophical reflection. In faithfulness to the Bible they upheld God's love for and grace upon us [...] They also wished to maintain that God entered freely into relationship with humanity and in grace saves us. [...] In addition they understood the incarnation to be a decisive action of God in human history that dramatically altered the course of world history [...] On the other hand, many of these same desires are in conflict with other guiding beliefs drawn from Greek metaphysics. If God is utterly transcendent and immutable, then every change in the relationship between God and humanity must be explained as a human change. God does not have the sort of relationship with his creation by which he can be affected by what he loves. This begins to undermine God's freedom and the reality of his action in history. The doctrine of simplicity exacerbates this tension, forming a gap between the God of biblical history and the God of theological reflection, between the God for us and God in himself. (Sanders 1994, p. 79)

Influenced by Greek philosophy, the Fathers considered having parts as an imperfection; therefore, God must be completely simple, with no part. However, this seemed in tension with the doctrine of Trinity according to which God is a communion of Three Persons in just one Substance, and thus He is a complex being. Protestant Reformation—with its renewed attention to the Biblical text—might have endorsed a concept of God closer to that conveyed by the Bible; however, often this did not happen. For instance, Calvin keeps defining God as self-existent, simple, impassible and immutable. Augustine's influence—in turn influenced by Neoplatonism—on Luther and Calvin is one of the factors explaining the permanence of the Greek concept of God until today.

Open theists acknowledge that the synthesis of these two views also had positive effects: "The inevitable encounter between biblical and classical thought generated many significant insights and helped Christianity to evangelize pagan thought and culture".[3] However, in order to reconcile

---

[3] Sanders (1994, p. 99).

this conception with the passages of the Scripture in which God is affected by the contingency of the world and He is angry or happy for what has happened, different hermeneutical strategies have been proposed: according to some of them, those episodes are vestiges of an anthropomorphic conception of God or metaphors designed for pedagogical purposes. Likewise, the passages in which God changes His own plans must be construed in a similar vein.[4]

According to open theists, the present cultural climate—in which change is usually seen as positive, while immutability and stasis are considered as synonyms of stagnation[5]—can lead the theological reflection toward a rethinking of divine attributes, rejecting some features of God inherited from Greek philosophy and adopting a conception closer to Scripture.

The intuitions of open theists stem from the acknowledgement that all the attempts of conciliating divine foreknowledge and human free will will fail. If God has an immutable knowledge of all that will happen in future, then the future is already predetermined and there is no place for free will. At the same time, they believe that the traditional theism too strongly emphasized the absolute sovereignty of God in the world. A world in which God decides everything—down to the last detail—is a world that cancels human freedom. According to Richard Rice, the key claim of Open Theism is that *God's experience of the world is open and not closed.* God is a temporal being who records in an infallible, but progressive, way what is happening.[6]

---

[4] One of the most discussed passages is the one where God seems to be sorry about His desire to destroy the city of Nineveh: "'Who knows? God may yet relent and with compassion turn from his fierce anger so that we will not perish.' When God saw what they did and how they turned from their evil ways, he relented and did not bring on them the destruction he had threatened" (Jonah 3, 9–10).

[5] See Pinnock (1994, pp. 103–105); see also Hasker (1994), who claims: "For us moderns, this preference for permanence over change is scarcely compelling. Indeed, it is arguable that in our intellectual life as well as in our general culture the pendulum has swung too far in the other direction, so that if anything at all remains constant for a while our response is one of boredom and impatience. Be that as it may, the extreme valuational preference for immutability has little hold on our thinking, and the appeal of theological doctrines based on this valuation is weakened accordingly" (p. 129).

[6] See Rice (2004, pp. 25–26).

Since the world is open and the relation between God and the world is open, open theists emphasize that one of the fundamental features that characterizes the relation that God has with human beings is that of *risk*. God cannot foresee what human beings will freely decide, and therefore He accepts the risk that they make up their minds contrary to His wishes. He accepts the risk that humans pull away from Him and, maybe, reject Him. In Hasker's words: "God takes risks if he makes decisions that depend on their outcomes on the responses of free creatures in which the decisions themselves are not informed by knowledge of the outcomes" (Hasker 2004, p. 125). It follows that God has to adjust His providential plan in accordance with what, from time to time, is happening in the world. Of course, the general objectives of God's plan are fixed: they consist in the universal salvation of all human beings and in their communion with Him. However, the particular decisions humans make in contingent situations can have an impact on the strategies God adopts in order to achieve His ends. So, on the one hand, God reacts to humans' choices; on the other hand, He changes as a consequence of such choices. God's reactions are emotional too: God can get angry, be disappointed, be delighted for human behaviour. According to Rice: "God is responsive to what happens in the creaturely world, [...] what happens there affects God somehow—by evoking a certain emotion, a change in attitude, a change in plans." (Rice 1994, p. 18). From a purely epistemic point of view, this entails that God can be *surprised* by unexpected developments of the history of the world. And the idea of epistemic surprise is at odds with the idea of omniscience.

This way of conceiving the relations between God and the world leads us to redefine certain divine attributes by emphasizing some of them at the expense of others traditionally ascribed to God. Certainly, love is the fundamental divine quality for open theists; God is a loving person: "From a Christian perspective, love is the first and last word in the biblical portrait of God. According to 1 John 4:8: 'Whoever does not love does not know God, because God is love.' The statement God is love is as close as the Bible comes to giving us a definition of the divine reality (Sanders 1994, p. 18)". Precisely because God is love, God is not totally immutable: "[L]ove is the most important quality we attribute to God, and love is more than care and commitment; it involves being sensitive and responsive as well. These convictions lead the contributors to this book to think of God's relation to the world in dynamic rather than static terms" (Sanders 1994, p. 15). Therefore, the attribute of immutability, cherished by classical theism, has to be redefined. Fair enough, it is not denied that God has a stable essence, but it is underlined that this does not entail His immutability. God's immutability must be construed, then, rather as *faithfulness*: God is faithful to His own loving nature, to the promises made to humans and to His plan of salvation: "God's character is faithful and reliable—he is a steadfast friend who binds himself to us and does not forsake us. His concern for the creature is constant and unaffected by anything. From the point of view of experience, however, God responds to the changing needs of his children and changes direction when necessary. God is changeless in nature, but his nature is that of a Creative person who interacts" (Pinnock 1994, p. 118). Also the *eternity* of God has to be reinterpreted. God has always existed and will exist forever and, in such sense, He is eternal; but it does not mean that He is out of time. Since God is subjected to change, He experiences the before and the after, as human beings: "When I say that God is eternal, I mean that God transcends our experience of time, is immune from the ravages of time, is free from our inability to remember, and so forth. I affirm that God is with us in time, experiencing the succession of events with us. Past, present and future are real to God." (Pinnock 1994, p. 120). Finally, there are divine attributes that, according to open theists, must not be reinterpreted but completely abandoned: *simplicity* and *impassibility*. Concerning the latter, they observe that "is the most dubious of the divine attributes discussed in classical theism, because it suggests that God does not experience sorrow, sadness or pain. It appears to deny that God is touched by the feelings of our infirmities, despite what the Bible eloquently says about his love and his sorrow" (Pinnock 1994, p. 118). The doctrine of divine simplicity seems to be incompatible with a changing God since change entails complexity. Moreover, it seems at odds with a personal God, who has intentions, thoughts and emotions and with the idea that God is triune, namely, a communion of three different Persons.

Open theists believe that omniscience is a traditional feature of God which has to be redefined but not abandoned. The redefinition of this attribute is necessary in light of the openness of the future. Open theists believe that the openness of the future has a crucial impact on the possibility of foreseeing it and, thus, on God's knowledge of future human actions. However, there are many senses in which the future is open, and these senses have an intricate net of connections. Given the centrality of this topic for this book and given the philosophical interest of this question, we will dedicate to it the next subsection. In Sect. 3.1.3, we will see to which senses of the openness of the future Open Theism and other theological conceptions are committed.

3.1.2 The Openness of the Future

In this section, we will take into account the different senses in which the future can be open, drawing on an interesting paper of Rhoda's (Rhoda 2011). He argues that the open God and the open world are two tightly connected concepts. A world with an open future entails an open God, who is able to react to the changes happening in the world; on the other hand, an open God, who wants to enter into communion with His creatures, entails the existence of an open future, which human beings are able, at least partially, to determine. But what does it mean to say that the world is open? According to Rhoda, there are at least five different meanings at play: causal, ontic,[7] alethic, epistemic and providential.

- The world is **causally** open if the past does not fully determine the future. According to our definition of determinism (see Chap. 1), the causal openness of the world is the negation of determinism: the present state of the world and the laws do not univocally determine what will happen in the future.
- the world is **ontologically** open "relative to time t if and only if the world state at t does not stand in an earlier than relation to a unique and complete series of subsequent world states" (p. 73). Rhoda remarks that

---

[7] Some authors use the term "ontic"; others, "ontological". Since the alleged difference of these two terms is probably rooted in the obscurities of phenomenology, we will use "ontic" and "ontological" indifferently.

an ontologically open world "implies a dynamic, non-eternalist theory of time—one which either denies the existence of future world states or admits their existence but denies that they constitute a unique and complete series" (p. 74).[8]

- The world is **alethically** open if at least one of the future tensed sentences is neither true nor false. The alethic openness of the world, as Rhoda understands it, is then incompatible not only with determinist views according to which it is already true that tomorrow φ will happen, since the state of the world and the causal laws determine what will happen tomorrow, but also with theories like **TRL** according to which, even if indeterminism holds, one of the future branches is privileged, since it is what will actually happen tomorrow.
- The future is, moreover, **epistemically** open if and only if there is (at least) a future tensed proposition (**F**φ), whose truth value is impossible to know even for an epistemically perfect being.
- Finally, the world is **providentially** open if and only if there are future states of affairs that have not been efficaciously ordained, where "for an agent S to efficaciously ordain X is for S deliberately to act in a way that guarantees the eventual occurrence of X and for S to know with certainty that in so acting he is guaranteeing the eventual occurrence of X" (*ibidem*, p. 76). Rhoda makes explicit that a providentially open world is a world where the so called meticulous providence does not hold; that is, a world in which not every tiniest detail has been either directly arranged by God or indirectly determined by putting human beings in certain situations in which they will make certain choices. In a providential open world, God has only *general* providential strategies.

---

[8] Here, it seems that Rhoda is confusing the ontology of time, its dynamics, and its topology. As we have seen in Sect. 2.5, it is possible to accept both Eternalism and branching time. In that case, at time t, there are many complete series of subsequent world states, but no dynamics at all. On the other hand, it is possible to endorse a Moving Spotlight Theory with no branching. However, in the following, Rhoda makes clear that he is thinking about Presentism or the Growing Block view or Erosionism (probably in a version similar to McCall's) as the metaphysics of time that make the future ontologically open. Let us notice, nevertheless, that the open theist views are compatible also with an eternalist dynamic view of time with an open future: for instance, a Moving Spotlight Theory with many future branches, in which it is not always determined which branch the light will illuminate.

Let us call **C**, **O**, **A**, **E** and **P** the theses according to which the world is respectively causally, ontologically, alethically, epistemically and providentially open. These theses are not independent of each other and are tightly interconnected. Rhoda has proposed a series of implications among them. As we will see, some of them are plausible, others are far less convincing. Rhoda claims that the following entailments hold:

A → **E**: According to Rhoda, this is a platitude since it stems from the principle that knowledge entails truth. If a proposition lacks truth value, it cannot be known. Actually, in Chap. 6, we will show that if God is out of time, this implication is not so plain as it could seem *prima facie*. Anyway, since in this context we assume that God is a temporal being, the principle holds.

E → **C**: If the world is causally closed (if it holds that ¬**C**), then an epistemically perfect being can know the future, by knowing the present state of the universe and its development laws. So, we have that ¬**C** → ¬**E**, from which, by logic, **E** → **C**.

E → **O**: If there is a unique series of future events that follow the present state of the world, then an epistemically perfect being should know that series and therefore the truth values of all future propositions. A future tensed proposition is true if and only if it is made true by the facts that happen in the future series.[9] Thus ¬**O** → ¬**E**, from which, by logic, **E** → **O**.

E → **P**: If God meticulously ordered all the future events, He knows these events in full detail. Therefore, ¬**P** → ¬**E**, from which, by logic, the principle follows.

Therefore, according to Rhoda, if one accepts the alethic openness of the future, one is also accepting the other four kinds of openness, that is **A** → (**E** ∧ **C** ∧ **O** ∧ **P**).

E → **A**: It follows from the assumption according to which an omniscient being knows all the true propositions. One could object by

---

[9] Let us notice that the existence of a unique series of future events is compatible with indeterminism and, therefore, with **C**. For instance, one could endorse a branching Eternalism and state that the events that happen at a certain point of the block do not causally determine those happening at the subsequent points; nonetheless, one could affirm that only one history actually exists, while alternative histories are pure possibilities.

arguing that there are true propositions that even an epistemically perfect being cannot know, just as there are actions that even an almighty being cannot perform.[10] For the moment, we assume this principle; in the following, we will discuss a possible criticism.

From $\mathbf{A} \to \mathbf{E}$ and $\mathbf{E} \to \mathbf{A}$, we can deduce $\mathbf{A} \leftrightarrow \mathbf{E}$, and from $\mathbf{A} \leftrightarrow \mathbf{E}$ and $\mathbf{A} \to (\mathbf{E} \wedge \mathbf{C} \wedge \mathbf{O} \wedge \mathbf{P})$, it is possible to deduce $\mathbf{E} \to (\mathbf{A} \wedge \mathbf{C} \wedge \mathbf{O} \wedge \mathbf{P})$.

If we are taking into account only an epistemically perfect temporal being, these conclusions are surely plausible. Moreover, Rhoda proposes further interconnections.

$(\mathbf{C} \wedge \mathbf{O}) \to \mathbf{A}$, $(\mathbf{C} \wedge \mathbf{O}) \to \mathbf{E}$, $(\mathbf{C} \wedge \mathbf{O}) \to \mathbf{P}$: In words: if we accept the causal and ontic openness of the future, it is necessary to accept also the other kinds of openness. Rhoda's argument for $(\mathbf{C} \wedge \mathbf{O}) \to \mathbf{A}$[11] is based on the assumption that (contingent) truth supervenes on being (**TSB**). In other terms, "According to **TSB**, every (contingent) difference in truth corresponds to a (contingent) difference in being, such that if anything that is true had not been true, then there would have been a corresponding difference in reality [...] In other words, reality must be sufficiently robust to discriminate propositions that are (contingently) true from those that aren't" (p. 82).

In the next chapter, when we analyse the possible combinations between TRL semantics and different metaphysics of time, we will show that the entailment defended by Rhoda is sound and that TRL semantics is in tension with Presentism and the Growing Block theory.

From $(\mathbf{C} \wedge \mathbf{O}) \to \mathbf{A}$ and from $\mathbf{A} \to \mathbf{O}$ it follows that $\mathbf{C} \to (\mathbf{A} \equiv \mathbf{O})$, and from $(\mathbf{C} \wedge \mathbf{O}) \to \mathbf{E}$ and from $\mathbf{E} \to \mathbf{O}$ it follows that $\mathbf{C} \to (\mathbf{E} \equiv \mathbf{O})$. Analogous claims hold also for **P**. Consequently, Rhoda comes to the conclusion that:

$$\mathbf{C} \to (\mathbf{O} \equiv \mathbf{A} \equiv \mathbf{E} \equiv \mathbf{P})$$

Thus, it is sufficient to prove that **C** entails at least one of the other kinds of openness to show that it entails all the other kinds of openness.

---

[10] Cf. Hasker (1998, p. 187), and Hasker (2001, pp. 110–111).
[11] Given that $\mathbf{A} \leftrightarrow \mathbf{E}$ and $\mathbf{E} \to \mathbf{P}$, it is sufficient to prove the first principle in order to get the other two.

Rhoda maintains that it is *probable* that at least one of these entailments is valid. However, there are reasons to doubt that it is actually so. Let us consider them one by one:

1. **C → O**: If this principle held, all the eternalist metaphysics that believe that the future exists but it is not determined would be incoherent. It would not be possible to conceive a scenario in which the past stages of the block do not determine the future stages. In other terms, it would exclude a branching time in which one of the future branches is actually existent while the others could have been actualized. Rhoda's answer is that there is no reason to affirm that one of the branches is privileged, since the future is indeterminate. The standard reply is that one of the branches is actually privileged since, contingently, it is what is going to happen. Of course, this line of thought can be resisted, but the implication is far from obvious.
2. **C → A**: If this were true, **TRL** semantics would be inconsistent. However, if one accepts a branching Eternalism such as that described in the previous point, **TRL** semantics is not only coherent but seems the only plausible option. Since, as said before, this metaphysical framework is not plainly false, the implication is not obvious.
3. **C → E**: If so, then all attempts to reconcile human free will and divine foreknowledge would be doomed to failure. But it is far from obvious that these attempts are false, so this principle is not obvious.
4. **C → P**: As we will see in Chap. 5, Molinism is precisely the attempt to reconcile human freedom with the idea of meticulous providence, that is, the idea according to which God ordered the facts in the world down to the smallest detail. Molinism is a controversial theory but it has intelligent advocates; therefore, this principle is far from trivial.

Since none of these implications is trivial, even if it is held that $C \rightarrow (O \equiv A \equiv E \equiv P)$, it does not follow that, given the causal openness of the world, one is forced to accept the other kinds of openness.

3.1.3 To What Openness Is the Open Theist Committed?

In this section, we will see what kinds of openness Open Theism is committed to. We will also compare Open Theism with other theological conceptions, which accept different levels of openness of the future. We will start by considering the more restrictive conceptions and we will then move to more and more liberal views before arriving at the most liberal of all, Open Theism.

Theological determinism is the position according to which God is the cause of every event in the world and, therefore, He determines the history down to the tiniest detail. Therefore, theological determinism is committed to ¬**C**, that is, a deterministic view of the world. So, it must assume a compatibilist conception of free will. Since **E** → **C** holds, theological determinism is also committed to the epistemic closedness of the world: God, ordering every detail of history, already knows what's going to happen. Consequently, theological determinism is committed to ¬**E**. Given that we assume **A** ↔ **E**, it is also committed to ¬**A**: every proposition about the future is true or false. Lastly, theological determinism is *a fortiori* committed to ¬**P**, since God causes everything that happens down to the last detail. The only openness of the future compatible with theological determinism is therefore **O**. The future can be seen as determined but not as actually existent.

As will be clear in Chap. 5, Molinism rejects ¬**C**, since it affirms a strong conception of freedom. However, it agrees with theological determinism in refuting **A**, **E** and **P**; Molinism claims (1) that all future tensed propositions—even those about free acts—are true or false, (2) that God knows the truth value of all these propositions and (3) that God has set up every detail of the world. However, Molinism, unlike determinism, does not state that God directly causes what happens, but that He has put human beings into conditions such that they will freely choose in a certain way. God, then, directly or indirectly (through free human actions) rules the world down to the last detail (meticulous providence). To sum up, the Molinist accepts **C** and can also accept **O**, if she likes the anti-realist metaphysical views about the future.

The so called theory of *simple foreknowledge*, compared to Molinism, denies that God can know what *possible* human agents will freely perform in every *possible* situation (it denies that God has *middle knowledge*) and therefore it accepts **P**: God cannot establish every detail of the world. However, God foresees what *actual* agents will do in the *actual* worldly situations. Therefore, this view is committed to ¬**E** and, consequently, given that we assume the temporality of God and that **A** → **E** does hold, it is committed to ¬**A** too. Consequently, the advocate of simple foreknowledge is committed to **C** and **P**; if her preferences about the future are anti-realist, she is also committed to **O**.

Finally, an open theist is committed to:

(a) a strong conception of free will—that is, a libertarian one—according to which the state and the context in which the agent finds herself do not determine what she is going to do in the future. The agent can do otherwise than she actually does.
(b) the view that God cannot foresee what human beings are going to do. He must know the free decisions of the agents *after* they are made.
(c) the negation of meticulous providence. God has a general providential plan for the world, but it does not include every last detail.

All open theists claim that these three commitments are intertwined and, in particular, that b. follows from a. and c. from b. It is in virtue of the strong conception of freedom that God cannot foresee the future in every detail, and from that it follows that meticulous providence is impossible. However, open theists differ about the reasons why b. follows from a. At least two paths are available. The first is adopted by William Hasker. He maintains the soundness of **C** → **E**,[12] but he denies **C** → **A** and consequently he does not accept that **E** ↔ **A**. In other terms, on the one hand, Hasker denies that even an epistemically perfect being is able to know the outcomes of free human actions; on the other hand, however, he does not exclude that the future is alethically closed, that is, that the propositions about the future contingents are true or false. Accordingly,

---

[12] As we have seen, this implication is not obvious.

there are true propositions that even an epistemically perfect being cannot know: for instance, the proposition that tomorrow Emma will drink a beer could already be true today, but God cannot know that it is true. He is, then, forced to redefine the attribute of omniscience:

Hasker's omniscience: God is omniscient $=_{def}$ it is impossible that God should at any time believe what is false or fail to know any true proposition such that his knowing that proposition at that time is logically possible (Hasker 1998, p. 187; see also Hasker 2001, p. 111)

To sum up, Hasker accepts at least **C**, **P** and **E**, but not **A**; if he assumes, as we do, that **E** $\rightarrow$ **O**, he should also accept **O**.

The second path from a. to b. claims that **C** $\rightarrow$ **A**[13] and then, through the equivalence **E** $\leftrightarrow$ **A**, it comes to **E**. In other terms, it is maintained that freedom in the libertarian sense actually entails that the future is alethically open; therefore, future contingents are neither true nor false, and even an omniscient being cannot know them.[14] If we go down this road, we can keep the equivalence between what an epistemically perfect agent can know and what is true:

Traditional omniscience: $K(a, p) \leftrightarrow p$

In words: a being a is omniscient if and only if for every true proposition p, a knows p and, trivially, every proposition p known by a is true. The left-to-right direction is analytic of the definition of knowledge.

What kind of Open Theism has better prospects? We agree with Rhoda that the second path is the more promising. If one accepts the view according to which the alethic closeness of the future is not incompatible with human freedom (in a libertarian sense)—that is, if one accepts a **TRL** semantics for the future—it is very hard to maintain that the *knowledge*

---

[13] As we have seen, this implication is not obvious in light of TRL semantics.
[14] Rhoda (2008, 2011) expresses his own preference for this view. It is also assumed by Lucas (1989) and by Sanders (1997), who states: "God's knowledge is coextensive with reality…the future actions of free creatures are not yet reality, and so there is nothing to know" (p. 198).

of that truth is not incompatible with free will. In other terms, if the truth of the proposition that Emma will drink a beer tomorrow is not incompatible with Emma's free will, why should the knowledge of this proposition be incompatible?

Moreover, the second kind of Open Theism is not forced to revise the traditional definition of omniscience. Hasker tries to justify his move by claiming that the manoeuvre transfers to the concept of omniscience what has been, usually, done with the concept of omnipotence. Just as omnipotence is not defined as the power of doing everything, but as the power of doing everything that is possible (e.g. God cannot draw a square circle because it is not possible to draw a square circle), so omniscience can be defined not as the knowledge of everything that is true, but as the knowledge of everything that it is possible to know. There are doubts about the cogency of this analogy. Drawing a square circle is not a possible action: not only does no action like that exist, but it cannot exist. Therefore, God cannot perform impossible tasks. However, knowing a true proposition is something possible, and therefore it is not clear why an omniscient being should be unable to know it.

Finally, the second kind of Open Theism is able to answer the classical theist criticism of giving up the "natural" concept of divine omniscience. Open theists can reply that their concept of omniscience is the traditional one: God knows all the truths. The difference with classical theism lies, instead, in the semantics of the propositions about future contingents which, according to Open Theism, lack truth values.

So, if we accept the second version of Open Theism, since we assume that $\mathbf{E} \rightarrow \mathbf{O}$, then we are committed to the openness of the future in all five senses here mentioned; according to the best version of Open Theism, the future is causally, providentially, epistemically, alethically and ontologically open.

3.1.4 Theological Difficulties

Both the conjunction of **C**, **P** and **E**—common to all open theists—and the conjunction of all five kinds of openness of the future are coherent and represent genuine metaphysical and semantic possibilities. It is a different story whether this view is a good description of the world. Open

Theism is immune to the fatalist argument; its difficulties are, instead, of a theological nature. In the following, we will briefly present those connected with the concepts of omniscience and providence. This is not, however, a book about theology, so we will touch upon these questions without any pretence of being exhaustive.

Difficulties Connected with E

Open theists believe that God does not foresee the future in every detail: the future is, then, epistemically open even for a perfect being such as God. Therefore, open theists have to interpret those biblical passages in which God (or one of His messengers) prophesies the outcome of human free choices. Secondarily, they must argue that the classical theist tradition, which is almost unanimous in conceiving God as omniscient in a strong sense, is wrong. Let us start with the first order of difficulties.

One of the most problematic points is, of course, prophecy. In the Bible, there are many examples of prophecies in which God—or a prophet—foresees the outcome of a free choice. Open theists construe the prophecies according to three possible lines of thought:

> Some prophecies—perhaps more than have generally been so recognized—are conditional on the actions of human beings. Others are predictions based on existing trends and tendencies, while still others are announcements of what God himself intends to bring about irrespective of the choices made by creaturely agents (Hasker 2004, p. 104)

About the first kind, Rice remarks:

> A prophecy may [...] express what God intends to do *if* certain conditions obtain. This is what a conditional prophecy represents—a prediction as to what will happen if human beings behave in one way rather than another. According to Jeremiah 18, prophecies of destruction will not come to pass if people turn from their evil ways, nor will prophecies of blessing be fulfilled if people disobey (Rice 2004, pp. 51–52)

About the second kind, Hasker says:

> A second important category [...] must include prediction based on foresight drawn from existing trends and tendencies. Even from our grossly

inadequate knowledge of such trends and tendencies, we invest enormous amounts of energy trying to make forecasts in this way; evidently God with his perfect knowledge could do it much better (Hasker 1998, pp. 194–195).

About the third kind of prophecies, again Rice:

> A prophecy may express God's intention to do something in the future irrespective of creaturely decision. If God's will is the only condition required for something to happen, if human cooperation is not involved, then God can unilaterally guarantee its fulfilment, and he can announce it ahead of time (Rice 2004, p. 51)

The obvious question is whether *all* the biblical prophecies can be interpreted in one of these three ways. To give a taste of the connected problems, let us take the most quoted example: Jesus predicts that Peter will disown him three times before the rooster crows. Hasker considers it a prophecy of the second kind:

> Jesus was able to predict Peter's betrayal because he knew something about Peter which Peter himself did not know, namely, that Peter, though brave enough in a fight even against the odds (as in the Garden of Gethsemane), lacked the specific sort of courage as well as the faith needed to acknowledge his allegiance in a threatening situation where physical resistance was impossible (Hasker 1998, p. 195)

In other words, Hasker maintains that Christ could predict Peter's betrayal because he knew his personality very well and, thus, he could prophesy what Peter would do in that situation. This response is puzzling in two respects. First, Hasker himself insists on several occasions that the character of a person can make *probable*, or even *very probable*, that she will behave in a certain way, but not *sure* or *necessary*. If it is sure or necessary that the agent will behave in a certain way, she is not really free, according to the libertarian view of freedom. By consequence, if Peter freely betrayed Jesus, it was not *true* before the betrayal that he would betray him; it was just *probable*. On this view, Christ's prediction should be read as stating not that it was true that Peter would betray him, but that the betrayal was probable. This interpretation is obviously disputable. The second point is even stronger. Jesus states that Peter will disown him three times before the rooster crows. Is it possible to foresee, only on the basis of Peter's personality, that he would disown Jesus *three times* and that he would do it *before* the rooster crows? The prophecy is too specific for being formulated only on the basis of Peter's personality. Such prophecy should consist of more generic assertions than Jesus' ones. Christ's prophecy seems to be based on a clear knowledge of what will happen and not on a hypothesis, however probable, about what might happen. Obviously, this single example does not prove that the open theist interpretation of prophecy is incorrect. However, it shows the kind of problems they must deal with.

The other family of difficulties, as we said before, concerns Tradition. Tradition is almost unanimous from the very beginning in ascribing to God full foreknowledge and control of the creation (Justin Martyr, Origen, Tertullian, Damascene, Chrysostom, Jerome, Augustine and Cyril are often quoted on this subject). Voices of opposition, if any, are very rare.[15] Open theists must state that Christianity has dropped a collective brick on this point. Naturally, the arguments that refer to Tradition are never decisive and their theoretical weight is, in turn, the object of debate. However, they cannot be set aside a priori.

Difficulties Concerning P

As open theists have argued repeatedly, **P** has unquestionable advantages. The advocate of the meticulous providence must concede that God planned also evil and suffering in the world. The problem is especially serious for theological determinists, according to whom God is the direct or indirect *cause* of all what happens in the world, and thus He is responsible for evil occurring in it. It is hard to understand how a morally perfect God can cause evil. The problem is slightly mitigated for theories such as Molinism according to which—as we will see in the following— the responsibility for moral evil is attributable to human agents. However, Molinists claim that God put human agents in certain circumstances *C* knowing, with absolute certainty, that, in those circumstances, they would

---

[15] For this line of argument, see for instance, Flint (1998, ch. 1).

freely choose to act badly. The question is why God did not choose to create human agents that, put in certain circumstances, always choose to do good or, at least, not do horrendous evils. Plantinga replied to this objection by means of his hypothesis of *transworld depravity*, that is, by means of the hypothesis that God did not have any choice but to create human agents that do wrong actions because no possible agent he could create would always act goodly. This hypothesis is, however, very demanding from the metaphysical point of view and, even if it were true, it likely would not solve the problem.[16] Here, it seems that open theists are in a better position: they claim that God has "only" a general salvific plan toward the creation and, therefore, He neither causes the moral evil in the world nor foresees it. Evil is, then, totally dependent on human beings.

However, **P** is puzzling for other reasons. By creating free human beings and being unable to foresee their actions, God runs the *risk* that they do horrendous evils. Moreover, He accepts the risk that nobody positively answers His call, that there is no Church, and nobody is saved.[17]

In other terms, God lacks full control of His own creation, and this seems to affect His *sovereignty* over the world. However, we would like a God who is in control of this creation, whose salvific plan will be brought to the end without any doubt or chance of failure. One of the reasons to trust God is the confidence that the world will proceed towards His Reign and that He is fully able to bring the world to this end. Critics of Open Theism underlined how **P** harms the absolute trust we are supposed to place in God. Bruce Ware is in this line of thought, for instance:

> [. . .] the hope of Scripture is based on the certainty of God's work and the unfailing accomplishment of his wise and good purposes and plans. Where

---

[16] For a detailed criticism of the hypothesis of transworld depravity, see De Florio and Frigerio (2013).

[17] "God allows the world to be affected by the power of the creature and takes risks accompanying any genuine relatedness. There is a paradox of strength and vulnerability of God according to the Scriptures. Though ontologically strong, God can be vulnerable because of the decision to make a world like this. The Lord of the universe has chosen to limit his power by delegating some to the creature. God gives room to creatures and invites them to be covenant partners, opening up the possibility of loving fellowship but also of some initiative being taken away from God and creatures coming into conflict with his plans" (Pinnock 1994, p. 115).

> Open Theism reduces our hope to something unavoidably fragile and weak, the Bible commends a hope that is strong, secure, fixed, and certain. Life is purposeful, and the God who gives himself to us is the conquering God who will lead us in his triumph. Our hope is secure, it is filled with joy and peace, and it will last eternally. [...] The openness God unavoidably makes all kinds of mistakes—mistakes in his guidance, mistakes in his dealings with free moral agents, mistakes in his own actions and responses—but the true God chooses perfectly, designs flawlessly, and accomplishes his will as he alone knows is best. The openness God cannot guarantee whether eternity will be what he hopes it will be, any more than he can guarantee that he'll get what he wants now, or in the immediate future, or in the distant future [...] The certainty of hope that is founded in the true and living God is simply diminished and defeated by Open Theism's understanding of God (Ware 2003, pp. 125–126)

To these criticisms, open theists have replied with two arguments:

1. Every love relationship, if genuine, does entail a certain amount of risk. Otherwise, it is not a love relationship but a form of absolute control.
2. The risk God is taking is, anyway, limited. By having unlimited resources, God will succeed in carrying out His general plan of salvation, even though some human beings pull away from Him. The failure of the divine plan is, then, limited to single cases but will never be general.

Concerning the first point, open theists argue that we have to choose between two conceptions of God: either that of an absolute monarch who reigns over the universe and human decisions or that of a father who enters into relation with His creatures. By accepting the second model, we accept at the same time that God takes the risk of being rejected. If we would like to avoid this risk, we must accept the first model:

> We may think of God primarily as an aloof monarch, removed from the contingencies of the world, unchangeable in every aspect of being, as an all-determining and irresistible power, aware of everything that will ever happen and never taking risks. Or we may understand God as a caring parent with qualities of love and responsiveness, generosity and sensitivity,

openness and vulnerability, a person (rather than a metaphysical principle) who experiences the world, responds to what happens, relates to us and interacts dynamically with humans (Pinnock 1994, p. 103)

Concerning the second point, open theists underline that divine omnipotence allows God to intervene in any situations and arrange things so that the world will go along with His desires. God's perfections (perfect knowledge, power of persuasion, infinite wisdom) should make us confident that the divine plan will be realized. A very illuminating metaphor is that of the Chess Master who plays against a beginner. The development of the match is not a priori predictable, and the Grand Master will adapt his moves to those of the beginner. But the outcome of the game is fully granted:

> God is the supreme Grand Master who has everything under his control. Some of the players are consciously helping his plan, others are trying to hinder it; whatever the finite players do, God's plan will be executed; though various lines of God's play will answer to various moves of the finite players. God cannot be surprised or thwarted or cheated or disappointed. God, like some grand master of chess, can carry out his plan even if he has announced it beforehand. "On that square," says the Grand Master, "I will promote my pawn to Queen and deliver checkmate to my adversary": and it is even so. No line of play that finite players may think of can force God to improvise: his knowledge of the game already embraces all the possible variant lines of play, theirs does not. (Geach 1977, p. 58)

Whether these answers are sufficient is the object of debate between open theists and their opponents concerning the acceptance of **P**.

3.1.5 Conclusions on Open Theism

Open Theism is a theological movement that aims to redefine the concept of God, by bringing it closer to the biblical understanding and abandoning the influences of Greek philosophy. As a matter of fact, the God of classical theism is an absolutely transcendent, immutable and impassible being. He is the sovereign of His creation, which He rules in every detail. Open theists, on the contrary, propose the image of a parent, who takes care of the creation by entering into relation with it; God is affected by the plans and desires of human beings, and He modifies His knowledge and His plans as a consequence of this love relationship.

We have analysed in which senses the future can be open, which interconnections exist among these senses and to which of them Open Theism is committed. We have argued that the most promising version of Open Theism accepts all five senses of openness of the future. From a conceptual point of view, the theses of Open Theism are coherent. Stating human freedom but denying that God foresees the outcomes of the free actions of human beings, Open Theism dissolves the foreknowledge problem by simply denying one of the horns of the dilemma. The difficulties of Open Theism are of different sorts, more theological than philosophical: is the concept of God advocated by open theists really in accordance with the God of the Bible?

As we said in the Preface, this is not a book on theology, and therefore our discussion about Open Theism is limited to its purely philosophical features. Moreover, we have no competence for taking a stand about the process of dehellenization of the Bible's God. We think, however, that the perfect being theology—with all its ontological and logical commitments—can provide a kind of *theological explanation* for some characters of God, which the very open theist wants to preserve. For instance, God is provident *because* He is omniscient, and He is able to unconditionally love *because* He is an absolute being, free from human imperfections. From this point of view, the ascription of perfection to God not only is not in contrast to His most "human" qualities; it is, in a certain sense, the ultimate ground of them.

3.2 Theological Determinism

Let us take into account, once again, the argument that aims to show the alleged incompatibility between divine foreknowledge and human free will:

1. Yesterday, God believed that *p*. [Divine foreknowledge]
2. If an event *e* occurred in the past, then it is accidentally necessary that *e* occurred then. [Necessity of the past]

3. It is accidentally necessary that yesterday God believed that p. [1, 2]
4. Necessarily, if God believes that p, p is true. [Infallibility of divine knowledge]
5. If r is accidentally necessary and if $\Box(r \rightarrow s)$, then s is accidentally necessary. [Transfer of Necessity Principle]
6. It is accidentally necessary that p. [3, 4, 5]
7. If p is accidentally necessary, then an agent a cannot do otherwise than p. [Definition of necessity]
8. a cannot do otherwise than p. [6, 7]
9. If, when she acts, an agent cannot do otherwise, then she does not act freely. [Libertarian freedom]
10. When a does p, a is not free. [8, 9]

Another way to block the argument, in some ways opposed to the Open Theism strategy, is to deny premise 9; that is, to state that one is free even if she is not able to do otherwise. In other terms, according to the advocates of this view, even if divine foreknowledge in some way *determines* the course of human actions, that does not entail that human beings are not free. *Compatibilism* is the view according to which human freedom is compatible with the impossibility of doing otherwise; *incompatibilism*, on the contrary, denies that freedom and impossibility of doing otherwise are compatible.

Therefore, the compatibilist can maintain a determinist view of the evolution of the universe. The topology of time is linear: given the conditions and the laws of the world at t_0, there is just one possible development of the history of the world at t_1. On the contrary, those who believe that free will requires the power of doing otherwise (and believe that there is actually free will) have to admit that the topology of time is branching and thus that the future is (at least partially) open.

While Open Theism strongly affirms human free will in the libertarian sense and it looks for a metaphysics of time, a semantics of future tensed sentences and a theology that are compatible with that key principle, theological determinism underlines God's foreknowledge (and, often, His full sovereignty over the universe) by proposing a concept of free will compatible with this other key principle. For that reason, we include this view among the extreme measures, although of opposite sign.

Open Theism is not a mainstream view; however, its advocates are not a tiny minority, and there exists a lively debate on the theoretical questions they emphasize. On the contrary, theological determinism is a position that, although it boasts illustrious predecessors (Augustine, Aquinas, Luther and Calvin are often considered to propose views akin to theological determinism), is very marginal in the current debate. This is a little bit paradoxical since in the wider debate about free will, compatibilism is surely a leading view, maybe more popular than incompatibilism. Since theological compatibilists—in order to argue that determinism is compatible with human free will—hinge on some theses defended by non-theological compatibilists, in the following, we will briefly sketch the key concepts of (non-theological) compatibilism (Sect. 3.2.1); then, we will apply those theses to the theological issues (Sect. 3.2.2).

3.2.1 Non Theological Compatibilism

There are at least two versions of (non-theological) compatibilism: *classical compatibilism* and *new compatibilism*. Let us start with the former, since it is the older version of this view.

Classical (non-Theological) Compatibilism
Classical compatibilism, which has among its founders philosophers such as Hobbes, Locke and Hume, focuses on the power (or ability) to do something and on the *constraints* or *impediments* that might prevent to do something. For instance, Emma could be prevented from going to the party tonight in many ways: by "inner" physical impediments (paralysis, disease), by "outer" physical impediments (she is in jail, someone has tied her up), by coercion (she has been threatened) or, finally, by lack of opportunity (the bus that should have dropped her at the party broke down). Compatibilists claim that she is free when she has the power or ability to do what she wants or desires to do. This implies an absence of constraints or impediments preventing her from doing what she wants to do. We can define compatibilist freedom as follows:

Compatilibist freedom   Agent a is free $=_{def} \mathcal{W}(a, \varphi) \rightarrow \varphi$

In words: that agent a is free means that if a wants φ, then φ. Let us notice that this definition is compatible with the fact that the agent cannot want differently from what she actually wants. Therefore, this notion of free will is compatible with determinism.

Some classical compatibilists, however, tried to account for the idea that freedom has to do with the power of doing otherwise. Let us suppose that Emma has to choose whether to go to the party or to stay at home reading a book. Let us further suppose that she decided to go to the party. What would have happened if the past had been different and she had decided to stay at home? What would have happened if she had had different reasons, beliefs or tastes and she had decided to do otherwise? The compatibilists state that a condition of Emma's freedom is that if Emma had chosen differently, Emma would have had the possibility to stay home. Therefore, Emma not only has the possibility to go to the party, if she chooses the party, but she also has the possibility to stay at home, if she chooses her home. All that, however, does not affect determinism. In determinism, it is impossible to have the same past and different futures. Different futures imply different pasts.

By means of possible world semantics, we can characterize the compatibilist position as follows. In the actual world, Emma chooses to go to the party and she has the power to go to the party. Emma's choice is determined, in the actual world, by the past states of this world and by the development laws. There exists, moreover, another possible world, among the closest to the actual world, in which Emma chooses to stay at home and in which she has the power to stay at home. This world necessarily has a different past, since Emma's choice is determined by the past states of the world. Formally:

Compatibilist freedom revisited Agent a is free $=_{def}$ 1) $\mathcal{W}(a, \varphi) \to \varphi$ 2) $\mathcal{W}(a, \psi) \,\square\!\!\to \psi$

where φ and ψ are, respectively, what agent a chooses to do and what she could have chosen to do. However, not all compatibilists agree that condition 2) is necessary. In fact, some (such as Harry Frankfurt) emphasize that individuals can be considered responsible for their actions even if there is no possible world in which they do otherwise.

The "New" Compatibilism

Classical compatibilism, being focused on the external impediments to will, ends up neglecting the internal dynamics of the human psyche, thereby blurring the difference with animals. It is easy to notice, for instance, that the definition of freedom given by classical compatibilism could easily be applied to the higher animals, provided that it is possible to attribute to them something like will and desires. Animals, too, could be defined as free in the case in which they obtain what the instinct forces them to desire.

The so-called new compatibilism tried to provide a remedy: Harry Frankfurt, while maintaining the compatibility between determinism and human freedom, has conceived a new definition of freedom. Frankfurt believes that it is necessary to distinguish first-order from second-order desires. Second-order desires are desires about other desires. For instance, the drug addict may have a first-order desire to take a drug. But she may also have the desire to not have this desire and can overcome the first-order desire in order to save her life. These desires concerning first-order desires are second order desires. Frankfurt argues that having second-order desires is what distinguishes human beings from animals and what makes humans persons (or selves). In other words, persons or selves are capable of "reflective self-evaluation", of reflecting upon and perhaps changing the desires they have rather than merely acting by following their desires instinctively. Therefore, Frankfurt considers that the drug addict is not free because she does not have the will she wants to have. A person is, on the contrary, free if she is able to get the will she wants to have. According to this new version of compatibilism, freedom can be defined as follows:

New compatibilism free will Agent a is free $=_{def}$ 1) $(W(a, W(a, \varphi))) \to W(a, \varphi)$ 2) $W(a, \varphi) \to \varphi$

In words: agent a is free if: (1) if the agent a wants to want φ, then a wants φ and (2) if a wants φ, then a achieves φ. Frankfurt's theory is compatibilist since it does not require that second-order desires can be different from what they are: second-order desires can be determined as much as first-order desires. What is crucial for freedom is that our will is able to control our desires.

New compatibilism adds a new component, concerning the internal dynamics of the human mind. It allows us to distinguish genuine human freedom from animal freedom; moreover, it allows to classify obsessed, drug addicted or mad people as not free. It is an improvement over classical compatibilism. However, libertarians do not think it is sufficient. The modern debate between compatibilists and incompatibilists concerns specifically second-order desires: compatibilists believe that to be free it is sufficient that first-order desires are determined by second-order desires; incompatibilists believe that this is not sufficient and that second-order desires must be self-determined by the agent. The following subsection gives a short account of this debate.

Freedom of Self-determination and Responsibility
Libertarians usually distinguish (at least) two kinds of freedom and argue that both are necessary if we want to consider someone actually free. They believe that compatibilists consider just one of these kinds, neglecting the other. The first is what Kane calls *freedom of self-realization*, the freedom to achieve one's own desires. Compatibilists identify freedom *tout court* with this kind of freedom. But, for libertarians, there exists another kind of freedom, which is behind the freedom of self-realization: the *freedom of self-determination*.

Kane defines it as "the power or ability to act of *your own free will* in the sense of a will (character, motives and purposes) of your own making—a will that you yourself, to some degree, were *ultimately responsible* for forming" (p. 172). It is not sufficient that we are able to achieve our desires if they come, so to speak, from the outside. When we choose which route to take, we form a purpose, that is, the desire to do something. But we are the ones who forge this desire (or purpose), who decide to desire this rather than that. According to libertarians, freedom entails a sort of self-determination of our desires which makes us, ultimately, responsible for our choices. If the second-order desires are imposed on us by our past, then we are not responsible for them and, ultimately, we are not responsible for our actions.

In order to have self-determination, indeterminism is needed. If the agent must be able to determine her own desires and purposes, it is necessary that they do not depend on the circumstances in which the agent is and on her past. They have to be something that is up to the agent, something she can determine one way or the other. Until an agent decides on her purposes, it must be undetermined what they are; for this reason, freedom of self-determination and determinism cannot coexist.

Summing up: both compatibilists and incompatibilists agree that freedom of self-realization is a necessary condition of freedom. For the former, however, this is also a sufficient condition, while for the latter, the freedom of self-determination is also necessary. The debate is focused, then, on the necessity of the freedom of self-determination for free will.

The notion of freedom of self-determination is crucial in the debate concerning responsibility and determinism. Libertarians argue that one cannot hold an agent responsible for an action if that agent cannot do otherwise. Therefore, responsibility and determinism are incompatible. Compatibilists try to show the opposite. Locke, one of the founder fathers of compatibilism, tried to prove that agents can be considered responsible for their actions even if they cannot do otherwise. Locke suggests the following example: some people are in a room and they must decide whether to stay there or to get out. Let us suppose they decide to stay. Unbeknownst to them, however, the room is locked from the outside and, therefore, *if they had decided* to get out, they could not have. Yet, we are inclined to consider them responsible anyway. So, Locke concludes that the possibility of doing otherwise is not necessary for the responsibility. Libertarians' answer is very natural. It could be objected to Locke that we consider those people responsible since they actually have the freedom of self-determination: they can *choose* to stay or to *try* to get out. They have, therefore, two alternatives in front of them. And they are able to self-determine their purposes one way or the other. Freedom of self-determination and the indeterminism it entails seem to be essential to the attribution of responsibility.

Harry Frankfurt tried to imagine situations in which there is no (at least, *prima facie*) freedom of self-determination, but the agent seems to be responsible for her actions. Frankfurt's examples have the following conceptual structure. Someone—Black let us say—wants that Thomas perform a certain action. Black is prepared to go to considerable lengths to get his way, but he prefers to avoid showing his hand unnecessarily. So he waits until Thomas is about to make up his mind and he does nothing unless it is clear to him that Thomas is going to do something other than what Black wants him to do. In that case, Black will block Thomas' choice. The modality by means of which the choice is blocked varies from case to case. We might imagine Black to have a potion that can be administered to work his will or imagine him as a neurosurgeon with direct control over Thomas' brain and intimate knowledge of Thomas' inclinations. If, however, Thomas makes his choice in accordance with Black's desires, then Black will not intervene. If so, we are intuitively led to attribute to Thomas the responsibility for what he did.

The main problem with Frankfurt's cases is whether the agent actually lacks the freedom of self-determination. Frankfurt claims that Thomas cannot self-determine his will since Black would block him. If Black noticed that Thomas' beliefs and character or the circumstances were inclining him to want something different from what Black wanted, Black would intervene to block the rising of that will.

The libertarian has, however, good chances to answer to Frankfurt's argument.[18] Either the world is deterministic or it is indeterministic. If the world is deterministic, then, at least from the point of view of libertarians, Thomas is not free. Regardless of Black's intervention, Thomas' desires are always determined by factors external to him, by past states of the world or by Black himself. As we have seen, libertarians insist that if we are not able to self-determine our desires, then it is difficult to state that we are responsible for our actions. If Thomas chooses what Black wants (that is, if Black does not intervene), Thomas is forced to perform this action by his past and the laws of the world. If, on the other hand, Thomas is choosing contrarily to Black's desires, Black will intervene and he will force Thomas to choose otherwise. In both cases, Thomas is not responsible for his actions from a libertarian point of view. If the world is indeterminist, then Black can intervene to modify Thomas' will only after Thomas has self-determined his own desires one way or another. Let us suppose, as in Frankfurt's case, that Thomas' beliefs and his character incline him to want something. If Thomas' choices are really self-determined, Thomas' beliefs and character and the circumstances cannot *determine* his choices. Else, they would not be really

---

[18] See Widerker (1995) and Wyma (1997), and Ginet (2017).

self-determined. But then Black *cannot* foresee Thomas' choice on the basis of these factors and he has to wait—so to speak—until Thomas makes his choice in order to block it. Consequently, Thomas is in a situation similar to Locke's room: he has actually the freedom of self-determination and, if he is permitted to do what he chooses, then he is actually free.

As it appears from these brief remarks, the freedom of self-determination is essential in the debate between compatibilists and libertarians about the attribution of responsibility to the agents. The details and the developments of this debate are outside the scope of this book. So, it is time to apply some of the previous considerations to the theological stuff.

3.2.2 Theological Compatibilism

As we have said, theological compatibilism invokes the arguments of non-theological compatibilism in order to defend the compatibility between free will and determinism. However, the reasons that inspire theological and non-theological compatibilists are very different. The aim of non-theological compatibilists is usually the reconciliation of, on the one hand, the intuitions about our freedom and the social institutions which seem to presuppose the responsibility of human beings for their actions and, on the other hand, naturalism, which seems to entail a deterministic image of the world (at least, at the macroscopic level). On the contrary, theological compatibilism is moved by a certain conception of the divine. There are essentially three reasons to embrace theological compatibilism:

1. *Omniscience*. God is omniscient and He foresees the future in every detail. But, according to theological determinists, divine omniscience entails the impossibility of doing otherwise.
2. *Providence*. Theological determinists maintain that God determines every feature of the world through His providence. The absence of a meticulous providence would compromise divine sovereignty. Therefore, everything, including human choices, must depend on God.
3. *Aseity*. In many theistic traditions, God is conceived as pure actuality, lacking every potentiality, and as impassable. So, God cannot be

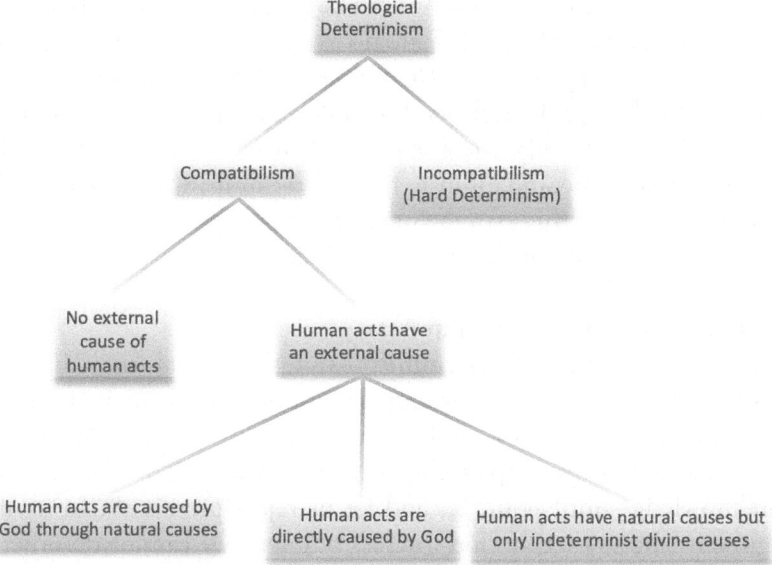

Fig. 3.1 Kinds of theological determinism

affected by the world and, in particular, God cannot *take note* of what human beings decide to do since this would entail a sort of dynamics in God's nature. God foresees the future because He determines it.[19]

Since there are many different reasons to embrace compatibilism—and theological compatibilism in particular—there are many kinds of theological compatibilism. In Fig. 3.1, some forms of these positions are classified.

---

[19] Aquinas conceived God as pure actuality; therefore, this thought is present in the Thomistic and Dominican traditions. See Garrigou-Lagrange (1934):

> If the divine causality is not *predetermining* with regard to our *choice* (…), the divine knowledge is fatally *determined* by it. To wish to limit the universal causality and absolute independence of God necessarily brings one to place a passivity in Him, a passivity in the *self-subsisting Being*, in the *self-subsisting intellect*. (Garrigou-Lagrange 1934, p. 538)

Firstly, the compatibilist solutions can be divided into two subgroups: the views according to which there are no external causes of human acts and the views according to which the human acts have external causes. The latter are further specified depending on the type of causality determining human choices. Finally, there exists a form of theological determinism that is actually incompatibilist: hard determinism, which is really an extreme version of this extreme measure.

Let us now see the main features of each view.

No External Cause of Human Acts

One can be a theological determinist—and, therefore, believe that human actions are necessitated—without assuming that there is a particular *cause* (divine or human) of those acts. Let us assume that we accept the argument of incompatibility between human free will and divine foreknowledge until point 8., and let us reject premise 9. In itself, the argument shows that, if God foresees our acts, we cannot do otherwise. It does not show that God *causes* our acts. One could still say that our acts are *determined* by past divine beliefs without being caused by them. If, moreover, one rejects premise 9—as all compatibilists actually do—the necessity of our acts would not be at odds with our freedom. It is easy to notice that all the theoretical weight of this view depends on how finely we are able to characterize the distinction between *determining* and *causing*.

This view is one of the three solutions that Linda Zagzebski proposes in her 1991 book—to be fair, it seems to be the view she advances with the least conviction.[20] Zagzebski insists that in Locke's and Frankfurt's cases—as well as in the theological determinist scenario—an agent's choice is not caused by the past state of the world and therefore, it is not counterfactually dependent on it:

> What is objectionable about determinism is that in a deterministic world, if the cause of an event had not occurred, the event would not have occurred either. For example, we can truly say that if some match had

---

[20] See Zagzebski (1991, pp. 154–162).

not been struck, it would not have lit. Given determinism, each choice is counterfactually dependent on the conditions that make it impossible to do otherwise. If those conditions had not obtained, the choice would not have been made. In the Frankfurt-Fischer[21] case, in contrast, [Thomas] seems free because his act would have occurred without the mechanism that prevented it from being otherwise. If Black had not inserted the mechanism into [Thomas]'s brain, [Thomas] would have voted for Reagan anyway. [Thomas]'s act is counterfactually independent of the mechanism that makes him unable to do otherwise (…) this difference is crucial to the kind of power necessary for free choice (Zagzebski 1991, p. 156)

If God, *per impossible*, were not omniscient and did not foresee that Thomas would vote for that candidate, Thomas would have voted, anyway, for that candidate. So, Thomas can be considered responsible for his vote.

There is, however, a difference between Locke's and Frankfurt's examples and theological determinism. We have seen that the libertarian can argue that, in Locke's and Frankfurt's cases, the attribution of responsibility to the agent arises from the fact that she seems to keep the freedom of self-determination. This is straightforward in Locke's case: the people in the room decided to stay inside, but they could have chosen otherwise and *tried* to get out. In other terms, the libertarian points out, they are faced with two *actual* alternatives: staying in or trying to get out; then, they self-determine their purposes in order to choose one alternative. Frankfurt's cases are structured so that the attribution of responsibility should be preserved even in the absence of freedom of self-determination. In fact, we have seen that it is dubious whether the agent has no real alternatives, even in these cases: if the world is indeterministic, it seems that we are effectively in the presence of two alternatives, one of which is blocked by Black as soon as Thomas takes it. But the assumption, according to which Thomas has the freedom of self-determination among various options, is preserved, or at least so the libertarian argues.

In theological determinism, things are different. Since it is predetermined that Thomas will vote for a certain candidate *before* Thomas

---

[21] Fischer's cases are very similar to Frankfurt's.

makes up his mind, Thomas lacks the freedom of self-determination among various options. Or, in other terms, there is no real indeterminism in the world and no real self-determination of the agent. In the case of theological determinism, the choice is determined *ex ante* by God's infallible beliefs and therefore the agent has no power of doing otherwise. In this case, we do not have two alternatives, one of which is blocked as soon as it is taken: just one alternative is available to the agent.

Zagzebski stresses that this determination is not causal. But it is important to investigate whether this is relevant, after all. What really matters, from a libertarian point of view, is whether the world is actually indeterminate until an agent's choice and whether the agent is able to determine it. This allows us to attribute to her the responsibility for her actions. If theological determinism is true, the world is determinate and therefore the agent has no freedom of self-determination but only freedom of self-realization. However, this latter is largely insufficient—from the libertarian point of view—to attribute responsibility since the agent has no alternatives. It does not seem relevant whether the agent cannot want otherwise because she is forced by God, by the nature or by some other kind of metaphysical necessity, as that arising from divine foreknowledge. When she loses the freedom of self-determination, she loses full-blooded free will, as it is intended by libertarians. So, we think that Zagzebski cannot appeal to the difference between causation and determination. Hence, the theological determinist cannot take this route and must invoke the usual intuitions of compatibilists, such as the idea according to which the freedom of self-realization or the freedom of determining our first-order desires are sufficient conditions for responsibility. The following subsections explore these attempts.

Human Acts Are Caused by God Through Natural Causes

Theological compatibilists can accept that God directly or indirectly causes our acts. Just as the fact that our acts are caused by natural causes does not prevent (non-theological) compatibilists from stating human free will, so the fact that God causes our acts does not prevent theological compatibilists from stating human free will. A first distinction regarding these compatibilist doctrines is whether God is considered a cause similar to natural causes or not. The first route is taken by Baker (2003). She defines compatibilism as follows: "An account of free will is *compatibilist* if and only if it entails that a person *S*'s having free will with respect to an action (or choice) *A* is compatible with the *A*'s being caused ultimately by factors outside of *S*'s control" (p. 460). After arguing that compatibilism provides many theoretical advantages to theism (for instance, the idea according to which divine providence extends to any aspects of the world and, obviously, an easy solution to our dilemma), she maintains that there is little difference for the theological compatibilist whether God directly causes the human actions or they are brought about by natural causes, since natural causes also depend, in the end, on God: "Compatibilism (in the relevant sense) is the view that the will can be free and caused; it is not a view that distinguishes between natural and supernatural causes" (p. 468).

Human Acts Are Directly Caused by God

The opposite option is to argue that God is a cause different from natural causes. For instance, McCann (1995, 2005) claims that while naturalistic determinism threatens human free will, theological determinism preserves it, since the way God causes events is different. McCann argues that if naturalistic determinism were sound, human beings would not be free: "We might even wish to say that if determinism is true then whatever the phenomenal appearances may be, we never really decide anything" (McCann 1995, p. 591). McCann affirms, however, that our decisions *must* have a cause, otherwise the principle of sufficient reason would be violated. That cause is God Himself. However, He is not a natural cause since He is the cause of my very being: "By willing that we engage in acts that have the intrinsic features of decision, God enables us to exercise spontaneous and voluntary control over our worldly situation, while at the same time His own involvement prevents the principle of Sufficient Reason from being violated" (McCann 1995, p. 592). In other terms, God creates my very decision; He does not operate on it. By creating it, He creates my decision as intentional and spontaneous, and therefore, as free. God's determination and my decision are the same thing.

To clarify the difference between divine and natural causality, McCann compares divine causality to the creation of a character by a writer. God's relationship with us

> is not analogous to that of the puppeteer to his puppet—which would indeed destroy our freedom—but rather to that of the author of a novel to her characters. The characters do not exist as an event-causal consequence of anything the author does. Rather, their first existence is in her creative imagination, and they are born and sustained in and through the very thoughts in which she conceives them, and of which they are the content. The interesting thing about this relationship is that it is too close to permit the author's creative activity to damage her characters' freedom. On the contrary, it is perfectly legitimate for her to present them as free and responsible beings (McCann 2005, p. 146)

Surely, divine causality is different from natural causality since the former is creation and not simply something that acts upon something other. However, it has to be shown whether this kind of causality is able to preserve human freedom.[22]

Although McCann emphasizes the close intimacy between creating divine will and created human will, it is clear that these are two distinct wills (unless we adopt a weird metaphysics according to which there is identity between God and human beings): if two agents are distinct, also their wills are. It is clear, moreover, that according to theological determinism, the divine will determines the human will. I want φ because God wants that I want φ. But then it is very hard to understand how McCann can state that it is up to me what I want, given that my will is something which does not depend on me, but on God.

Moreover, the comparison with the characters of a novel is theoretically rather weak. The characters of a novel have no autonomy: they do what they do because the author decides in some way about their destiny. Of course, we represent them as free, but because we *pretend* that they are

---

[22]For a criticism of McCann's view, see Rowe (1999). For an answer to Rowe's criticisms, see McCann (2001).

free as well we *pretend* that they exist. We know, on the contrary, that they have no autonomy and ontological consistency outside the novel.

Human Acts Have Natural Causes but Only Indeterminist Divine Causes

There exists a third kind of theological compatibilism which is, curiously, quite the opposite of McCann's. It argues that if God were the direct cause of our acts, then we would not be free. On the contrary, if our acts have natural causes, then the compatibility between determinism and free will can be preserved. This view has been advocated, for instance, by Turner (2013). Turner calls *historical compatibilism* the view that

> the property of acting freely is, like the property of being a Rembrandt or a genuine one-dollar-bill, a *historical* property. A counterfeit dollar or Rembrandt may be an intrinsic duplicate of a genuine one; what makes it a counterfeit is that it has the wrong history. A dollar bill is genuine only if it was produced in the right way and under the authority of the US Mint; a Rembrandt is genuine only if it was Rembrandt who put its pigment on canvas. According to historical compatibilism, whether an action is free or not depends on the history that led up to the action. (Turner 2013, p. 130)

Thus, according to the historical compatibilist, causes are not on a par: some of them, despite determining human actions, preserve the freedom of those actions; others, on the contrary, restrict human freedom. There are as many possible versions of historical compatibilism as possible causes of a human action. Turner is interested in one of these versions. He calls it *independent compatibilism*. The advocates of independent compatibilism endorse the following principle:

Determination   If S's arranging matters in way w would result in T's being causally determined to A, and if S knows this and arranges matters in way w in order to get T to A, then T does not freely A.

In other terms, if an agent intentionally sees to it that another agent acts in a certain way, thus determining his behaviour, then the second agent is not free. Therefore, agents are free only if their actions are not *intentionally* determined. According to independent compatibilists, if God intentionally sets our actions, then human beings are not free. We are free, however, if those actions are determined by natural causes, whose causal power lacks intentionality and consciousness.

Now, one could ask in which sense independent compatibilism can still be *theological*, since it excludes divine causality. However, this is not Turner's conclusion. He claims that if God decided to create a world in which every tiny aspect is dependent on His will, then, according to independent compatibilists, human beings would not be free. But God could create by disjunctive decree; He could say "Let there be world w_1 or world w_2". Furthermore,

> He can presumably also give essentially probabilistic decrees: he can say "Let there be a cat with likelihood .75 or a mouse with likelihood .25, at which point either a cat or a mouse will pop into existence, and the objective chance of the decree's giving rise to one or the other is .75 and .25, respectively. If this is right, then God could make general "chancy" decrees (Turner 2013, p. 133)

Thus, on this view, God does not determine which world exists and, then, He does not determine our choices. However, each of the worlds the divine decree lets be is a natural determinist world. As rather implausible as it may seem, an independent theological compatibilist has the possibility of adopting a free will defence in theodicy, which is usually precluded to other versions of theological determinism: God is not responsible for evil since He does not directly determine human actions. The responsibility for these actions rest on human beings (where, of course, the concept of responsibility at play is compatibilist).

Hard Determinism
It is worth mentioning, in the diverse family of theological determinists, hard determinism. The views so far analysed are all compatibilist because they state that, although our actions are determined, they are nevertheless free. If, on the other hand, we accept an incompatibilist standpoint, according to which determinism and free will are actually *incompatible*,

we face a theoretical alternative: either we accept free will and, then, we deny determinism (libertarianism) or we accept determinism and, then, we deny free will (hard determinism). The large majority of theological incompatibilists embrace the first solution; hard determinism is a minority position. It is not hard to see why: denying free will, this view must affirm that human agents are not morally responsible for their acts. And this seems completely at odds with the conceptual core of classical theism.

However, Pereboom (2011, 2016) tried to defend a form of hard theological determinism. For sure, hard theological determinism cannot maintain the idea of the agent's responsibility, but many other core notions of theism can be preserved. For instance, Pereboom claims that the attitudes of blame, guilt, forgiveness, repentance, gratitude and love can be maintained in his theoretical framework. It must be rejected that the notion of blame "presupposes that the agent being blamed is morally responsible" (Pereboom 2011, p. 266), but a concept of blame constituted by a certain belief-desire pair can be assumed: the belief that the agent has acted badly or is a bad person and the wish that he did not perform his bad act or did not have his current bad character. Both this belief and this desire are compatible with hard determinism.

Also, a particular notion of guilty—which seems tightly connected with the idea of moral responsibility—can be maintained within the framework of hard determinism:

> Suppose that you do wrong, but because you believe that hard determinism is true, you reject the claim that you are blameworthy. Instead, you accept that you have done wrong, you feel deeply sad, sorrowful, or pained that you were the agent of wrongdoing (…) Furthermore, because you have a commitment to doing what is right, and to moral improvement, you would resolve not to perform an action of this kind again, and perhaps seek out help to make this change (Pereboom 2011, pp. 268–269)

According to Pereboom, all these attitudes are compatible with hard determinism. Finally, love and gratitude are also attitudes that can be included in his perspective. *Prima facie* one could think that love has value only if it is the outcome of a free choice. However, love for one's children is hardly interpretable as a free choice but, not for that reason, whoever is beloved considers it valueless. Pereboom concludes that the value of love and gratitude can be preserved in his theoretical framework.

The hardest point to accept from a theistic point of view is the idea that God rewards or punishes human beings for acts for which they are absolutely not responsible. Moreover, this punishment, or reward, is ultimate. Maybe, one can try to accommodate our legal system within the hard determinist framework[23]: exactly as someone who is infected by a virus is pushed away from society and placed in quarantine, even if it is not at all her fault, in the same vein someone who has criminal inclinations can be legitimately isolated from the society since she is dangerous to the very society, even if she has no responsibility for her criminal behaviour. But it is difficult to think that God eternally punishes someone faultless and, analogously, eternally rewards someone with no actual merits. Classical theism seems to be intimately connected with the idea that we will be punished or rewarded because we are responsible for our actions. Therefore, the compatibility of this view with classical theism is at least dubious, while it seems clearly incompatible with Christianity.

Conclusions on Theological Determinism

Theological determinism has both philosophical and theological difficulties. From a *philosophical* point of view, since the majority of theological determinists are compatibilists, they have to face all the objections brought against non-theological compatibilism. In particular, one can doubt that the freedom of self-realization and the freedom of reflective self-control can account for the notions of human freedom and responsibility. But there are also *theological* difficulties. First of all, the great theistic traditions seem to presuppose, at least *prima facie*, the free will of human beings: it is up to us to follow God. And the value of this choice—which is surely *also* a choice of faith—lies in some form of "power of doing otherwise". After all, the destiny of our soul (its eschatology) is connected to our choices in the worldly life. Obviously, there are aspects of our existence that are *not* up to us and that the believer must accept. But even this "stoic" tolerance is the fruit of a brave and very often painful choice.

---

[23] On this, see Pereboom (2006).

Secondarily, in a determinist view, the responsibility of evil must be attributed to God. Actually, one of the most common strategies in theodicy is the so-called free will defence: since human beings are free, they can choose. If they choose wrong, the blame can be put on them. But this train of thought is precluded to theological determinists, since—according to them—our choices are, directly or indirectly, determined. It does not mean that the determinist has no argument: she can make appeal to the fact that this is the best of all the possible worlds or, alternatively, she can argue that every evil is for a greater good (even if this is not evident), adopting, for instance, a form of soul-making theodicy (Hick 2010) according to which God allows evil and suffering in the world in order to convert humans into virtuous creatures capable of following His will. However, with no free will defence, the task of conciliating the existence of an omnipotent, omniscient and morally perfect God with the existence of evil certainly becomes more difficult.

In the next two chapters, we will assume both libertarianism and divine foreknowledge of human choices. So premises 1. and 9. of the fatalist argument are preserved. If one wants to resist the conclusion, she must focus on the other premises. As we will see, both Ockhamism and Molinism attack premise 2. about the necessity of the past.

References

Baker, L.R. 2003. Why Christians should not be libertarians: An Augustinian challenge. *Faith and Philosophy* 20(4): 460–478.

De Florio, C., and A. Frigerio. 2013. God, evil, and Alvin Plantinga. *European Journal for Philosophy of Religion* 5(3): 75–94.

Flint, T.P. 1998. *Divine providence: The Molinist account*. Ithaca: Cornell University Press.

Garrigou-Lagrange, R. 1934. *God, His existence and His nature*. London: B. Herder Book.

Geach, P. 1977. *Providence and evil: the Stanton lectures 1971–1972*. CUP Archive. Cambridge: Cambridge University Press.

Ginet, C. 2017. In defense of the principle of alternative possibilities: Why I don't find Frankfurt's argument convincing. In *Moral responsibility and alternative possibilities*, ed. D. Widerker, 87–102. Abingdon: Routledge.

Hasker, W. 1994. A philosophical perspective. In *The openness of God: A biblical challenge to the traditional understanding of God*, ed. C. Pinnock, R. Rice, J. Sanders, and W. Hasker, 126–154. Westmont: InterVarsity Press.

Hasker, W. 1998. *God, time, and knowledge*. Ithaca: Cornell University Press.

Hasker, W. 2001. The foreknowledge conundrum. In *Issues in contemporary philosophy of religion*, ed. E.T. Long, 97–114. Berlin: Springer.

Hasker, W. 2004. *Providence, evil and the openness of God*, vol. 3. Psychology Press.

Hick, J. 2010. *Evil and the God of love*. Berlin: Springer.

Lucas, J.R. 1989. *The future: An essay on God, temporality, and truth*. Oxford: Blackwell Publisher.

McCann, H.J. 1995. Divine sovereignty and the freedom of the will. *Faith and Philosophy* 12(4): 582–598.

McCann, H.J. 2001. Sovereignty and freedom: A reply to Rowe. *Faith and Philosophy* 18(1): 110–116.

McCann, H.J. 2005. The author of sin? *Faith and Philosophy* 22(2): 144–159.

Pereboom, D. 2006. *Living without free will*. Cambridge: Cambridge University Press.

Pereboom, D. 2011. Theological determinism and divine providence. In *Molinism: The contemporary debate*, ed. K. Perszyk, 262–280. Oxford: Oxford University Press.

Pereboom, D. 2016. Libertarianism and theological determinism. In *Free will and theism: Connections, contingencies, and concerns*, ed. K. Timpe, and D. Speak, 112–131. Oxford: Oxford University Press.

Pinnock, C. 1994. Systematic theology. In *The openness of God: A biblical challenge to the traditional understanding of God*, ed. C. Pinnock, R. Rice, J. Sanders, and W. Hasker, 101–125. Downers Grove: InterVarsity.

Rhoda, A.R. 2008. Generic open theism and some varieties thereof. *Religious Studies* 44(2): 225–234.

Rhoda, A.R. 2011. The fivefold openness of the future. In *God in an open universe: Science, metaphysics, and open theism*, ed. W. Hasker, and D. Zimmerman, 69–93. Eugene: Wipf and Stock Publishers.

Rice, R. 1994. Biblical support for a new perspective. In *The openness of God: A biblical challenge to the traditional understanding of God*, ed. C. Pinnock, R. Rice, J. Sanders, and W. Hasker, 11–58. Downers Grove: InterVarsity.

Rice, R. 2004. *God's foreknowledge and man's free will*. Eugene: Wipf and Stock Publishers.

Rowe, W.L. 1999. The problem of divine sovereignty and human freedom. *Faith and Philosophy* 16(1): 98–101.

Sanders, J. 1994. Historical considerations. In *The openness of God: A biblical challenge to the traditional understanding of God*, ed. C. Pinnock, R. Rice, J. Sanders, and W. Hasker, 59–100. Downers Grove: InterVarsity.

Sanders, J. 1997. Why simple foreknowledge offers no more providential control than the openness of God. *Faith and Philosophy* 14(1): 26–40.

Turner, J. 2013. Compatibilism and the free will defense. *Faith and Philosophy* 30(2): 125–137.

Ware, B.A. 2003. *Their God is too small: Open Theism and the undermining of confidence in God*. Wheaton: Crossway Books.

Widerker, D. 1995. Libertarianism and Frankfurt's attack on the principle of alternative possibilities. *The Philosophical Review* 104(2): 247–261.

Wyma, K.D. 1997. Moral responsibility and leeway for action. *American Philosophical Quarterly* 34(1): 57–71.

Zagzebski, L.T. 1991. *The dilemma of freedom and foreknowledge*. Oxford: Oxford University Press.

4

God Knows the True Future: Ockhamism

4.1 Introduction

In the previous chapter, we looked at the spectrum of views that can be considered extreme measures taken to address the problem of divine foreknowledge and human free will. The reason for this label is straightforward: if the compatibility between an omniscient entity and free agents is understood as a dilemma, the previously advanced solutions radically revisited one of the horns (even negating the current meaning). Thus, for instance, an advocate of Open Theism is ready to put under discussion the very concept of omniscience, claiming that God can be omniscient even if He does not know what is going to happen tomorrow.[1] Analogously, the compatibilist views try to argue that an agent who cannot do otherwise is notwithstanding free, following the authoritative path of compatibilist scholars.

These theoretical manoeuvres actually work. They have, however, a cost and, as it is easy to imagine, the cost is rather high. We tried to

---

[1] In particular, and less roughly, God is ignorant about the future events that depend on the free choices of agents.

© The Author(s) 2019
C. De Florio, A. Frigerio, *Divine Omniscience and Human Free Will*, Palgrave Frontiers in Philosophy of Religion, https://doi.org/10.1007/978-3-030-31300-5_4

show the limits of these proposals. In this chapter and in the next two, we will deal with solutions to our problem that can be considered *moderate* (in, albeit ideal, opposition to those described as *extreme*) or, if this did not create some confusion, *compatibilist*. The grounding idea of these approaches is that it is possible to provide an account able to preserve both a *prima facie* acceptable conception of divine omniscience and a *prima facie* acceptable conception of human free will. The three frameworks we are going to discuss are Ockhamism, Molinism and the Timeless Solution.[2] To the first, we dedicate this chapter; the second and the third will be discussed in Chaps. 5 and 6.

It is possible to distinguish Ockhamism and Molinism on the one hand and the Timeless approach on the other. The difference between these approaches has to do essentially with the relationship God has with the temporal dimension of reality. A little roughly, the problem is the following: is God within or out of time? This is a *metaphysical* question and the fundamental options are two. Either God is in time or not. In both cases, the riddles are challenging. In the temporal case, we need to clarify the modalities of His persistence: is God constituted by temporal parts (as the perdurantist orthodoxy prescribes)? Or, on the contrary, does He wholly exist at any instant (according the endurantist orthodoxy)? Or maybe God's persistence conditions are special—not comparable with any other worldly entity. For instance, God could be an *extended simple*, with a duration but lacking temporal parts. After all, the existence of temporal parts of God could be a problem if compared with another feature of His nature, His alleged absolute *simplicity*.

On the other hand, whoever advocates God's timelessness has other problems in her metaphysical agenda. How to characterize this timelessness? Is God's timelessness similar to the atemporal existence of some categories of entities such as abstract objects (numbers, propositions and so on)? Or is much more theory packed within the concept of eternity—as it seems to suggest Boethius' definition: "simultaneously full and perfect possession of interminable life"?

---

[2] Sometimes we will use the label "Eternity" to indicate the timeless existence of God. Of course, this must not be confused with the Eternalism discussed in the metaphysics of time.

Moreover, there is a family of questions about the relationships between a timeless God and a (temporal) world. Many truths of classical theism presuppose the possibility of such relationships. The problem is then to characterize these alleged relationships. In the end, according to many adversaries of the timeless God, His being personal, and His having a life, is at odds with timeless immutability. In other terms, as we have seen in the previous chapter, critics say that a timeless, impassible, simple God is a conceptual artefact of Greek philosophical thought, far from the God revealed in the Biblical Tradition, source of Love and Meaning for human existence.

In spite of these difficult and deep metaphysical questions, we believe it is possible to provide a sketch of the distinction between these general views—the former including Ockhamism and Molinism, the latter, the Timeless conception—which does not take into account these problems. In particular, our account does not presuppose a complete analysis of the relationships between God and time. Thus, in order to see how this criterion works, let us consider the two following sentences:

(1) Napoleon was defeated at Waterloo, on 18 June 1815
(2) The sum of the interior angles of the triangle ABC was equal to $180°$, on 23 March 1655

Sentence (1) seems perfectly plain; it describes a historically important event and it contains a date. Moreover, it is a past tensed sentence: from today's perspective, Napoleon's defeat is a past fact. On the contrary, things are not so straightforward about sentence (2). Although (2) is not meaningless—we are able to understand it and we can, at least partially, attribute to it a truth value—it is, doubtless, a *weird* sentence. The reason is that predications concerning structural properties of objects, and in particular of abstract objects, seem to be tenseless predications: the triangle ABC always has that property and therefore it is strange to specify a precise instant of history at which the triangle has the sum of its angles equal to $180°$. Two remarks on this.

Tenseless predications do not seem a prerogative of the domain of abstract entities; in the sentence "Socrates is a man", for instance, the (essential) property of being a man is predicated in a tenseless way to the individual Socrates, who belongs, no doubt, to the past. The case of abstract objects, obviously, is paradigmatic: it is plausible to maintain that mathematical objects (abstract objects *par excellence*) have *only* structural properties and then that all predications about them are tenseless. Actually, there are controversial cases. Let us think about the famous example "the number 27 has been thought by Euler on 12th April 1770 at 3 pm"; in that case, the property as being thought by Euler at a certain instant of time is predicated to an abstract object. It is, however, controversial that this is a *genuine* property of the number 27: after all, many argue that it is just a Cambridge property which indicates, at most, an (intentional) relation between an epistemic subject and an abstract entity. This relation—which surely has a temporal feature—does not affect the nature of 27: its essential intrinsic features are "eternally" present.

One could argue that a sentence such as (2) is not so strange, after all; if it is *always true* that the triangle ABC has the sum of its angles equal to 180°, *a fortiori* it is true at a certain instant of time, which we called 23 March 1655. What strikes us is simply the specification, useless at a closer look, of an instant t at which Pa holds when, given the very nature of Pa, we know that it holds *at every* t. This stance is possible but we believe that it fails to grasp an intuition about this distinction. The reason according to which (2) sounds effectively strange is that, at least *prima facie*, it is similar to a categorical mistake: it is a sort of metaphysical confusion to consider the geometrical properties of triangles as relativized to a time.

Let us try to apply the considerations just sketched to the problem of God's knowledge. We can, at least partially, neglect the other properties of God and, thus, focus on His modalities of knowing. What matters for our aims is whether God's knowledge is temporally collocated, not whether His existence or some other attributes are in time. Therefore, in order to distinguish the Ockhamist and Molinist approaches on one side from the Timeless approach on the other side, it is sufficient to investigate the temporality (if any) of God's knowledge. In other terms, we can remain reasonably agnostic about the temporal features of God's existence and, nevertheless, have a good account of the temporality (if any) of His knowledge. Thus, let φ be a proposition (of any complexity) which is object of divine knowledge; we have, then:

(a) God (timelessly) *knows* that φ.
(b) God *knew/knows/will know* that φ.

(a) is advocated by the *Timeless* approach. As we will see in more detail in Chap. 6, whoever defends this position claims that God's knowledge is in a timeless dimension: God did not know, does not know now or will not know tomorrow; He eternally, timelessly knows.

Although (a) is, maybe, the most common position in classical theism, there are scholars who believe not only that (b) is consistent but that it is even the most faithful description of God's knowledge. The reasons to defend a temporal account of God differ in kind: they can be *metaphysical, theological, mixed*. From a purely metaphysical point of view, a serious tensionalist might state that absolutely nothing is timeless. Consequently, God and abstract objects, if they exist, should be accommodated within a purely temporal metaphysical framework. This position is analogous to that adopted by those who consider sentence (2) as acceptable, that is, who consider the timeless predications as limit cases of temporal predications. From a theological point of view, on the other hand, some have argued that there are reasons which decree the end of Timeless God: in order to consider God as a Person in relation with human beings (through Incarnation and Revelation), it is necessary that He inhabits the temporal dimension.[3]

Lastly, there are, say, mixed reasons to consider God temporal. Craig (2001) authoritatively advocated that, in order to preserve God's omniscience, He must be temporal. Craig's argument is the following. God is omniscient (and, in a sense, one could say that this premise has a theological nature) and the world is tensed, described by the A-theory of time (and this is a metaphysical point). It follows that God must be able to know all the features of the world and, among them, there are tensed features; for instance, God must be able to correctly answer the

---

[3] *The End of Timeless God* is the title of a book by Mullins (see Mullins 2016), where the author provides good theological arguments to defend the temporality of God.

question "What time is it?", otherwise He loses omniscience. However, God has to bear temporal relationships in order to have access to tensed states of affairs; it follows that God has temporal location.[4]

In this and the next chapter, we will examine the solutions that assume option (b); this, as we will see, has both some advantages and theoretical costs we will critically discuss. In particular, in the remaining part of this chapter we will focus on Ockhamism. In Sect. 4.2 we will sketch the keystones of this solution, while in Sects. 4.3 and 4.4 we will focus on two particular aspects of Ockhamism: the idea that there is a true future and the idea that some past facts are determined by future facts. In Sect. 4.5, we will see that these features of Ockhamism seem to commit this solution to a particular metaphysics of time. Section 4.6 concludes this chapter.

4.2 The Ockhamist Solution

Although some modern Ockhamists overtly refer back to William of Ockham (see, for instance, Plantinga (1986)), the relationship between modern Ockhamism and Ockham's historical contribution is a subtle and, in a way, thorny question. We do not further investigate this question, leaving it to an historical research program.[5]

---

[4] In De Florio et al. (2017), we will provide a model according to which it is possible to maintain that God timelessly knows tensed features of reality *contra* Craig. We will review this model in Sect. 6.5.

[5] For some scholars, the relationship between Classical and Modern Ockhamism is almost a lexical coincidence: according to Arthur Prior, for example, a semantics is Ockhamist if it evaluates propositions with respect to times and histories. On the contrary, others maintain that it can, nonetheless, be useful to point out at least some intuitions that can be ascribed to William of Ockham and that are fundamental in current Ockhamism.

> Ockham advocates the determinateness of the truth of future contingent propositions. For Ockham, future contingent propositions are determinately true or false because the states of affairs to which they correspond will determinately be or not be actually present. (cf. Ockham *Tractatus de praedestinatione et de praescientia dei respectu futurorum contingentium*, 1.O–P and Craig (1988, p. 148)).

4 God Knows the True Future: Ockhamism

Modern theological Ockhamism builds on John Turk Saunders' and Marilyn McCord Adams' works in the Sixties.[6] These works have been conceived as answers to the fatalist argument formulated by Pike (1965). Pike's argument, which presupposes that God is an everlasting but temporal being, goes as follows. If God is omniscient, then He believes at time t_1 that Emma will do φ at time t_3. If, at time t_2, Emma could refrain from bringing about φ at t_3 (where $t_1 < t_2 < t_3$), then at time t_2 either (a) it is within Emma's power to render some of God's beliefs false; (b) it is within Emma's power to act in such a way that God does not believe something at t_1; or (c) it is within Emma's power to act in such a way that God does not exist at t_1. Pike rejects these three alternatives and concludes that, at t_2, Emma cannot refrain from bringing about φ at t_3 and, accordingly, she is not free in the libertarian sense of the term. Pike rejects alternative (b) because it seems to imply that it is within Emma's power to change the past: if it is within Emma's power at t_2 to change God's beliefs at t_1, then Emma has the ability to modify something that has already happened. However, this conflicts with our understanding that the past is fixed and so cannot be changed.

Ockhamism is the defence of alternative (b) above. Ockhamists distinguish two kinds of facts concerning the past: hard and soft facts. While human beings (and presumably God as well) cannot change hard facts, they can operate on soft facts. Therefore, the fundamental idea of Ockhamism is to deny that the necessity of the past holds for all facts. There are some facts, the so-called soft facts, with respect to which the accidental necessity does not hold. Crucially, the fact that God believes at t_1 that Emma will perform φ at t_3 is considered by Ockhamists a soft fact at t_2. Let us consider the fatalist argument (once again):

1. Yesterday, God believed that p. (Divine foreknowledge)
2. If an event e occurred in the past, then it is accidentally necessary that e occurred then. (Necessity of the past)
3. It is now necessary that yesterday God believed p. (1,2, *modus ponens*)

---

[6]See, for instance, Saunders (1966), Adams (1967).

4. Necessarily, if yesterday God believed p, then p. (Infallibility of divine foreknowledge)
5. If r is accidentally necessary and if $\Box(r \rightarrow s)$, then it is accidentally necessary that s. (Principle of transfer of necessity)
6. So it is now necessary that p. (3,4,5)
7. If it is now necessary that p, then you cannot do otherwise than p. (Definition of necessary)
8. Therefore, you cannot do otherwise than p. (6,7, *modus ponens*)
9. If you cannot do otherwise when you do an act, you do not do it freely. (Principle of Alternate Possibilities)
10. Therefore, when you do p, you will not do it freely. (8,9, *modus ponens*)

Ockhamists deny premise 2: not all past facts are accidentally necessary.[7] It seems, *prima facie*, rather implausible that past facts can be influenced by human actions. The past, as Pike states, is conceived as something closed, which cannot be changed. Ockhamists, however, claim that certain past facts have a sort of "orientation" toward the future and are determinable by human beings. One important point on the Ockhamist agenda is understanding this orientation and how soft facts can be distinguished from hard facts. On this, Ockhamists do not share a common view. We have shown in De Florio and Frigerio (2018) that there are two different definitions of soft facts in literature. The first definition is based on examples such as:

SF1   Thomas writes a letter 2000 years after Caesar's death

It seems that it is in Thomas' power to write or not write a letter *now* and, by means of that, it is in Thomas' power to make true SF1.[8] However, in De Florio and Frigerio (2018), we showed that the facts described by sentences such as SF1 are not past facts but meta-facts constituted by relations between two facts located at two different temporal positions (in

---

[7] As we will see, Molinism also rejects premise 2 of the fatalist argument, and this connects these two views.
[8] Adams (1967), Freddoso (1983), Hoffman and Rosenkrantz (1984), Zemach and Winderker (1987) and Todd (2013) exploit example such as SF1, in order to provide a definition of soft fact.

the example, Caesar's death and Thomas' writing of the letter). Yet, divine beliefs about future human actions are different from the facts depicted by SF1; thus, the Ockhamist gains little advantage by exploiting these examples.

Other Ockhamists have advanced a different idea to block the fatalist argument: past divine beliefs are counterfactually dependent on future human actions. On this view, God believed yesterday that Emma will drink a beer because Emma will drink a beer tomorrow. If Emma had decided otherwise in the future, God would have believed otherwise in the past. This idea is at the basis of the second definition of soft fact. According to this definition, a soft fact is a past fact that depends counterfactually on a future fact. For example, Plantinga (1986) defines a soft fact in the following way: p is a proposition that describes a soft fact at t iff "p is true at t and it is (…) possible both that p is true at t and that there exists an action A and an agent S such that (1) S has the power at t or later to perform A and (2) *necessarily* if A were to perform S at t or later, then p would have been false" (p. 259). Thus, soft facts depend counterfactually on agents' future actions. Craig (1986) is even more explicit regarding this point: a "fact is soft iff it is a past or present event or actuality which is counterfactually dependent upon some future event or actuality in such a way that the earlier event or actuality is a consequence of which the later event or actuality is the condition. A fact is hard iff it is a past or present event or actuality which is not so dependent" (p. 83). In the next two sections, we will see that this definition of soft fact naturally follows from the main tenet of Ockhamism: the negation of premise 2 of the fatalist argument. So we will adopt this notion of soft fact and we will analyse its theoretical weight and consequences in Sect. 4.4.

Let us remember that Ockhamists reject only premise 2 of the fatalist argument. On the contrary, they accept both premise 1:

1. Yesterday, God believed that p

and premise 4:

4. Necessarily, if God believes that p, p is true

From these two propositions, it follows that if p describes a future fact which will happen tomorrow, then it was already true yesterday that tomorrow p will happen. The Ockhamist, then, accepts that future tensed propositions are true or false. At the same time, she also accepts a libertarian conception of free will and thus the openness of the future. We will see in the next section that these two features combine into the idea of a true future among many possible futures.

4.3 The True Future

As you recall, the problem of divine omniscience and human free will hinges on the compatibility between two features of reality: the existence of free subjects, in a libertarian sense, and the existence of an omniscient entity. To ensure the first requirement, we argued, the topology of time must be branched: there must exist at least two really possible alternatives open to the agent's choice. That means, a little more formally, that—at least for some instants of time t—there exist two (or more) histories which branch off from t.

The Ockhamist accepts this assumption, but she enriches it with the hypothesis that, among these possible futures, one is *alethically privileged*: it is the future which will happen, the true future. Emma can drink a beer or a Coke; the course of the world bifurcates, then, into two alternative branches. But eventually, Emma will make up her mind and, in fact, she will have a beer (or a Coke). And that future that will happen is the true future. Let us notice that, for Ockhamism, the notion of true future is radically anti-epistemic: it could be totally opaque to our knowledge what the true future is. But there is one.

As we have seen in Sect. 2.6.4, the **TRL** semantics accounts for this intuition. Those structures have three elements: a non empty set of instants of time (T), an order relation ($<$) and a privileged history (**TRL**). The Thin Red Line is the actual history of the world: what has happened, what happens, and what will happen. It is then straightforward to connect the Thin Red Line to the idea of true future: given a moment t from which two histories, h_1 and h_2, stem, one of these is the **TRL**, that is, the history that will happen.

At a closer look, the idea of **TRL** is rather intuitive. Let us imagine a concrete case. We throw a die. There are six possible outcomes (in the cases in which the die is not fair, the probability of these outcomes can vary but this is not relevant here), and we assume that we have absolutely no idea about which number will come up. However, we know, right now, that a determinate outcome will obtain. We can represent the outcomes as a finite disjunction: $1 \vee 2 \vee \ldots \vee 6$. One of these will happen. Therefore, it is already true that there exists a history that will happen. The point is that, according to Ockhamism, it is already true now *which* is the future history. Again, the train of thought is the following: even if we do not know which number will come up, the outcome is already determinate. Thus, there exists a true future even if it is not the only one.

There are alternative futures, in which, for instance, Emma drinks something else than what she will actually choose. The presence of these alternative futures, according to the advocates of the **TRL**, ensures the openness of the future, although it is already true today that one determinate future will become real. The fact that a certain number come up does not exclude that other numbers could have come up. The fact that Emma will choose, for instance, to have a beer does not exclude that Emma could have had a Coke. The advocates of **TRL**, then, claim the full compatibility of the truth of $\mathbf{F}\varphi$ with $\Diamond(\mathbf{F}\neg\varphi)$. According to Ockhamism, the presence of many future histories excludes that the future is *necessary* and then deterministic; at the same time, the fact that there is a true future ensures that future tensed propositions have a truth value. Is it the existence of a true future with an open future plausible? We will discuss this question in depth in Sect. 4.5. Before that, we will combine the idea of **TRL** with the idea of divine beliefs and we will see how, from this combination, the concept of *soft fact* naturally originates—that is, a fact counterfactually dependent on a future fact.

4.4 Soft Facts

As we said in the introduction to this chapter, the Ockhamist considers meaningful the ascription of tensional properties to the divine epistemic states. In other terms, according to this approach, saying "God *knew* from the beginning of time that Emma would go to the party" is not only meaningful but it reflects the modality through which God foresees the facts of the world.

To introduce soft facts and the related issues, first we will discuss a kind of soft facts that is philosophically harmless, *semantic soft facts*. Let us suppose that at t_1 Emma decides to go to the party. In line with what was said before, the proposition "Emma will go to the party" ($\mathbf{F}\varphi$) was *already* true at t_0. It is the choice that Emma will make at t_1 that makes this proposition true at t_0; the fact that a proposition is true or not is a semantic fact that depends on our choices. The fact that at t_0 certain propositions are true because the agents will choose in a certain way at a later time t_1 is consistent with one of the most common argumentation paths against logical fatalism (see Sect. 1.3): the fact that yesterday it was true that today there would be a sea-battle is *grounded* on the fact that today there is a sea-battle. In other terms, the truth of a proposition that concerns the future depends on the actuality of some future fact. Merricks (2009) insisted on the dependence of the truth of propositions on the actuality of the facts:

> Despite the many controversies surrounding truth, it should be uncontroversial that a claim, if true, is true because the world is the way that claim represents the world as being, and not vice versa. Again, it should be uncontroversial that *that there are no white ravens* is true because there are no white ravens, *that dogs bark* is true because dogs bark, that *there were dinosaurs* is true because there were dinosaurs, and so on. (pp. 30–31)

Therefore, the fact that yesterday it was true that tomorrow there will be a sea-battle does not entail fatalism because that truth depends on a future fact and not vice versa.

Let us call *semantic soft fact* the fact that the truth of a proposition at one time depends on what the agents will choose at a later time. Soft facts differ from hard facts: the former are facts of the past that an agent can determine by her present actions; the latter are facts of the past that an agent cannot affect any more. The fact that it was true yesterday that Emma would drink a beer today is a semantic fact determined by the fact

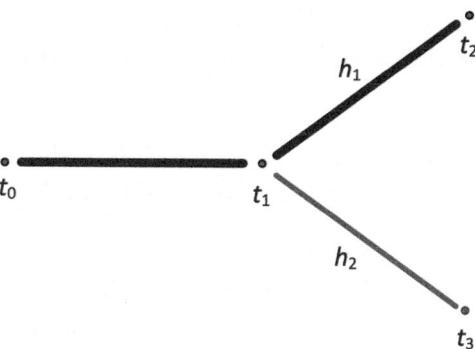

Fig. 4.1 TRL schema

that Emma, today, decided to have a beer. Since it is determined by the *future* decision of an agent, such a semantic fact is soft.

Normally, semantic soft facts are considered innocuous. Things become more complex when one passes from semantic soft facts to epistemic soft facts. Let us consider the following example: at t_0, a moment of the remote past, God knew that Emma would go to the party at t_2. Let us enrich the semantic framework depicted in Sect. 2.6.4 with some small additions: let K_G be an epistemic operator whose intended meaning is being known by God; φ describes the state of affairs such that Emma is at the party. We have then that:

$$\mathcal{M}, t_0 \models^{\mathsf{TRL}} K_G(\mathbf{F}\varphi)$$

By the factivity of the knowledge operator, we have $\mathcal{M}, t_0 \models^{\mathsf{TRL}} \mathbf{F}\varphi$, that is, it was true since ancient times that Emma would go to the party; this means that $\exists t' > t_0, t' \in \mathsf{TRL}$ and $\mathcal{M}, t' \models^{\mathsf{TRL}} \varphi$. In Fig. 4.1, the Thin Red Line is the history h_1. And this formally characterizes the idea according to which God is really omniscient about the future: He knows all the true propositions, namely, the Thin Red Line.

But this is just a half of the history. In order to *ensure* that Emma is really free, we need to introduce a sort of counterfactual dependence, that is:

(Alt) If Emma had made a different choice, then God would have known from ancient times that she would act differently.

(Alt) is essential if we want Emma to be really free, that is, if we want that the identity of the **TRL** is determined by her choice. The Ockhamist is then forced to accept a kind of counterfactual dependence. In other terms, Emma was not necessitated to go to the party; she freely chose to go to the party and God knew it, but if *she had made a different choice*, God would have known it (from ancient times). So, we can represent this situation by confronting two models, $\mathcal{M}_1$ and $\mathcal{M}_2$: in the first one Emma decides to go to the party, in the second one not.

$$\mathcal{M}_1, t_0 \vDash K_G(\mathbf{F}\varphi)$$
$$\mathcal{M}_1, t_1 \vDash \varphi$$
$$\mathcal{M}_2, t_0 \vDash K_G(\mathbf{F}\neg\varphi)$$
$$\mathcal{M}_2, t_1 \vDash \neg\varphi$$

In model $\mathcal{M}_1$, Emma decides to go to the party (and God knew that); analogously, in model $\mathcal{M}_2$, Emma decides to stay at home (and God knew that). Now, these states—Emma's choice and God's epistemic state—are always correlate: there never exists a model in which there is discrepancy between Emma's decision and God's belief. Regularities, as scientists and philosophers of science know very well, require *explanations*, and the most natural is that regularities are due to some form of *causal nexus*.[9] Moreover, the causal relationship is oriented—at least *prima facie*—from the past toward the future: the cause precedes the effect.[10] Thus, the natural answer

---

[9] Clearly, not all the correlations are signs of deep causal relationships, as several fallacies show very well.

[10] Much ink has been spent on this point. There are accounts of causation that relax this condition, including, for instance, causes contemporary with their effects or forms of backwards causation. We will see these options in a moment.

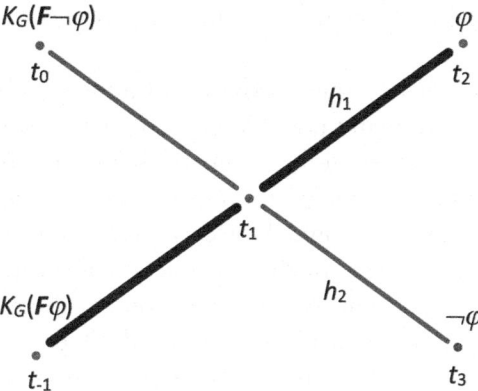

Fig. 4.2 Butterfly schema

to construe the correlation between God's state of knowledge and Emma's free decision is that God, in some way, causes Emma's choice. Anathema! The Ockhamist absolutely rejects this conclusion, which precludes the agent's freedom. It is Emma, again, who is the cause of her own choice. So, the Ockhamist must claim that the reason why the states are always correlated is that the free agent's choice influences God's knowledge even if the former follows the latter.

The Ockhamist is forced to accept a "butterfly" topology of time such as that represented in Fig. 4.2; the branching is not only toward the future but also toward the past (from a formal point of view, this feature is characterized by the property of *convergence*). In the classic branching time structures, all the instants before a given instant t are linearly ordinate. That is: if $t_1 < t_0$ and $t_2 < t_0$, then $t_1 < t_2 \lor t_2 < t_1 \lor t_1 = t_2$. As we have seen, the branching toward the future tries to grasp the intuition according to which the future is, somehow, open and indeterminate *unlike* the past; apart from their ontological consistency, future and past are not on a par. Even if one is eternalist—and therefore she grants the same ontological status to the past as to the future—the branching differentiates the past from the future: the future of the world at t is, in a sense, indeterminate since different and mutually incompatible possible future courses of events stem from t. On the contrary, the past of

t is fixed; things have gone in a certain way and they cannot be modified any more.

On the other hand, the Ockhamist butterfly schema revises this intuition. There are many possible pasts, that is, there are at least two past histories with respect to t_1: in one of them it is true that God knew that Emma would go to the party; in the other it is true that God knew that Emma would stay at home. However, precisely as possible futures are not all on a par, since one of them is the actual future of the world, so also possible pasts are not on a par, since one of them is the actual past of the world, what has in fact been actualized. One of the histories of the world is marked because it is the history that has been actualized and that will be actualized. The other histories, with different pasts and futures, are histories that could have actualized but they did not.

The Ockhamist, thus, is committed not only to the semantic soft facts (which many are ready to accept), but also to other, more robust, kinds of soft facts. In particular she must claim that divine beliefs about future free human choices are soft facts since they depend on such future free human choices. The Ockhamist's problem is, thus, to show how a worldly fact—as a belief—can depend on a future fact. Beliefs are much more robust facts than the semantic facts, and it is far from clear whether they can be soft.

Ockhamists are usually very careful to specify the sense in which we can determine and manipulate the past. In particular, they want to avoid the following, very weird, metaphysical view of the openness of the past: it is possible that a fact is a past fact until t and it is no longer a past fact *after* t. Namely, the fact that Thomas ate a pizza is a fact of the past just until a certain instant of time, and then this fact changes its deep metaphysical nature and it becomes no longer past. Ockhamists usually claim to be committed not to the statement that it is metaphysically possible to *change* the past but to the statement that it is metaphysically possible to *determine* it.

That said, the Ockhamist can move from the argument rejecting logical fatalism by means of semantic soft facts to the argument rejecting theological fatalism by means of the idea that God's beliefs are soft facts. This passage might seem rather natural: if it is true that yesterday it was true that Emma tomorrow will drink a beer (provided that Emma will actually drink her beer), and if it is true that God believes all true propositions, then it is also true that yesterday God believed that tomorrow Emma will drink a beer. The argument can easily be extended from logical fatalism to theological fatalism. Merricks (2009) actually makes this extension:

> My objection to this argument builds on an idea that goes back at least to Origen, who says: "…it will not be because God knows that an event will occur that it happens; but, because something is going to take place it is known by God before it happens." Similarly, I say that God has certain beliefs about the world because of how the world is, was, or will be — and not vice versa. For example, God believes *that there are no white ravens* because there are no white ravens, and not the other way around. And God believed, a thousand years ago, *that Jones sits at* t because Jones will sit at t, and not the other way around. (p. 52)

Ockhamists, then, do not claim that the past is in a certain way until t and then in another way after t. Rather, they say that the past is determined by and dependent on future human actions. The fact that tomorrow Emma will drink a beer does not change the truth of the proposition that tomorrow Emma will drink a beer. This proposition is not first false and then true. Rather, the fact that tomorrow Emma will drink a beer determines the truth of the proposition that tomorrow Emma will drink a beer. This proposition is true *because* tomorrow Emma will drink a beer. The same applies to God's beliefs: they are not modified by our actions. It is not the case that until yesterday God did not believe two centuries ago that tomorrow Emma would drink a beer, whereas today the past is changed and it is now true that God believed two centuries ago that Emma would drink a beer tomorrow. Rather, some past divine beliefs are dependent on our future free actions. The fact that God believed two centuries ago that Emma would drink a beer tomorrow is determined by the fact that Emma will drink a beer tomorrow.

Ockhamists' main idea is precisely such: by our decisions we determine *some* future facts and *some* past events. This idea—that we cannot change but we can determine the past as we can determine some future events—has been clearly expressed by Mavrodes (1984):

When people speak of the impossibility of changing the past what they generally have in mind is this. To change the past would be to bring it about that at a certain time the past contained a certain event, and then at a later time did not contain it. If, for example, the past from 1943 to 1982 contained the Second World War, and then after 1982 *no longer* contained that tragic event, then the past would have changed in the way said to be impossible. To put it in the formal mode of speech, a change in the past would involve a time at which it was true that *E has occurred*, and a later time at which it was not true that *E* has occurred. I, at any rate, have no intention of denying this alleged impossibility. It seems to me to be quite correct. What is envisaged here is absolutely impossible, and neither God nor man can do it. And, for what it is worth, the future seems to me to be unchangeable in a thoroughly parallel way. That is, it is not possible that there be a time at which *E will occur* is true and an earlier time at which *E will occur* is not true. But the impossibility of changing the past in this sense is not relevant to the thesis we are considering here. For we need not be considering a case of changing the past, but rather one of determining or affecting the past. And that is a different matter. (pp. 136–137)

Mavrodes argues that if it is not possible to change the past, it is not possible to change the future either. However, we can determine or affect the future. In the same way, he says, we can determine or affect some past events, even though he admits that he has no idea of which past events we can actually determine.

Notice that our butterfly schema accounts for this Ockhamist intuition. In the **TRL**, that is, in the actual history of the world, the past is never changed. It is what it is. However, some past facts *depend* on future facts. Even though the past is never changed, it could have been different, meaning that there is a possible history of the world, different from the actual history, in which in the past things different from those that actually occurred occurred because, in the future, things different from those that will actually occur will occur.

Still, even with these specifications, which render the thesis less implausible, Ockhamism is committed to a sort of backward causation in which future events cause past events. This seems to be in conflict with our intuition that the past determines the future, but the future does not affect the past. Backward causation is not, by itself, logically contradictory or *conceptually* impossible[11]—after all, even the possibility that something happens with no cause is consistent—but it is not clear whether it is *metaphysically* possible. The examples that can be brought about in favour of the metaphysical possibility of backward causation, such as pre-cognition, tachyons or time travel, are very doubtful.[12] Ockhamists often rebut the charge of being compromised with peculiar metaphysical possibilities by claiming that they are just committed to the counterfactual dependence of the past with respect to the future, but not to the causal dependence of the past with respect to the future.[13] In other words, Ockhamists claim to be committed to the thesis that *if* the future had been different from the actual future, then also the past would have been (partially) different from the actual past, but not to the thesis that the future *causes* the past to be what it is. It is not clear, however, whether this distinction between counterfactual and causal dependences is genuine. For instance, many theories account for the concept of causal dependence by means of the concept of counterfactual dependence.[14] So, the distinction between counterfactual dependence and backward causation has a price: either the price of embracing a non-counterfactual theory of causation or the price of postulating some conditions which exclude the fact that the counterfactual dependence of divine beliefs on human actions is a causal dependence. Furthermore, it is not clear whether the concept of counterfactual dependence of the past with respect to the future is, from a metaphysical point of view, more respectable than the concept of backward causation. One could argue that the concept of backward causation is doubtful just because it entails a metaphysical dependence of the past with respect to the future. It is this dependence that is doubtful. So, the concept of backward causation is just a particular case of a more general problem.

---

[11] It is contradictory only if a view is embraced whereby the temporal order of events is determined by the causal order of events. For such a view, see Reichenbach (1956).

[12] For a discussion on the idea of backward causation, see Craig (1991, pp. 94–157).

[13] On this line of thought, see Craig (1986, 1991), Merricks (2009, 2011) also claims that his approach is not committed to backward causation.

[14] For instance, Lewis (2013) says: "If c and e are two actual events such that e would have not occurred without c, then c is a cause of e" (p. 563).

4.5 Metaphysics of Time and Ockhamism

In the previous section, we showed which conception of soft fact the Ockhamist is committed to. In this section, we will try to evaluate how problematic is the other assumption of the Ockhamist project: the existence of a **TRL**. About the Thin Red Line much has been written.[15] From an indeterministic point of view, there could be perplexities about the existence of an actual course of events. As we mentioned in Sect. 2.6.4, about the logic of the future, there is a sort of disagreement among scholars. Some believe that indeterminism is incompatible with the idea of a **TRL**. Rather than repeating their arguments, here, we want to investigate the question by connecting it to the problem of the ground of future tensed propositions and of the metaphysics of time. In particular, we would like to show whether the notion of true future is more in tune with an eternalist metaphysics of time than with other metaphysical frameworks.

In fact, if one had an argument that showed that, for instance, Ockhamism is *incompatible* with a certain metaphysics of time, say, Presentism, this would be a problem for those who want to embrace Presentism (or other A-theories) and Ockhamism. On the other hand, let us hypothesize we have established that Ockhamism *requires* a certain metaphysics of time—Eternalism, say. If we have independent arguments to reject Eternalism, this, in turn, becomes a problem for Ockhamism. In general, *any* proposal to solve the problem of divine omniscience and human freedom has a theoretical advantage in being *compatible* with more metaphysical options.[16] We will show that this is not the case. To anticipate: we will show that the Ockhamist view is not, in fact, compatible with a presentist metaphysics and with the other A-theoretic metaphysical frameworks. Probably, our arguments are not decisive but we think that the burden of proof is on the presentist Ockhamist

---

[15] See, for instance, the collection of excellent essays in Correia and Iacona (2012).

[16] A situation similar, in some respects, is Tarski's famous remark in his Tarski (1944); as is well known, Tarski claims that his conception of truth is compatible with various epistemological and metaphysical views. One can be a realist, idealist and so on and, nevertheless, accept what the semantic theory of truth says about the notion of truth and its formal properties.

shoulders. So, we vindicate Rhoda's claim (see Sect. 3.1.2) according to which if one accepts the causal and ontic openness of the future, she must also accepts its alethic openness.

One of the key points of Ockhamism is that there exists a true future among the many possible futures and that this future is known by God from the beginning of time. If we analyse this intuition from the point of view of its ontological commitment, it seems natural to assume that there exist now future states of affairs that make future tensed propositions true. It then seems natural to assume that the following entailment holds:

- Ockhamism $\Rightarrow$ Eternalism

Finch and Rea (2008) agree. They call q_S the proposition that agent S will perform A in a future instant t and they state that:

> The presentist [...] insists that the only time that exists simpliciter is the present time. She believes that the only concrete events that exist simpliciter are the events that are currently taking place and the only concrete objects that exist simpliciter are those that exist now; she cannot abide an ontological distinction between what exists simpliciter and what exists at the present time. So, according to the presentist, S's performance of A exists only if S is performing A at the present time. Since the presentist denies that S's performing A exists when other times—times at which S is not performing A—are present, she obviously cannot say that the truth value of q_S depends on anything that S is doing or has done. For, again, q_S was true (and unchangeably so) nearly a billion years before S ever existed; so its truth value does not depend on S's existence. (p. 13)

Obviously, if this were the case, it would shrink the theoretical range of Ockhamism. What if, for independent reasons, we do not want to adopt an eternalist metaphysics?

However, although we agree with Finch and Rea's conclusion, we believe that they have given insufficient reasons to support it. Saying that future states of affairs do not exist in the presentist framework is not enough to demonstrate that Ockhamists cannot be presentists. After all, presentists have similar problems with past tensed sentences: they think that past states of affairs do not exist, but this does not mean that they reject the truth of past tensed sentences. As we will see, this is a complex question which requires a sort of *detour* about the relationship between truth and time. We will show that there exist two ways to account for past truths in a presentist context, which will be examined in Sects. 4.5.1 and 4.5.2, respectively; in the following three sections the combinations between Ockhamism and Eternalism, Presentism and other A-theories are examined. We will see that, while Ockhamist Eternalism is a coherent position, the strategies to ground the truth of past tensed sentences within Presentism cannot be extended to future tensed sentences. This extension is *precluded* by an essential component of Ockhamism. Comparable problems also bother the other A-theories. Our conclusion is that Ockhamists are committed to Eternalism.

4.5.1 Presentism and Truth

As frequently happens in philosophical debates, we are in the presence of a tension between basic intuitions we are not ready to easily give up. Here, the two intuitions are the following:

Presentism   Everything that exists is present.[17]
Truth   The truth of a proposition *depends* on how things are.

Since Presentism has been analysed in Sect. 2.1, we will focus on **Truth**. From a very general point of view, one can say that it codifies the common sense principle, according to which truth has to do with reality. Philosophically, this intuition is captured by the Aristotelian correspondentist conception of truth. This is a very long-lived philosophical thesis; many centuries later, the same idea is roughly expressed by the *Grounding Intuition*:

Grounding   Every true proposition depends for its truth on the world.[18]

---

[17] There are problems with the very formulation of the presentist thesis. See Meyer (2005) and Mozersky (2011).
[18] This is Alex Baia's formulation (see Baia 2012).

Although **Truth** and **Grounding** are quite plausible, they do not *explain* very much. Specifically, they do not say how the dependence relationship between being and truth is. As we will see, there are more possible interpretations of **Truth** and **Grounding**. The following exploits the notion of *truth-maker*:

Truth-making A proposition is true because there exists something that makes it true.

The concept of truth-making has been heavily discussed starting with the seminal paper (Mulligan et al. 1984). We deliberately leave undetermined the metaphysics of truth-making, that is, the kind of entities that make propositions true. In the following, for convenience, we refer to *facts* as truth-makers. Those who claim that *any* true proposition is true in virtue of a fact embrace a form of *Truth-making maximalism*, a quite committal view in metaphysics. Much discussed counterexamples are necessary truths—which seem to be true without the contribution of any (contingent) fact—and negative truths.[19]

Basing on a certain ontological economy, Lewis (2001) and Bigelow (1988) proposed a modification of **Truth-making** that is able to account for negative and necessary truths with no inflation of the base ontology. The idea is to exploit the concept of *supervenience*: truth supervenes on being. If the subvenient basis is modified, the class of truths will be modified as well. And vice versa, it is not possible to have a difference in truth without changing what exists (or what is instantiated) in the subvenient basis. A little more formally:

TSB For any proposition p and any worlds w_1 and w_2, if p is true in w_1 but not in w_2, then either something exists in one world but not the other, or else some object instantiates a property or a relation in one world but not the other.

---

[19] This is a problem already known by Plato: what makes the proposition "Theaetetus does not fly" true? The alleged negative fact that Theaetetus does not fly? But are there such facts? The truth-making problem also concerns mathematical (a particular case of necessary truths), ethical and aesthetic truths. We are in the Procrustes bed: it is complicated to give up a robust notion of truth in those fields of investigation, but, at the same time, it is committal to buy ontologies that include ethical, mathematical and aesthetic facts.

TSB (Truth Supervenes on Being) allows one to solve the case of negative and necessary truths: in a sense, it is the totality of existent things that allows the supervenience of these truths.[20] In any case, **TSB**—as well as more demanding forms of truth-making—are incompatible, at least *prima facie*, with Presentism. Let us consider, indeed, the following true past proposition:

(3) Napoleon was defeated at Waterloo

In light of **TSB**, this proposition is false unless there is some difference in existing things. Obviously, the eternalist—according to whom the past exists as the present—has no problem here. (3) is grounded by the past states of affairs. Things are different for the presentist, who, by assumption, confines what exists to the present; thus, (3) is false unless there is some difference in present things. But it is possible that the present is exactly how it is now and that Napoleon was not defeated at Waterloo. Therefore, the present scenario is not sufficient to account for the truth of (3). However, the presentist has at her disposal just the present as subvenient basis for the truth. It follows that the presentist cannot account for past truths such as (3). Now, since giving up past truths is "epistemically repugnant" (paraphrasing Michael Dummett), one concludes that Presentism should be dropped.

The same point can be analysed reasoning on possible worlds. Let us imagine two presentist possible worlds: w_1 and w_2. By hypothesis, w_1 and w_2 are identical at the present instant. However, it is not hard to imagine a case in which, in w_2, say, it is false that Napoleon was defeated at Waterloo. As an extreme situation, one can imagine that w_2 is a Russell's world, that is, a world that came into existence just three minutes ago and is totally indistinguishable, by hypothesis, from the actual world at the present moment. In Russell's world, the past has never existed, and all the traces of the past (memories, photographs, historical documents, etc.) are fake. But then, there is nothing in the present which can make true in w_1

---

[20] Clearly, the opponents could attack this account on the basis of the poor explanatory power of this view (see, for instance, Jago (2013)) But this debate is out of our goals.

and false in w_2 that Napoleon was defeated at Waterloo, since w_1 and w_2 are indistinguishable.

The presentist is in danger: on the one hand, she does not want to give up her metaphysics of time (which has, as we have seen in Sect. 2.1, undeniable advantages); on the other hand, this is in tension, at least *prima facie*, with a hardly negotiable principle of truth. What are the possible answers to this problem? In the debate, there are two big families[21] of answers. The first approach tries to *enrich* the present in order to have a strong enough base for the supervenience of truths; the second approach, in a sense more radical, liberalizes the **TSB** principle and tries to show that the general intuition that the truth is grounded on being can be maintained even without **TSB**. In the following, we take into account mainly the second approach. But, first, let us take a look to the strategy of enriching the present.

According to some scholars, since **Truth-making** and **Presentism** are in tension, it is the latter that must be revised; only the present exists, but what is present is, in fact, metaphysically richer than it appears at first sight. There are many variants of this strategy. Some claim that the universe acquires some complex tensional properties such as *being such that Napoleon was defeated at Waterloo*. These properties are presently instantiated by the universe: this should save both Presentism and truth-making.[22] Others posit the existence of an *ersatz structure*, that is, a B-series of propositions that describe the past, present and future states of the world. For example:

> Abstract times, on this view, are presently existing abstract objects. One of these abstract times represents how things are, others represent how things were, and still others represent how things will be. To distinguish past, present, and future, we need to suppose that, unlike abstract worlds, abstract times stand in a linear order, one induced by a being earlier than (or a being later than) relation that holds between abstract times. (Sanson and Caplan 2010, p. 32)

---

[21] As often happens, some positions that belong to the same general strategy of solution are, actually, very different.
[22] See, for instance, Bigelow (1996).

There are, moreover, thinkers who advocate the existence of abstract entities (*haecceitas*), which, being abstract, exist at any time, and then also at the present; according to this approach, Napoleon does not exist but his *haecceitas* does and it instantiates the property of being defeated at Waterloo.[23] Other philosophers try to enrich the present without using abstract entities; let us hypothesize that all things are constituted by some fundamental elements (atoms, strings or whatever) that, as such, are essentially indestructible and unchangeable. By "Napoleon" we mean, actually, an extremely complex configuration of these particles (again, their real physical nature is clearly unessential for the argument). Now, Napoleon does not exist but the particles that composed him in the past exist and they instantiate a series of properties that are sufficient to make true the past proposition that Napoleon was defeated at Waterloo.[24]

There are at least two criticisms against this strategy of enrichment of the present:

1. The manoeuvre is extremely expensive from the ontological point of view. This is ironic since one of the advantages of Presentism over Eternalism is its alleged economical simplicity: according to the presentist, there are no past and future facts. But, in order to save **Truth-making**, the presentist invokes a series of quite strange entities, which are at odds with her ontological sobriety. Moreover, it is not clear that the so enriched present, after all, does not coincide with the whole four-dimensional manifold, removing, thus, the difference with Eternalism.
2. The manoeuvre seems to be inadequate from the *explanatory* point of view. Let us see why, by adapting Sanson and Caplan (2010)'s example. Let φ be the proposition "Emma is blonde" and $\mathbf{P}\varphi$ the past tensed proposition "Emma was blonde".

---

[23] For *haecceitas* as truth-makers of past propositions, see Keller (2004, pp. 96–99).
[24] For a similar theory, see Keller (2004, pp. 99–101).

Now, let us take into account two explanations of the truth of $\mathbf{P}\varphi$:

(a) The proposition that Emma was blonde is true *because* Emma has the property of *having been blonde*.
(b) The proposition that Emma was blonde is true *because* Emma *had* the property of being blonde.

It is easy to notice the difference between (a) and (b). In the first case, the tensional feature is downloaded onto the property and it cannot be otherwise since, according to **TSB**, what is true supervenes to what is present, in this case, the present instantiation of a past property. Now, there can be doubts about the existence of past properties ("having been blonde", "having been defeated", etc.) but the main problem is another. The main point is that (a) properly does not explain why $\mathbf{P}\varphi$ is true; or better, its explanatory contribution is dependent on (b). It is because Emma had a certain property that we are allowed to claim, in a derivative and almost parasitic way, that Emma has the property of having been blonde. The explanatory asymmetry is clear if we invert the direction of explanation. Let us suppose that one argues as follows: Emma was blonde because Emma has (now) the property of having been blonde. This seems absurd; it is because things have gone in a certain way that the present has, now, the traces of the past. The explanatory asymmetry can be applied to the most debated cases of enrichment of the present: the entities that enrich the present and serve as truth-makers for past truths are explanatorily dependent on what happened in the past.[25] Thus, it seems that this strategy of keeping **TSB** is unpromising.

Some other scholars[26] chose to modify **TSB**. However, the amendment must not be too much revisionary about the original grounding intuition. There is no doubt that, when an anti-realist theory of truth is assumed, the problem does not arise. But this is at odds with the original link between truth and being.

---

[25] This point has been advocated in great detail by Tallant and Ingram (2015).
[26] For instance, Sanson and Caplan (2010), Tallant (2009a, 2010), Baia (2012), and Tallant and Ingram (2015).

4.5.2 TSB Revisited

Let us consider, once again, the truth-making principle:

Truth-making A proposition is true because there exists something that makes it true.

The existence of a truth-maker explains the truth of the proposition at issue. It is not difficult to notice that the principle is formulated in a tenseless way: the reason why the proposition at play is true is that something that makes it true *exists* tenselessly. But the presentist reads the verbal present tense as "ontological" present; therefore, she is forced to claim that something that makes true a past proposition must exist presently. Hence, the strategy of enrichment we have just seen. But, it is possible to block the argument by focusing on the tenseless character of the truth-making principle. If a past tensed proposition is true, so the presentist argues, then the truth-maker of that proposition *existed*; analogously (and we will return on this point in the following), if a future tensed proposition is true, then the truth-maker of that proposition *will exist*. The truth-making principle is, thus, formulated from a tensed point of view:

Tensed Truth-making A proposition is true because something that makes it true exists or existed or will exist.

In this case, the presentist is not committed to the present existence of truth-makers: Napoleon does not exist anymore, but he did, and the event of his defeat at Waterloo makes true the past tensed proposition "Napoleon was defeated at Waterloo" The supervenience principle too can be revisited in a tensed way:

(TSTB) For any worlds w_1 and w_2, let φ be the proposition that something exists in one world but not the other, or else some object instantiates a property or a relation in one world but not the other. For any proposition p, if p is true in w_1 but not w_2, then φ or $\mathbf{P}\varphi$ or $\mathbf{F}\varphi$.[27]

Let us recall what we said about Lewis' and Bigelow's argument for supervenience. In that case, the worlds w_1 and w_2 were indistinguishable (from the present perspective) but, in the first one, it is true that Napoleon was defeated at Waterloo while in the other this is not true (maybe because w_2 was created *ex nihilo* five minutes ago). In the case of **TSTB** (Truth Supervenes on Tensional Being), the worlds *are* different since in the first one Napoleon *was defeated* at Waterloo and in the other he was not.

There are, of course, criticisms to the tensed version of **TSB**. Some insist on a rather debated charge to Presentism: its difficulty in accounting for cross-temporal relations. The proposition that Emma is smaller than Napoleon has a cross-temporal nature: a *relatum* (Emma) is presently existent, but she maintains a relation with another entity (Napoleon) which does not exist (any more). Therefore, according the presentist who accepts **TSTB**, the truth-maker of this proposition should be mixed, being constituted by entities that exist and those that do not exist (even if they existed). It is, doubtless, a strange truth-maker. A possible way out is paraphrasing; when one says that Emma is smaller than Napoleon, she *actually* says something more complex, that is:

- Emma has a certain height (and this proposition is made true by how things are arranged at the present)
- Napoleon *had* a certain height (and this proposition is made true by how things *were* arranged in the past).
- From the previous propositions, it follows that Emma is smaller than Napoleon.

To give support to the third point, it is necessary to assume a principle concerning Truth-making and Entailment: if a certain proposition has a

---

[27] For a defence of **Tensional TSB**, see Tallant (2009a,b, 2010), Sanson and Caplan (2010), Baia (2012), Tallant and Ingram (2015). For criticisms to this principle, see Torrengo (2013, 2014), Asay and Baron (2014), Baron (2015).

truth-maker, then that truth-maker will make true all the propositions that logically follow from it (if $S \vDash \varphi$ and $\varphi \rightarrow \psi$ then $S \vDash \psi$).[28]

It is beyond our goals to continue the analysis and the defence of the **TSTB** principle. Rather, we would like to evaluate which metaphysics of time Ockhamism is compatible with and what the possibilities of grounding future tensed propositions are.

4.5.3 Eternalist Ockhamism

The debate about the grounding of temporal propositions has been mainly focused on the propositions that describe past things. This is perfectly understandable. There are very few disposed to renounce the truth of "Napoleon was defeated at Waterloo". What about the future? As for the past, the eternalist has no problem in providing a truth-maker for future tensed propositions: $\mathbf{F}\varphi$ is true if the future history of the world makes φ true. Such a history is actual and then also the fact that makes such a formula true is actual. The eternalist, then, can also endorse **TSB** for the propositions about the future.

Must the eternalist be determinist? No, as we have seen in Sect. 2.5. The eternalist conceives the whole history of the world as actually existing, but she need not accept that every stage t of this history (together with the laws of nature) univocally determines any following stages t'. Thus, Eternalism is fully compatible with a strong conception of freedom.[29] As we have seen, one of the most plausible representations of the world for the eternalist, who accepts the openness of the future, is the following. There exists an actual history of the world in which, however, not every instant determines the subsequent ones. At the points of indeterminateness, alternative histories branch off; they are histories that could have happened but they did not. Let us suppose that the world at t leaves two possibilities open: Emma can drink a beer or not. And let us suppose that the history in which Emma drinks her beer is actual. In the eternalist libertarian framework, the reason why the history of the world

---

[28] For a discussion, see Armstrong (2003) and Restall (1996).
[29] For a defence of the compatibility of Eternalism and libertarian free will, see Ocklander (1998).

in which Emma decides to have her beer is actual *depends* on Emma's choice.

It is easy to understand how this ontological view fits well with the Ockhamist's preferences. In this framework, it is easy to take on board a semantics of the future fully in line with Ockhamists' desires. A formula such as $\mathbf{F}\varphi$ is true if in the actual future φ is true. The actual future is the Thin Red Line: the future that will happen. The Ockhamist eternalist can, thus, preserve **TSB** and, at the same time, provide a ground for future tensed propositions since there are future facts that make these propositions true. Thus, the Ockhamist eternalist need not liberalize **TSB** through **TSTB**.

The Ockhamist has to add the soft facts, namely, alternative pasts. Therefore, any possible history that departs from the instant t has not only a different future but also a different past—the past in which God has different beliefs. So we return to the butterfly schema (see Fig. 4.3).

For the Ockhamist eternalist, the **TRL** is wholly composed by actual facts. In this case, the divine belief at t_{-1} that in future φ will be true and the fact that at t_2 φ is true are both actual. The alternative history, in which God believes that φ will be false and in which indeed φ is false, is just possible, but not actual. The possibility of a semantics like this refutes the implication $\mathbf{C} \to \mathbf{O}$, which Rhoda considers correct (cf. Sect. 3.1.2).

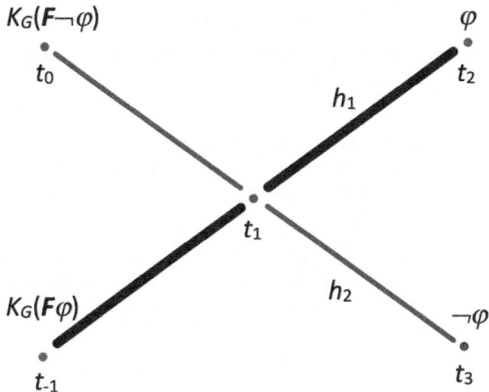

Fig. 4.3 Butterfly schema (again)

That the future is ontologically closed (i.e. that there is a unique existent future) does not imply that it is causally closed (i.e. is compatible with indeterminism).

4.5.4 Presentist Ockhamism?

Ockhamism is entirely compatible with an eternalist framework. Is it also compatible with a presentist metaphysics? We have seen that Finch and Rea (2008) deny this since future tensed propositions would lack truth-makers. One could ask whether this conclusion is premature. The presentist has different strategies to ground past truths, as we have seen. Why not transfer these theoretical manoeuvres to future truths?

We saw that the presentist has at her disposal two main strategies to ground past truths; either she keeps **TSB** and enriches the present through the addition of entities that make past truths true or she liberalizes **TSB** through **TSTB** and she claims that a proposition like $P\varphi$ is true because, in the past, a truth-maker of φ existed. One can also try to apply these two strategies to future truths such as $F\varphi$.[30]

As we have seen, the first solution is very expensive from the ontological point of view and, moreover, it is not explanatory, given that the present facts that should ground past truths seem to be, in turn, explained by the fact that certain past states of affairs existed. If applied to future truths, such a strategy is still more expensive. For instance, Bigelow (1996) claims that the tensed properties that the universe possesses—such as

---

[30] Actually, the presentist has at her disposal a third option: she can endorse determinism. This is Markosian (2013)'s view, who states that the grounding of future truths must lie in the present state of the world and the laws that rule it. He argues:

> This is the short version of my proposed solution to The Truthmaker Problem. If things now are such that it is a deterministic matter that there will be Martian outposts in 1000 years, then I say [that this proposition is] true now. Otherwise, I say, let [this proposition] be false now. [...] In this way, the truth about the past and the future will be determined by the way present things are right now, in accordance with Presentism and The Truthmaker Principle. (Markosian 2013, p. 7)

We do not discuss this view since it cannot be defended by the Ockhamist: Ockhamism is, in fact, an indeterminist position. If it were not so, the very concept of **TRL** would make no sense.

the property of being such that Napoleon was defeated at Waterloo—are traces that past events left in the present. It is because Napoleon was defeated at Waterloo that, now, the universe has that particular property. Now, this train of thought is not clearly applicable to the future: it is hard to imagine that the future leaves traces in the present. Of course, this is not a decisive argument against these theories, but it is a further cost.

Much more promising is the second strategy, based on the liberalization of **TSB** and on the assumption of **TSTB**. One could argue as following. By adopting **TSTB**, the presentist can easily respond to Finch and Rea (2008)'s criticism: as in the past case, a proposition such as $F\varphi$ is true even if no present state of affairs that makes φ true exists; for its truth, it is sufficient that a fact that makes φ true *will exist* in the future; the truth of $F\varphi$ is grounded on what will happen and, in our cases, on what the agent will choose. This is a way out which could—at least *prima facie*—make Ockhamism compatible with Presentism: it is true that Emma will go to the party because a certain future situation in which Emma goes to the party will exist. Being is confined (so to speak) to the present, but truth supervenes to the things that existed, that exist, and that will exist. This approach adopts, from the point of view of the truth-making theory, a symmetry between past and future.

However, this second recovery strategy for future truths is probably doomed to failure. The Ockhamist cannot consider the past and the future in the same way since the future is, contrarily to the past, open. When we refer to the truth-maker of a proposition, we think that it must be some determinate entity, for instance, a certain fact. This can be a present or a past fact, but it is, in any case, determinate. However, things are different in the case of branching. Let us think about the proposition "Emma will go to the party". This sentence is true if a determinate fact will exist. But if a determinate fact will exist, then there is a unique future and no branching.

Let us consider a simple bifurcation, at instant t. t has two future histories. Let us suppose that in one history it is true that φ and in the other it is not. How to explain the truth of $F\varphi$? The presentist Ockhamist might claim, by symmetry with the past, that such a proposition is true if a truth-maker of φ *will exist*. But the point is that, at the moment, it is indeterminate whether there will be such a truth-maker. It is not determinate which history will become real. The presentist who accepts **TSTB** can argue that a proposition such as **P**φ has a truth value because a truth-maker of φ existed. But for the future, things are different. Not only is there no present truth-maker for **F**φ but it is indeterminate whether this truth-maker will exist. There is nothing at the present time that can say which history stemming from the present instant will become real; therefore, one cannot rely on the fact that a truth-maker will make φ true, since there is a future history that contains no truth-maker for φ.

The presentist Ockhamist could insist on the very idea of **TRL**, that is, of the true future. It is already true or false that **F**φ *because* there will be or will not be a truth-maker of φ in the true future history of the world. One or the other history will become real, even though we do not know which one, and this history makes **F**φ true or false *now*. However, this reasoning is not convincing. Based on the supervaluationist intuition, one might say that the Ockhamist presentist is right in believing that one or the other history will become the actual history of the world, so that **F**$\varphi \vee$ **F**$\neg\varphi$ is true now; however, it would be wrong to conclude that **F**φ is true or that **F**$\neg\varphi$ is true now. These formulas are both indeterminate because there exists a history in which they are true and a history in which they are false.

We believe to have shown that the presentist Ockhamism—that is, the view according to which the future is ontologically and causally open, but alethically closed—tends to be unstable. Using Rhoda's symbols (Sect. 3.1.2), we believe that $(\neg\mathbf{A} \wedge \mathbf{C}) \rightarrow \neg\mathbf{O}$, that is, if the future is alethically closed but causally open, then it is ontologically closed. This principle is equivalent to $\mathbf{O} \rightarrow (\mathbf{A} \vee \neg\mathbf{C})$, that is, if the future is ontologically open, then either it is alethically open or it is causally closed. In other words, if the future does not exist yet, only determinism can ensure the truth of future tensed sentences.

4.5.5 Growing Block and Spotlight Ockhamism

In this section, we shall briefly discuss whether it is possible to combine Ockhamism with the Growing Block view or the Moving Spotlight Theory. We will show that the Growing Block and the Spotlight Ockhamist share the same problems of their presentist cousin but, in addition, they have some more troubles.

Let us begin by showing that the Ockhamist who accepts the Growing Block or Spotlight ontology of time shares the same problems with the presentist. According to the Growing Block theorist, all past facts exist but there is no future. So, the indeterminist Growing Block theorist claims that at the moment there are many open histories such that the current state of the world together with its laws does not univocally determine which one will be the future. However, the Ockhamist is forced to state that one of the possible future histories is the TRL, that is, the true history of the world. In particular, the Ockhamist has to provide truth-makers for truths such as $F\varphi$. But, since no future possible history is actual, it is easy to notice how the indeterminist Growing Block theorist, who admits a true future, is in the same position as the Ockhamist presentist.

For the MST theorist, the discourse is similar *modulo* some changes due to the different ontology. According to her, there are many future histories, and they are constituted by actual facts. But it is indeterminate on which of these possible paths the light of the present will travel. Let us suppose, for instance, that the light of the present illuminates t and that from t two histories stem: in one history, Emma drinks a beer; in the other, Emma drinks a Coke. Both these facts—Emma's drinking her beer and Emma's drinking her Coke—are existent, but it is indeterminate, now, which history the light of the present will illuminate. If the light will illuminate a certain fact, then φ will be true. Else, another proposition will be true. But, again, it is hard to reconcile this ontological framework with the idea that future tensed propositions *do* have a truth value.

In addition to these difficulties, the MST Ockhamist has another problem. She must accept—as any good Ockhamist—that the universe has a butterfly structure. There are many alternative pasts, only one of which has been illuminated: it is the "true past history". The MST Ockhamist is committed to the truth of counterfactuals such as the following: "If Emma had chosen to drink a Coke (rather than a beer), God would have believed something different from what He actually believed". If Emma had chosen otherwise, the light of the present would have traced a different path. By consequence, the fact that the light of the present illuminated a certain past fact (and not another) depends on Emma's free choices. But being illuminated by the light of the present seems to be a substantial fact of the world: it is a fundamental feature of the reality. However, the MST Ockhamist is forced to claim that such a fact is a soft fact which depends on the free choices of the agents. It is a consequence rather hard to swallow.

The Ockhamist has her natural place among eternalists. Although we do not claim to have provided a knock-down argument against the presentist (or the Growing Block theorist or MST theorist) who also accepts Ockhamism, we believe that these theoretical alternatives are rather implausible. This results in a further cost for Ockhamism, since it could be not endorsed by any advocate of those metaphysics of time.

4.6 Conclusion: Is There Really an Ockham's Way Out?

In this chapter, we have analysed the Ockhamist solution to the foreknowledge dilemma using the TRL semantics. Such a semantics posits the existence of a "true future" within a topologically open structure; this is what the Ockhamist needs in order to maintain, on the one hand, the idea according to which future contingents are known by God and, on the other hand, human free will. Moreover, Ockhamism maintains that, even if it is true that the future is semantically settled, nevertheless, this is a contingent fact and the future could be different. However, if the future were different, the past too would have been different.

The main theoretical costs of this view are two:

1. Past divine beliefs depend on future human decisions. There is, so it seems, a sort of backward causation. But that the future can cause the past is metaphysically suspect. Some Ockhamists deny being committed to some form of backward causation and claim that their view entails just a counterfactual dependence of the past on the future. The problem is that many authoritative analyses of the notion of cause exploited the very notion of counterfactual dependence in order to construe the relation of causation.

2. Ockhamism seems to entail Eternalism. Contrary to Finch and Rea (2008), we do not think that the simple admission of future truths entails Eternalism. Presentists have the theoretical resources to affirm that there are past truths, even if the past does not exist. What is problematic is the combination of an open future with the statement that the future does not exist: in this situation, there is no ground for future truths.

In the next chapter, we shall take into account a solution very close to Ockhamism: Molinism. It has some advantages compared to Ockhamism, but it adopts an even more complex and, therefore, ontologically expensive temporal model.

References

Adams, M.M. 1967. Is the existence of god a "hard" fact? *The Philosophical Review* 76(4): 492–503.
Armstrong, D. 2003. Truthmakers for modal truths. In *Real metaphysics*, ed. H. Lillehammer, and G. Rodriguez-Pereyra, 20–32. London: Routledge.
Asay, J., and S. Baron. 2014. The hard road to presentism. *Pacific Philosophical Quarterly* 95(3): 314–335.
Baia, A. 2012. Presentism and the grounding of truth. *Philosophical Studies* 159(3): 341–356.
Baron, S. 2015. A bump on the road to presentism. *American Philosophical Quarterly* 52(4): 345–356.
Bigelow, J. 1988. *The reality of numbers: a physicalist's philosophy of mathematics*. Oxford: Clarendon Press.
Bigelow, J. 1996. Presentism and properties. *Philosophical Perspectives* 10: 35–52.
Correia, F., and A. Iacona. 2012. *Around the tree: semantic and metaphysical issues concerning branching and the open future*, vol. 361. London: Springer.
Craig, W.L. 1986. Temporal necessity; hard facts/soft facts. *International Journal for Philosophy of Religion* 20(2–3): 65–91.
Craig, W.L. 1988. *The problem of divine foreknowledge and future contingents from Aristotle to Suarez*. Leiden: Brill.
Craig, W.L. 1991. *Divine foreknowledge and human freedom: the coherence of theism I: omniscience*, vol. 19. Leiden: Brill.

Craig, W.L. 2001. *God, time, and eternity: the coherence of theism II: eternity*. London: Springer.
De Florio, C., and A. Frigerio. 2018. Two kinds of soft facts. *Grazer Philosophische Studien* 95(1): 34–53.
De Florio, C., A. Frigerio, and A. Giordani. 2017. Tense and omniscience. In *Logic and philosophy of time: Themes from Prior*, ed. P. Hasle, P. Blackburn, and P. Øhrstrøm, vol. 1, 189–205. Aalborg: Aalborg Universitetsforlag.
Finch, A., and M. Rea. 2008. Presentism and Ockham's way out. In *Oxford studies in philosophy of religion*, ed. J. Kvanvig, vol. 1, 1–17. Oxford: Oxford University Press.
Freddoso, A.J. 1983. Accidental necessity and logical determinism. *The Journal of Philosophy* 80(5): 257–278.
Hoffman, J., and G. Rosenkrantz. 1984. Hard and soft facts. *The Philosophical Review* 93(3): 419–434.
Jago, M. 2013. The cost of truthmaker maximalism. *Canadian Journal of Philosophy* 43(4): 460–474.
Keller, S. 2004. Presentism and truthmaking. In *Oxford studies in metaphysics*, ed. D.W. Zimmerman, 83–104. Oxford: Oxford University Press.
Lewis, D. 2001. Truthmaking and difference-making. *Noûs* 35(4): 602–615.
Lewis, D. 2013. *Counterfactuals*. New York: Wiley.
Markosian, N. 2013. The truth about the past and the future. In *Around the tree*, ed. F. Correia, and A. Iacona, 127–141. London: Springer.
Mavrodes, G.I. 1984. Is the past unpreventable? *Faith and Philosophy* 1(2): 131–146.
Merricks, T. 2009. Truth and freedom. *Philosophical Review* 118(1): 29–57.
Merricks, T. 2011. Foreknowledge and freedom. *Philosophical Review* 120(4): 567–586.
Meyer, U. 2005. The presentist's dilemma. *Philosophical Studies* 122(3): 213–225.
Mozersky, J.M. 2011. Presentism. In *The Oxford handbook of philosophy of time*, ed. C. Callender, 122–144. Oxford: Oxford University Press.
Mulligan, K., P. Simons, and B. Smith. 1984. Truth-makers. *Philosophy and Phenomenological Research* 44(3): 287–321.
Mullins, R.T. 2016. *The end of the timeless God*. Oxford: Oxford University Press.
Ocklander, N. 1998. Freedom and the new theory of time. In *Questions of time and tense*, ed. R. Le Poidevin, 185–205. Oxford: Oxford University Press.
Pike, N. 1965. Divine omniscience and voluntary action. *The Philosophical Review* 74(1): 27–46.
Plantinga, A. 1986. On Ockham's way out. *Faith and Philosophy* 3(3): 235–269.

Reichenbach, H. 1956. *The direction of time*. California: University of California Press.
Restall, G. 1996. Truthmakers. entailment and necessity. *Australasian Journal of Philosophy* 74(2): 331—340.
Sanson, D., and B. Caplan. 2010. The way things were. *Philosophy and Phenomenological Research* 81(1): 24–39.
Saunders, J.T. 1966. Of God and freedom. *The Philosophical Review* 75(2): 219–225.
Tallant, J. 2009a. Ontological cheats might just prosper. *Analysis* 69(3): 422–430.
Tallant, J. 2009b. Presentism and truth-making. *Erkenntnis* 71(3): 407–416.
Tallant, J. 2010. Still cheating, still prospering. *Analysis* 70(3): 502–506.
Tallant, J., and D. Ingram. 2015. Nefarious presentism. *The Philosophical Quarterly* 65(260): 355–371.
Tarski, A. 1944. The semantic conception of truth: and the foundations of semantics. *Philosophy and Phenomenological Research* 4(3): 341–376.
Todd, P. 2013. Soft facts and ontological dependence. *Philosophical Studies* 164(3): 829–844.
Torrengo, G. 2013. The grounding problem and presentist explanations. *Synthese* 190(12): 2047–2063.
Torrengo, G. 2014. Ostrich presentism. *Philosophical Studies* 170(2): 255–276.
Zemach, E.M., and D. Winderker. 1987. Facts, freedom and foreknowledge. *Religious Studies* 23(1): 19–28.

5

Molinism

This chapter is devoted to Molinism, a solution to the dilemma of divine foreknowledge that has many points in common with Ockhamism. However, in the face of higher theoretical costs, Molinism is able to provide a theodicy and a solution that reconciles absolute divine sovereignty over the world with human freedom. Our aim in this chapter is to identify precisely these costs and to distinguish them from other costs usually attributed to Molinism, which are not such in our opinion. In particular, we will see that Molinism must suppose that time has the **TRL+** structure, in which every instant is part of a **TRL** relative to that instant. Molinists must also suppose that all the worlds among which God must choose before the creation have this structure. We will show that this structure implicates higher costs with respect to Ockhamism. By contrast, some criticisms levelled against Molinism, like that of circularity, turn out to be surmountable once this temporal structure is assumed.

The plan of this chapter is the following. Section 5.1 introduces the notion of conditional of freedom (CF), which is central in the Molinist view; Sect. 5.2 argues that **TRL+** is the temporal model implicitly assumed by this notion; Sect. 5.3 surveys the costs that this temporal model entails; Sect. 5.4 shows that, once this structure is assumed, Molinists need not pay further costs that have been charged to this approach. Section 5.5 concludes this chapter.

5.1 Conditionals of Freedom

Contemporary Molinism is inspired by the solution provided by the Spanish Jesuit Luis de Molina to the problem of divine foreknowledge in the sixteenth century. Part IV of the most important of his writings, entitled *Concordia liberi arbitrii cum gratiæ donis, divina præscientia, providentia, prædestinatione et reprobatione* (Lisbon, 1588) [The Compatibility of Free Choice with the Gifts of Grace, Divine Foreknowledge, Providence, Predestination, and Reprobation], was translated into English by Alfred Freddoso in 1988. This translation and Freddoso's long introduction, in which he explains the cornerstones of de Molina's view and defends it from some objections and misunderstandings, has sparked a lively debate within philosophy of religion. As a result, Molinism is one of the main solutions to the dilemma of divine prescience on the market today.

de Molina's view had also triggered a heated debate in the years in which his volume was published. His doctrine was virulently attacked by the Spanish Dominican Domingo Bañez, who accused him of denying efficacious grace. The controversy between defenders of de Molina and his opponents was so intense (Molina was even denounced to the Spanish Inquisition) that Pope Clement VIII imposed silence upon the contending parties in 1594 and established a special commission to settle the controversy. Initially, the commission expressed a very negative judgement on the Molinist doctrine, but the Pope was not satisfied by this result and ordered the commission to resume the work. The generals of the Dominicans and Jesuits were invited to appear before the commission in Rome with some of their theologians to state their cases. The generals defended, respectively, Bañez' and de Molina's positions before the commission: Jesuits accused Dominicans of advancing a theory of predestination incompatible with human freedom; Dominicans accused Jesuits of Pelagianism (the heretical doctrine according to which salvation was attainable in this life without the assistance of divine grace). Clement VIII died in 1605 and the commission continued its work under Pope

Paul V. In 1607, the commission finished its work without any decision about which of the two doctrines was correct. The Pope's decree, communicated on 5 September 1607 to both Dominicans and Jesuits, allowed each party to defend its own doctrine, prohibited each from censoring or condemning the opposite opinion, and ordered them to await the final decision of the Apostolic See. That decision, however, has never been reached, and both orders, consequently, maintained their respective theories. The echoes of the polemic between Jesuits and Dominicans have never been extinguished since then and have continued until today, albeit in a less vigorous way.

Here, we are not interested in either the reconstruction of the polemic or the exegesis of de Molina's writings; instead, we wish to analyse the theories of the contemporary scholars who are inspired by de Molina, independently of the question of whether or not these theories are faithful reworking of de Molina's doctrine.[1]

The notion of conditional of freedom is at the centre of Molinism, and the particular divine knowledge required for knowing these conditionals is called *scientia media* [middle knowledge] by de Molina. The typical form of a conditional of freedom (CF) is the following:

(CF) If agent a were in circumstances C, a would freely perform the act φ

CF states that if an agent were in certain circumstances, she would freely perform a certain action. Circumstances must be intended as the context in which an agent a has to make a choice. Such context includes at least the different options among which a can decide, her motivations, her physical and mental state, the chances of success if a certain course of action is undertaken, the physical and psychological context in which the decision is made and so on. If anything, the circumstances C can be interpreted as the state of the world at the moment at which the agent has to take a decision. Notice that a's choice of opting for φ is free.

---

[1] For a defence of the Molinist position, see, Flint (1998). For a collection of papers that discuss the Molinist view, cf. Perszyk (2011).

This freedom is intended to be in a libertarian sense: there is more than one possibility among which a has to choose, and the state of the world (namely, C) does not determine which of these options the agent will choose. Therefore, φ is just one of the options that a has at her disposal.

Molinism states that for every possible agent and for every set of possible circumstances in which the agent has to make a choice, there is one and only one true CF. From the alethic point of view, it is never indeterminate what a possible agent will do in a possible circumstance. Human beings do not know the truth value of a large number of CFs, but this is due to limits intrinsic to their knowledge. God lacks these restrictions and, therefore, He knows the truth of every CF through His *middle knowledge*.

This name comes from the fact that middle knowledge is halfway between the knowledge of eternal truths (called by de Molina *natural knowledge*) and of contingent truths (called by de Molina *free knowledge*). The knowledge of eternal truth and middle knowledge are pre-volitional, that is, they are possessed by God before the creation of one of the possible worlds. The knowledge of contingent truths is post-volitional and is grounded on the fact that God has created a certain possible world, in which certain contingent truths rather than others are true.

Before the creation of the world, God knows all necessary truths—for instance, mathematical truths—and all CFs. Necessary truths and CFs determine the space of possibilities in which God can perform His creative choice. For example, God cannot create a world in which $2 + 2 = 4$ is false; neither can He create a world in which an agent freely chooses differently from the way in which she has freely chosen. In other terms, if the CF "agent a would freely perform φ in circumstances C" is true, God cannot create a world in which agent a *freely* chooses something other than φ in circumstances C. God can certainly create a world in which a is *determined* to do something different, for instance, a world in which the agent is determined to choose ψ rather than φ. However, a's choice will *not* be free because she is determined to do what she does and she cannot do otherwise. What God can do is limited by human freedom: God cannot determine an agent to do *freely* something against her will. The free choices of an agent depend at least in part on her will.[2]

In the space of possibilities opened by eternal truths and CFs, God has chosen to create the world that He, in His wisdom, has considered as most satisfactory for His aims. In creating a world, God creates some agents and some circumstances in which these agents make their choices; these agents and circumstances *can* differ from world to world. Obviously, God can create a world devoid of free agents, in which every choice is determined by His will. But, if God decides to create a world with free agents, He must also choose which possible free agents to create and in which circumstances they will make their choices. God infallibly knows how human agents will act because He knows the truths of every CF and, on the basis of His creative choices, which agents will act in which circumstances.

Molinists can claim to have reconciled divine prescience and human freedom. By means of His middle knowledge and of His free knowledge, resulting from having created this world, God knows the actions that free agents will freely perform. Moreover, these actions are free because the truth of CFs (and, therefore, the knowledge of CFs) is not in contrast with human freedom. Although it is true that agent a will choose to do φ, many possibilities are open to the agent, and the circumstances in which she chooses do not determine her choice. The agent has *contingently* chosen to do φ: she might have chosen otherwise, if she had wished.

Molinism not only has the ambition to reconcile human freedom and divine prescience; it also aims to reconcile divine sovereignty and human freedom and to provide a theodicy. Let us see briefly how. The Molinist God cannot be surprised by the course of the world as the open-theist's God is because, in creating a world, God knows its outcomes in every detail. This knowledge is not in contrast with human freedom. This reconciliation of human freedom and divine prescience is a result that Molinists share with Ockhamists. However, the Ockhamist foreknowl-

---

[2] This principle is called by Plantinga *Leibniz' Lapse*: according to Plantinga, Leibniz's mistake is to consider divine omnipotence as the power to actualize every possible state of affairs. However, the states of affairs in which an agent acts in a way different from that prescribed by CFs are logically possible states of affairs that God cannot actualize. See Plantinga (1977).

edge is *simple* foreknowledge: although God foresees what human beings will do, Ockhamism cannot rule out that that human beings make choices against God's will and that the world takes a direction that He does not like. In a sense, the Ockhamist God can only take note of human beings' choices, even if in advance. He cannot intervene to change these choices because, if He did, His prescience would no longer imply knowledge of what will happen in the future: if God *knows* that a will do φ in the future, and if, as a result of His intervention, a will not do φ any more, then His knowledge of what a will do was not knowledge after all because knowledge entails truth. If God knows that a will do φ, then it is true that a will do φ and this truth cannot become a falsity in the development of the world, if we do not want to deny divine prescience. Ockhamists have, then, the problem of providing a plausible account of providence, given their solution to the foreknowledge dilemma.[3]

Molinists can say something more than Ockhamists. In particular, Molinists can offer a good explanation of divine providence and the government of the world. Moreover, Molinists can offer a theodicy. Let us start from the last point. As we have said, God knows all the possible arrangements of the world that He can actualize. He also knows, on the basis of CFs, that if He creates free agent a in circumstances C, a will freely choose to perform φ. God can "weigh" the different scenarios from

---

[3] The question of the uselessness or usefulness of simple foreknowledge has ignited an interesting debate within the analytic philosophy of religion. William Hasker and John Sanders have claimed that simple foreknowledge has no providential usefulness because it comes "too late": once God has taken note that the agent will act in a certain way, He can do nothing to ensure that the agent will choose differently (cf. Sanders (1997) and, for instance, Hasker (2004, pp. 188–193)). On the other hand, if God uses His knowledge of the fact that the agent will do φ to induce the agent to do φ, then a loop will be engendered: God knows that the agent will do φ because the agent will do φ and the agent will do φ precisely because God foreknows that she will do it. However, David Hunt has endorsed the thesis of the usefulness of simple foreknowledge for divine providential action. Hunt acknowledges that divine prescience that φ will occur in the future cannot be used to prevent or bring about φ, but his knowledge can be useful for operating in other areas of the world. For instance, foreseeing that Thomas will fall in love with Emma in the future, God can advise Emma not to marry Thomas because their marriage would be unhappy. If Emma listens to God's advice and marries Robert, then God's simple foreknowledge about Thomas will have a providentially efficacious result without engendering a loop and without preventing an already true future (see Hunt 1993a). A lively debate has arisen between these two opposite positions. For a criticism of Hunt's stance, cf. Basinger (1993), Kapitan (1993), Robinson (2004), Hasker (2009). For Hunt's replies to some of these objections, cf. Hunt (1993b, 1996, 2004).

the moral point of view: in some scenarios the agents behave well, in some scenarios the agents behave badly. It follows that, being perfectly good, God will actualize the best logically possible world, *given* CFs. This can also partly account for the fact that it is not difficult to imagine a better world than ours: for instance, a world in which heinous human choices have not led to massacres, genocides, tortures and so on. Such a world is possible from the logical point of view, but it does not satisfy CFs. Molinist theodicy is a revised version of Leibniz' theodicy: God has created the best world He *could* create.

Molinists can explain also the idea of providence and the divine government of the world. If God does not wish that an agent performs a certain action, and if God, on the basis of His middle knowledge, knows that a will perform that action in circumstance C, God can create a world in which a will never take any decision in circumstance C. Alternatively, God can refrain from creating a and create another agent b who will, in C, perform not that action but another action that pleases God. If, on the other hand, God wishes that an agent performs a certain action, and if He knows that a will perform that action in C, God can create a world in which a has to take a decision in C. In this way, the Molinist God can exercise full control over His creation and direct it towards His aims. However, this does not limit the freedom and autonomy of human beings. Suppose that ψ is the state of affairs that God may want to actualize (say, peace and harmony among all human beings). It might happen that no sets of possible agents would freely choose to actualize ψ: this rescues the Molinist from the idea that human beings are puppets in God's hands.

This last point is important for responding to an objection addressed to Molinism: God is jointly responsible for the evil committed by human beings. This objection follows from the Molinist view that God puts human beings in the position to choose wrongly, even if He knows that they will choose wrongly. One may wonder whether there is much difference between doing evil and putting somebody in the condition to do it.[4] However, Molinists might answer that, as a matter of fact, there is no world in which no agent behaves badly in the space of possibilities

---

[4] For an argument of this kind, cf. Hasker (1998, pp. 199–205).

open to God by eternal truths and CFs. So, God cannot create a world without evil. According to this hypothesis, every possible agent does at least one bad deed in every possible world.[5]

Since the focus on this book is divine prescience, we will not discuss this theodicy (for some comments and criticism, we refer the reader to De Florio and Frigerio (2013)). Instead, we will analyse CFs and the structure of the world needed for grounding their truth.

5.2 The Structure of the Molinist World

The aim of this section is to model the structure of the Molinist world. In Sect. 5.2.1, we will see that the structure **TRL+** is needed to ground the truths of CFs. In Sect. 5.2.2, we will present some extensions of this structure in order to model the Molinist world in a more fine-grained way. In Sect. 5.2.3, we will discuss which of the premises of the fatalist argument Molinism denies. Finally, in Sect. 5.2.4, we will show that **TRL+** is a better interpretation of CFs than Lewis' semantics of counterfactuals.

5.2.1 Local TRL

Ockhamism is committed to the existence of a true future: among the different possible futures, one is privileged because it is what will occur. Metaphorically, Ockhamists are committed to the existence of a **TRL**, which is the history of the world in which human beings perform the actions they *actually* decide to perform, even though they could act otherwise.

Molinism is also committed to the existence of a **TRL**. However, as Molinism accepts that *every* CF has a truth value, it is committed to a more demanding model than that of Ockhamism. For Molinism, it is not only true that a certain actual agent a will actually perform φ in the

---

[5] This hypothesis is defended by Alvin Plantinga, who calls it the hypothesis of transworld depravity. Cf. Plantinga (1977, ch. 3).

future when she will find herself in circumstances C; it is also true that if a found herself in circumstances different from C—for instance, in the counterfactual circumstances C'—she would freely choose in a certain way.

To illustrate, we can return to an example we have already seen in Chap. 2: suppose that Mary has invited Emma to a party. Emma must decide whether to accept the invitation or stay home and read a novel. Suppose Emma decides to dedicate herself to reading. According to Ockhamists, it was already true before Emma's decision that she would choose to stay at home. In more technical terms, $\mathbf{F}\varphi$, where φ is the proposition that Emma dedicates herself to reading, is true in the **TRL**. However, suppose we ask: what would Emma have done if she had gone to the party? She would have had to decide whether to drink a beer.

In Fig. 5.1, moment t is the moment at which Emma decides to stay at home and read a novel (φ) or to go to the party. As Emma will choose to read a novel, history h_1 is marked. However, if Emma had gone to the party, she would have had to decide whether to drink a beer (ψ) or not ($\neg\psi$)—that is, to make h_3 or h_2 true. What would she have done in such a circumstance? Molinists acknowledge that this question has a definite answer. It must be true or false that Emma, if she had to decide

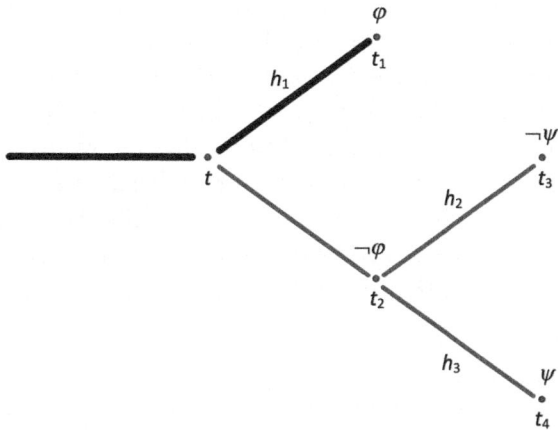

Fig. 5.1 Emma's case (again)

in certain circumstances what to drink, would choose to drink a beer. In fact, a sentence such as:

(1) If Emma had gone to the party, she would have drunk a beer

is a CF. The **TRL** model we have used in the previous chapter to account for the Ockhamist semantics is insufficient for Molinism because it cannot assign a truth value to $\mathbf{F}\psi$ when evaluated at the instant t_2. We need a different semantics based on a structure where every instant of the tree is part of a **TRL**.

The semantics **TRL+** by Øhrstrøm, which we have analysed in Sect. 2.6.4, will suit for the Molinist. Recall that this semantics introduces a function **trl** that assigns a specific Thin Red Line to every instant of time. Going back to Fig. 5.1, the function **trl** will assign h_1 to time t—in which Emma has not yet decided whether to go the party or to stay at home—because it is true at t that Emma will choose to stay at home, even if she could have chosen to go to the party, that is to make the histories h_2 or h_3 true. The same function **trl** assigns h_2 or h_3 to time t_2, at which Emma is at the party and has not decided yet whether to drink a beer or not. For concreteness's sake, let us suppose that (1) is true and that Emma would drink a beer if she went to the party. Then, the function **trl** assigns the history h_3 to t_2 because in this history Emma performs action ψ, that is, she drinks beer. The same happens for every fork of the tree: the function assigns one of the histories of the fork to the times immediately preceding the fork. This is the "true history" with respect to those times, that is, the history that the world would take if it arrived at those times. The time t that immediately precedes the fork can be intended as the circumstances C in which the decision of the agent occurs.[6] The history assigned by the function to time t is the history that contains the decision that the agent will contingently take if she should

---

[6]Alternatively, one may consider the circumstances as a proper part of the stage of the world in which the decision occurs, that is, as a proper part of t. However, there are reasons to reject this interpretation and to believe that C coincides with the whole stage of the world in which the decision of the agent takes place. For arguments in favour of this, cf. Wierenga (2011) and Zimmerman (2009).

find herself in t. Øhrstrøm's model is, therefore, particularly appropriate to account for the truth of CFs.

Recall the clause for the future in the **TRL+** structure (cf. Sect. 2.6.4):

$$M, t \vDash^{\mathsf{TRL+}} \mathbf{F}\varphi \Leftrightarrow \exists t'(t' > t \wedge t' \in \mathsf{trl}(t) \wedge M, t' \vDash \varphi)$$

In words: the formula $\mathbf{F}\varphi$ is true at the instant t iff in the **TRL** assigned by the function **trl** to t, φ is true at an instant t' subsequent to t. For example, it is true that Emma will drink a beer at t iff in the **TRL** assigned to t, Emma drinks a beer at an instant subsequent to t.

5.2.2 Many Worlds and Normal TRL

In this section, we introduce some complications to our model to account for any aspect of the Molinist solution. So far we have considered only the decisions of actual agents, both the decisions that they will actually take and the decisions that they could have taken. However, Molinism needs to account not only for these decisions, but also for the decisions that every possible agent could take in every possible situation. To do this, we have to enrich our model, even if, as we will see, it is just a quantitative and not a qualitative enrichment.

To simplify the framework, suppose that the world is open solely because there are free agents.[7] Therefore, the forks arise only on the occasion of free agents' choices. Suppose that, in creating the actual world, God has created a set of initial conditions and a set of agents. These agents have performed some free actions and have begotten some other agents, who in turn have performed other free actions and have begotten some other agents and so on. This succession of agents, of situations in which they have to take decisions, and of decisions is the actual history of the world that we want to represent. The structure **TRL+** is able to provide a model of the actual world. The tree pictures every decision of every agent of the actual world: every fork represents a choice, and the instant

---

[7]This is a simplification because the world is probably open for other reasons, for example, for aspects concerning the physics of elementary particles. We will ignore these aspects here.

that precedes the fork represent the conditions in which the agent has to take a decision, that is, the state of the world at the moment at which the agent chooses what to do. Obviously, two different agents can make two different choices at the same time. Supposing that the agents' choices are binary, four histories will depart from that instant, corresponding to the four possible combinations of choices. For instance, if agent a has to decide whether to do φ or not and agent b has to decide whether to do ψ or not, then the following histories will depart from that instant: the history h_1 in which a brings about φ and in which b brings about ψ, the history h_2 in which a brings about φ and in which b does not bring about ψ, the history h_3 in which a does not bring about φ and b brings about ψ and the history h_4 in which a does not bring about φ and b does not bring about ψ. If there is a larger number of agents or if they have more than two possibilities, the number of histories increases. Whatever the number of the histories stemming from an instant of time is, one of them will be marked as the local **TRL**: it is the history containing the combination of choices that the agents will actually make.

However, God could have created a world different from the actual world. In the model we are analysing, this means that God could have created either different initial conditions in which the actual agents would have had to decide what to do; or agents different from the actual ones, putting them in the initial conditions of the actual world; or agents different from the actual ones, putting them in initial conditions different from the actual ones. Anyway, every possible Molinist world has **TRL+** branching structure, similar to that of the actual world, in which some free agents take some decisions in some situations. Every free choice corresponds to a fork in this structure: the history that an agent makes actual by means of her choice is marked by the function **trl** so that the structure makes true the CFs relative to that agent. The set $\mathfrak{U} = \{w_0, w_1, \ldots, w_n, \ldots\}$ of the possible worlds among which God chose the actual world is such that every element m_j has a tree structure, in which the bifurcations correspond to free choices taken by some free agents.

The elements of $\mathfrak{U}$ are the different scenarios among which God has to choose the actual world: they are, so to speak, *alternatives of creation*. One might affirm that actually these scenarios are possible evolutions of a unique universal history and that the first free choice is just God's creative choice. In this case, $w_0, w_1, \ldots$ would be the names of the branches of a unique gigantic tree. This leads us to think that there might be true CFs regarding God's free choices:

CDF If God were in conditions C, He would decide to create world w

If the conditionals of divine freedom (CDFs) are true or false, God should know them in advance because He knows every true proposition. Moreover, as divine knowledge is infallible, if God knows that He would create the world w in conditions C, then He will actually create the world w in C. This may be a problem because God would know His choices before taking them. For this reason, de Molina argues that there are no true or false CDFs before the divine creative act. God knows His deliberations *after* the volitional act by which He creates the world, and not before it. The CDFs are objects of free knowledge and not of middle knowledge because they become true or false after the creation of the world.[8] Thomas Flint agrees with de Molina's opinion on this question[9] and so do almost all Molinists. However, Cohen (2016) objects that there is no reason to deny that God knows the CDFs *before* the creation. Indeed, Molinists believe that the knowledge of the CFs concerning human beings is not in tension with their freedom. The fact that God knows that Emma would drink a beer if she went to the party is not in conflict with Emma's freedom in taking her decision. If this is true for human beings, it should apply also to God. Divine knowledge of CDFs should not be in contradiction with divine freedom and with the possibility of doing otherwise: if God infallibly knows that He will create world w_0, this knowledge should not impinge upon the freedom of the creative act and the possibility of choosing another world. One may object that the knowledge of a CF is puzzling when it is reflexive, that is, when the knowledge of a CF is relative to the subject that knows it. However, Cohen argues, this objection disregards the fact that it is difficult to see how gaining knowledge can reduce one's abilities. If anything, the opposite is true: gaining knowledge can enhance one's abilities.

---

[8] See Molina, *Concordia*, Quaestionis XIV, Art. XIII, Disputatio LII.
[9] Cf. Flint (1998, pp. 55–65).

We will not take a stance on this question.[10] We will leave indeterminate whether there exists a world that is marked because it is the world that God would choose if He would create a world. Hence, we will leave indeterminate whether the worlds of the set $\mathfrak{U} = \{w_0, w_1, \ldots, w_n, \ldots\}$ are branches of a gigantic tree whose root corresponds to God's creative decision. We will presuppose only that the worlds of this set are possible scenarios among which God had to choose the actual world and that each of them has the structure **TRL+**.

We conclude this section by introducing another important notion for the Molinist framework, that of *normal* **TRL**. It will be useful for clarifying the options among which God had to actually choose. As we have seen, every world w can be modelled as a tree that bifurcates in correspondence with the decisions of the agents. However, every w models not only the decisions that the agents will contingently take in that world, but also the decision they would have taken if they had made other choices earlier. Suppose that in w Emma has to choose whether to go to the party or to stay at home. She will stay at home, but if she had chosen to go to the party, she would have had to decide whether to drink a beer or not. Therefore, tree w models not only the choices that Emma will contingently make in that world (to stay at home or to go to the party), but also what she would have done if her previous choices had been different. The structure of w makes true or false the CF "If Emma had gone to the party, she would have drunk a beer" because the function **trl** assigns a particular history to the moment at which Emma has to decide whether to drink a beer or not at the party.

We can distinguish the choices that Emma will actually make in w from the choices she could have made if she had decided differently in previous stages of the world. This difference can be extended to the other agents of this world. Generalizing, we can distinguish the choices effectively made by the agents of w from the choices they would have made if they had chosen differently previously.

---

[10] Cohen (2016) underlines that God's pre-volitional knowledge of CDFs is puzzling if one accepts the principle that for taking any decision a subject must not be absolutely certain that she will make a certain choice. If God infallibly knows the CDFs before creating the world, God cannot *deliberate* on which world to create. This implication is very costly, according to Cohen.

Consider only the bifurcating points of the tree w corresponding to the choices that the agents will *actually* take in w and the local **TRL**s assigned by the function **trl** to those points. In other words, at the first fork in w, consider the **TRL** assigned by **trl** to this fork. At the following fork, choose again the **TRL** assigned by **trl** and go on in this way till the end of the tree. We have identified the history that would occur if w were chosen by God as the actual world. Let us call this history the *normal* **TRL** of w. We can formally define the normal **TRL** of a world as follows[11]:

Normal TRL The history h^* is normal with respect to the world w iff $\forall t \in h^* \, \mathbf{trl}(t) = h^*$

In words: the history h^* is a normal **TRL** if the function **trl** assigns precisely h^* to every instant of h^*. For every world w, we can identify only one normal **TRL**. God knows all CFs and, therefore, also the choices that the agents would have made if their decision had been different in previous stages of the world; however, to make a choice among the different possible worlds, God can consider only the normal **TRL**s of these possible worlds. In fact, the normal **TRL**s indicate which course of events would occur, if a certain world had been created. By observing the normal **TRL** of a world, God can consider the set of choices of free agents in that world and evaluate whether such choices are in agreement or not with His will and aims. Comparing the normal **TRL**s of every world, God can decide which He considers as the closest to His purposes and create the world that, in His wisdom, He judges as the best one.

The Molinist world has, therefore, the structure sketched in Fig. 5.2. In this figure, it is supposed that God can choose among three possible worlds: (w_0, w_1, w_2). Every possible world is represented by a branching tree, in which the forks correspond to the choices of the agents. The normal **TRL**s are marked: they are the histories that model the decisions that the agents will actually take in each world. Every tree has further forks in correspondence with the choices that the agents could have made if

---

[11]The name "normal **TRL**" was used for the first time by Braüner et al. (1998). Barcellan and Zanardo (1999) call this **TRL** "real".

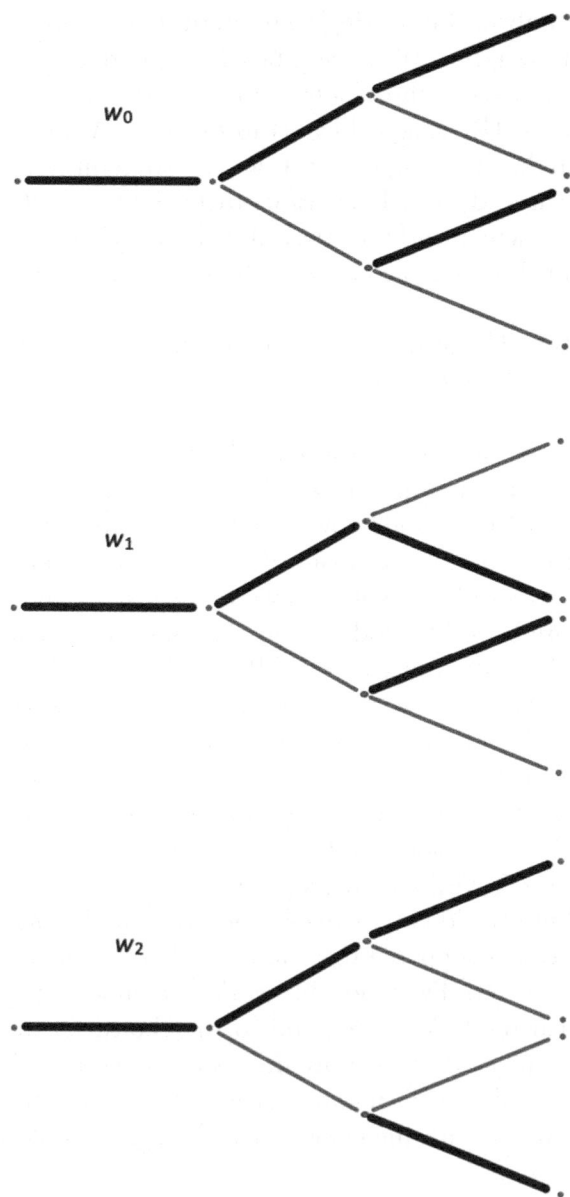

Fig. 5.2 Molinist universe

they had decided differently in earlier stages of the world. The function **trl** assigns a history to each of these forks. Also these histories are marked in red in the figure: they are the histories that the agents would have chosen if they had had to take those decisions. However, as they had decided differently in earlier stages of the world, they would never have had to make those choices, if that world had been created. Although God knows the CFs regarding these choices, He can consider only the normal **TRL**s of each world when He must decide which world to create. Calling $h^*_{w_i}$ the normal **TRL** of the world w_i, the real set of the alternatives at God's disposal is $\mathfrak{U}^* = \{h^*_{w_0}, h^*_{w_2}, \ldots, h^*_{w_n}\}$.

5.2.3 What Answer to the Fatalist Argument?

In this and the following subsection, we will investigate two further issues concerning the Molinist framework. The first one is which premise of the fatalist argument the Molinist does not accept; the second one is a possible alternative interpretation of CFs by means of Lewis' semantics of counterfactuals.

Let us start with the first issue. It is not clear which of the premises of the theological fatalist argument the Molinist rejects. Many Molinists have not even addressed this question; the scholars who have done it have indicated premise 5 of the argument, that is, the transfer of necessity principle (cf., for instance, Freddoso (1988, pp. 57–58), Zagzebski (1991, pp. 131–133))[12]:

1. Yesterday, God believed that p. (Divine foreknowledge)
2. If an event e occurred in the past, then it is accidentally necessary that e occurred then. (Necessity of the past)
3. It is now necessary that yesterday God believed p. (1,2, *modus ponens*)

---

[12] It is not clear whether de Molina denied this principle. He seems to do so in Disputation 52, paragraph 34 of the *Concordia*, or, at least, this is Freddoso's interpretation, followed also by Zagzebski (1991) and John Martin Fischer (cf. Fischer 2008). For an alternative interpretation of de Molina's passage, cf. Jäger (2011, 2013). Instead, Zagzebski (2017) says that "Middle Knowledge does not entail the falsehood of any premise of the basic [fatalist] argument".

4. Necessarily, if yesterday God believed p, then p. (Infallibility of divine foreknowledge)
5. If r is accidentally necessary and if $\Box(r \to s)$, then it is accidentally necessary that s. (Principle of transfer of necessity)
6. So it is now necessary that p. (3,4,5)
7. If it is now necessary that p, then you cannot do otherwise than p. (Definition of necessary)
8. Therefore, you cannot do otherwise than p. (6,7, *modus ponens*)
9. If you cannot do otherwise when you do an act, you do not do it freely. (Principle of Alternate Possibilities)
10. Therefore, when you do p, you will not do it freely. (8,9, *modus ponens*)

If this were true, it would be bad news for Molinists because the transfer of necessity principle is a very solid and intuitive logical principle of modal logic.[13] If r and $r \to s$ are true in every possible accessible world, then it is clear that s is also true in every possible accessible world. To reject this, one must either deny that *necessary* means "true in every possible accessible world" or deny that *modus ponens* is a valid logical rule. However, the first denial questions the standard interpretation of modal logic, the second one of the most basic logical principles.

Fortunately for Molinists, we do not believe that their view questions premise 5, but, again, premise 2, that is, the necessity of the past. This should be clear in light of the very fact that the Molinist framework is an extension of the Ockhamist one. However, let us see this issue in more detail. Molinists are explicit in acknowledging the fact that God cannot determine the truth values of CFs. They are less explicit about the fact that the truth values of CFs depend on the choices of human beings, but it is easy to see that this is the case. A CF is true because the agent would freely decide in a certain way if she were in circumstances C. As this choice is free, the agent could decide differently in C. If the agent did so, the CF would be false and another CF would be true. So,

---

[13] The transfer of necessity principle, which from $\Box r$ and $\Box(r \to s)$ infers $\Box s$ is valid in every modal logic system, in which the axiom **K**: $\Box(r \to s) \to (\Box r \to \Box s)$ is a rule. From $\Box(r \to s)$ and **K**, it follows by *modus ponens* that $\Box r \to \Box s$ and from this formula and $\Box r$, $\Box s$ follows, again by *modus ponens*. Since **K** is the weakest normal modal logic, the transfer of necessity principle is valid in every normal modal system.

the truth value of a CF is determined by the free choice of an agent. Agents have a counterfactual power in regard to CFs: if they decided differently from what they contingently decide, then the truth values of CFs would change. Now, God knows all true CFs and, therefore, if the agents decided differently from what they contingently decide, God would know different things. God's knowledge about CFs depends counterfactually on the free choices of human beings.

As regards the **TRL** of the actual world, things are very similar to the Ockhamist case: in a future situation C (let us suppose, the party tomorrow), Emma will choose to drink a beer. Her drinking a beer is part of the local **TRL** assigned by the function **trl** to the time t, that is, to the party time. Since Emma's choice is free, she could choose differently: in this case, the function **trl** would assign an alternative history to t, in which Emma does not drink a beer. Another CF would be true, for instance: "If Emma were in C, she would drink a Coke" and God would know the truth of this CF before creating the world. Then, the world would have a different past, in which God would believe things differently from those He believes: in particular, He would believe that Emma will drink a Coke at the party.

However, unlike the Ockhamist, the Molinist can repeat this remark for *every* fork in the tree, including for those forks that do not belong to the normal **TRL** of the actual world and also for those that do not belong to any normal **TRL**. If the agents chose differently from how they contingently choose in a certain scenario—true or hypothetical— then other CFs would be true and God would have known different propositions from those He has known since the days before the creation of the world. The "butterfly" scheme of the Ockhamist framework should be repeated for *every* branch of the tree: the histories not selected by the function **trl** all have a different past from those selected by the same function because in their past God believes different things with respect to the histories marked as local **TRL**s.

Molinism is committed to epistemic soft facts, as Ockhamism is. In this sense, it is not a more costly option than Ockhamism. However, as we will see in Sect. 5.3, there are other aspects of the Molinist framework relating to the grounding of CFs that make Molinism a more demanding theory in comparison to Ockhamism.

5.2.4 CFs as Counterfactuals?

CFs are usually interpreted in literature according to Lewis' semantics of counterfactuals (Lewis 2013). By contrast, in the model we have proposed, we have not used the machinery of counterfactuals and we have interpreted CFs as propositions that describe a free act of the agent—interpreted at a time t, that is, at a certain stage of the world.

We believe that our interpretation of CFs is better than that which uses Lewis' semantics of counterfactuals.[14] Firstly, counterfactuals state what *would happen* if some aspects of the world were different from how they actually are (their name derives from this). However, CFs are known by God before the creation of any world, that is, when no world was actual. CFs, then, do not necessarily describe how the world would be if some actual conditions did not take place.

Secondly, CFs remain true, when the actual world is created. In particular, there are true CFs concerning the choices that actual agents make in the actual world. For example, suppose that Emma is an actual agent and that she has to decide whether to go to the party or to stay at home and to read a novel. God knows that, when Emma will take her decision, she will choose to stay at home. The CF that describes what Emma will do when she will have to make a choice is not really a *counter*factual. It describes what Emma will *actually* do, not what she would do in counterfactual circumstances. Certainly, Lewis' semantics assigns truth conditions to the counterfactuals with true antecedent. If the antecedent is true, counterfactuals become simple material conditionals.[15] Such truth conditions arise from Lewis' semantics, which dictates that a counterfactual $\varphi \;\square\!\!\rightarrow\; \psi$ is true if in the worlds most similar to the actual world in which φ is true, ψ is also true. As the world most similar to the actual world is the actual world itself, if φ is true in the actual world, then, according to this semantics, the conditional is true if and only if ψ is also true in the actual world.

---

[14] Some of the following arguments are adumbrated by Zimmerman (2009).
[15] Cf. Lewis (2013, pp. 26–31).

Such conditionals with factual antecedents are, however, defective in some ways. If Emma has actually gone to the party, it is odd to affirm: "If Emma had gone to the party, then Emma would have drunk a beer". According to Lewis (2013), conditionals of such kind are only *pragmatically* infelicitous: they convey the idea that the antecedent is false, and then they sound odd if their antecedents are true. Nevertheless, Lewis believes that they are not *semantically* defective and it is possible to assign them truth conditions. But one can suspect this is not the case. In light of some counterexamples, some criticisms have been made against the thesis that counterfactuals are true if both their antecedent and consequent are true.[16] Many theories of counterfactuals have been proposed in order to avoid the assignment of a truth value in the case of true antecedents.[17] The debate on counterfactuals with true antecedents is complex and intricate and we are not interested in following it here. It is sufficient to observe that the interpretation of the counterfactuals with true antecedents is a controversial question and that Lewis' semantics is not straightforward on this point. However, the CFs with true antecedents are especially important for the Molinist because God knows what will happen in the actual world in light of them. Using such a controversial semantics in the treatment of these CFs does not seem to be a good idea.

Finally, Lewis (2013, pp. 21–24) defines the so-called might counterfactuals (such as, e.g. "if Emma went to the party, she might drink a beer") as follows:

Might counterfactuals $\varphi \diamondsuit\!\!\rightarrow \psi =^{def} \neg(\varphi \,\square\!\!\rightarrow \neg\psi)$

---

[16]McDermott (2007) makes this counterexample: a coin is to be tossed twice; before it is tossed, I bet that it will come up heads both times; it does and I win. Now consider:

(i) If at least one head had come up, I would have won

Both the antecedent and the consequent of (i) are true in the hypothesized scenario: it is true both that at least one head came up (actually, two heads came up) and that I won. So, (i) is true in the Lewisian semantics of conterfactuals. But (i) is intuitively false. So, the Lewisian semantics of counterfactuals fails when the antecedent is true.

[17]For a review of these semantics and for their assessment, cf. Walters (2016).

It follows from this definition that if $\varphi \;\square\!\!\rightarrow\; \psi$ is true, then $\varphi \;\Diamond\!\!\rightarrow\; \neg\psi$ is false. For instance, if it is true that "if you had lit a match, you would have caused a fire", then it is false that "if you had lit a match, you might not have caused a fire". This is a problem for the interpretation of CFs through Lewis' semantics: if we interpret the CF "if Emma went to the party, she would drink a beer" by means of this semantics, then "if Emma went to the party, she might not drink a beer" would turn out to be false. As a result, if Emma went to the party, it would be necessary that she drinks a beer, and she could not do otherwise. As Molinists accept the libertarian conception of freedom, they must maintain that the option of not drinking a beer is really open to Emma and that she might not drink it. If we analyse Lewis' semantics of counterfactuals, it is easy to see why it has this unfortunate consequence for Molinists: a counterfactual such as $\varphi \;\square\!\!\rightarrow\; \psi$ is true iff *every* φ-world belonging to the sphere of the worlds most similar to the actual world is also a ψ-world. If the counterfactual is true, in no φ-world that is most similar to the actual world in which ψ is false. By consequence, in *every* world most similar to the actual world in which Emma goes to the party, she drinks a beer. This result cannot satisfy Molinists because they want to leave open the possibility that Emma goes to the party and does not drink a beer.[18]

This objection to the interpretation of CFs through Lewis' semantics is known to Molinists. However, most scholars have failed to distinguish between the objection to the use of Lewis' semantics for interpreting CFs and the rejection of Molinism based on Lewis' semantics. For instance, some critics of Molinism have contended that Molinists deny a libertarian conception of freedom because Lewis' semantics of counterfactuals entails that if $\varphi \;\square\!\!\rightarrow\; \psi$ is true, then $\varphi \;\Diamond\!\!\rightarrow\; \neg\psi$ is false.[19] On the other hand, some Molinists have tried to show that the interpretation of CFs by means of Lewis' semantics does not imply the denial of libertarian freedom. To this

---

[18] That Lewis' semantics of counterfactuals expresses a necessary link between the antecedent and the consequent is underlined by many scholars; for instance, Pollock (1976, p. 34) claims that "all counterfactual conditionals express necessitation" and Stalnaker (1981, pp. 87–104), commenting on the Lewisian semantics, points out that "the antecedents of conditionals act like necessity operators on their consequents".

[19] For instance, cf. Hasker (1994, p. 145) and Van Inwagen (1997).

aim, they argue that if a CF is true, then the worlds in which that CF is true are more similar to the actual world than the worlds in which that CF is false. For instance, if it is true that Emma would freely drink a beer if she went to the party, then the worlds in which Emma goes to the party and drinks a beer are more similar to the actual world than the worlds in which she goes to the party and does not drink a beer. By consequence, only the former worlds are included in the sphere of the worlds that must be taken into consideration to evaluate the truth value of the CF. As only the worlds in which Emma drinks a beer are to be considered, the CF "Emma would freely drink a beer if she went to the party" turns out true. However, there are possible worlds—not included in the set of the worlds most similar to the actual one—in which Emma goes to the party and does not drink a beer, and this warrants Emma's freedom of drinking a beer or not at the party.[20]

How can Molinists justify the thesis that the worlds in which Emma goes to the party and drinks a beer are more similar to the actual world than the worlds in which Emma goes to the party and does not drink a beer? Surprisingly, the Molinists advocating the analysis of CFs through counterfactuals respond that the former worlds are more similar to the actual world than the latter worlds because they have in common with the actual world the truth of the CF "if Emma went to the party, she would freely drink a beer", while the latter worlds do not. Alvin Plantinga points out that the similarity among different worlds is often also evaluated on the basis of physical laws: the worlds that share the same physical laws are

---

[20]For example, Craig (1991, p. 252) considers the CF:

1. If I had asked, the butcher could have refused to sell me a pound of ground beef

    and claims that it is incompatible with the truth of:

2. If I had asked, the butcher might not have sold me a pound of ground beef.

    He comments:

    This is not deterministic, however, since [the CF] remains true; the butcher could have not sold me the meat, though it is false that he might have not sold me the meat, that is, that it is true that he would have sold me the meat. He *could* have refused to sell me my pound of *Fleisch*, but he *would* not have refused.

considered more similar than the worlds that do not share them.[21] Now, physical laws can be interpreted as counterfactuals. As the counterfactuals describing physical laws are taken into consideration in the evaluation of the similarity among worlds, why cannot CFs also be considered in the evaluation of this similarity?[22]

This Molinist answer has the flavour of circularity. A CF is true because it is true in the most similar worlds and these worlds are the most similar because that CF is true in them. To evaluate the truth of a CF, we have to consider the worlds most similar to the actual worlds and see whether the consequent is true in them. But the worlds most similar to the actual world are those in which the consequent is true. The worlds in which the consequent is false are *for this reason* considered not similar enough to the actual world to be included among those to be considered for the evaluation of the CF. With a similar method, we can make *every* counterfactual true: it is sufficient to say that only the worlds in which the consequent is true are the most similar to the actual worlds and to judge the counterfactual only in those worlds.

Notice that Plantinga is right in pointing out that physical laws, and thus some counterfactuals, are taken into consideration in the evaluation of the similarity among worlds. But these counterfactuals are considered

---

[21] Physical laws are central in the evaluation of a counterfactual such as:

1. If I dropped the glass, it would fall to the ground

We judge this sentence true even though there are worlds with physical laws different from those of the actual world—in which, for instance, masses are not attracted to each other by the gravitational force. These worlds are regarded as very different from the actual world and are thereby not part of the sphere of the worlds most similar to the actual world in which the antecedent is true.

[22] Cf. Plantinga (2012, pp. 377–78). This argument is repeated and approved by Craig (1991, pp. 256–258). Although in a less clear way, this also seems to be the argument proposed by Wierenga (1989, pp. 140–143), who argues that a CF such as "If a were in C, a would perform φ" is not compatible with (i) "if a were in C, a might not perform φ", but it is compatible with (ii) "if a were in C, a retained the power to do other than φ" and with (iii) "it's possible that a be in C and not do φ". This compatibility derives from the fact that the possible world in which the antecedent of the CF is true and the consequent is false is not among the worlds most similar to the actual world; this is because in the evaluation of the similarity among worlds, we have to take into consideration not only the segment of world that precedes the choice of the agent but also what follows, in particular the choice of the agent and its consequences. Flint (2011, pp. 38–39) even finds it "astounding" that after Wierenga's reply the argument of the might-counterfactuals is still offered by the anti-Molinist scholars.

in the evaluation of *other* counterfactuals, in some ways connected to the former, not in the evaluations of those counterfactuals themselves. In evaluating the truth of a counterfactual such as "If I dropped the glass, it would fall to the ground", we can consider only the worlds in which the law of universal gravitation is in force because only these worlds are sufficiently similar to the actual world. However, counterfactuals used to evaluate the similarity among worlds are *different* from those under examination and form a sort of background against which the latter are judged as true or false.[23]

The Molinist answers based on the similarity among the possible worlds seem to be quite unsatisfactory. However, in contrast to many anti-Molinists, we do not conclude that Molinism *per se* implies the denial of the agents' possibility of doing otherwise. More modestly, we conclude that the interpretation of CFs by means of Lewis' semantics of counterfactuals results in serious problems because it seems to imply that agents cannot do otherwise. Our interpretation through the TRL+ semantics does not have these problems. We will therefore use this framework to evaluate the costs of Molinism. As we will see, this framework also permits us to evaluate the costs of Molinism with greater precision than that based on Lewis' semantics of counterfactuals.

5.3 The Costs of Molinism

Having illustrated the structure of the Molinist universe, we can now evaluate its costs. As we will see, Molinism is a more costly approach than Ockhamism: many semantic and metaphysical options open to the Ockhamist are closed to the Molinist.

One of the main objections to Molinism is the groundlessness of CFs: it is difficult to see how they can be true or false and what could ground their truth.[24] As we have seen in Sect. 4.5.1, there are weak and strong

---

[23] For the charge of circularity, cf. Hasker (1999a) and Cowan (2003). For a Molinist reply, cf. Flint (1998, pp. 136–137).

[24] Probably, this objection was raised for the first time by Robert Merrihew Adams: see Adams (1974, 1977). William Hasker has insisted on this objection on many occasions; see, for instance, Hasker (1998, pp. 29–39) and Hasker (2011, pp. 26–29).

versions of the grounding principle, but the main idea is that we do not want truth to be able to float free of any constraints from reality. Our propositions are representational entities, and we find appealing the idea that their truth depends not only on how they represent reality but also on how reality is. As we have seen, the grounding principle is often expressed as follows:

Grounding   Every true proposition depends for its truth on the world.

The challenge for the Molinist is to find something in reality that can ground the truth of CFs. What makes it true that Emma would freely decide to drink a beer if she went to the party? As pointed out by Adams (1974, 1977), CFs cannot be grounded in a necessary link between their antecedent and consequent. In other terms, the situation of the world at the instant at which Emma decides to drink a beer or not cannot necessitate or cause the fact that Emma drinks a beer. Libertarian freedom is based on the assumption that the stage of the world at which the decision is taken does not determine the outcome of the decision. At most, the character, the desires, the intentions of an agent and the situation in which the agent finds herself can make a decision *probable*, but cannot determine it necessarily. Then, we cannot say that it is *true* that Emma will drink a beer at the party because she will be thirsty and she usually drinks beer. At most, we may say that, given these circumstances, it is *probable* that Emma will drink a beer. Molinists must find another candidate for the grounding of CFs.[25]

We have seen in the previous section that some Molinists' use of the Lewisian semantics of counterfactuals for grounding the truth of CFs is

---

[25] Sometimes Molinists dismiss the objection of groundlessness: in light of the advantages of Molinism, CFs can remain ungrounded. For instance, Thomas Flint says that:

> Given that the cost for the libertarian of rejecting Molinism is the demolition of the traditional notion of providence, the "grounding" objection gives the orthodox Christian insufficient incentive to pay so high a price. (Flint 1998, p. 137)

> But this is not a good response to the problem. To renounce the idea that our propositions must be grounded means to give up the idea that they must have a link with reality, understood in the widest sense. The price to pay for this link is never too high.

not a good move. Plantinga, Craig and Flint appeal to the fact that worlds in which they are true are more similar to the actual world than the worlds in which they are false with the aim of grounding their truth. However, we have shown that this is circular because in this way they ground the truth of CFs on the similarity among worlds and the similarity among worlds on the truth of CFs. Therefore, this solution cannot be adopted. What other chances to solve the grounding problem do Molinists have? We will see in Sect. 5.3.1 that if a strict interpretation of **Grounding** is assumed, there is no solution for the Molinist (in contrast to the Ockhamist). The only possibility seems, then, to be to liberalize **Grounding**. However, in Sect. 5.3.2, we will see that the liberalizing of **Grounding** is also not an easy route for Molinists to pursue.

5.3.1 The Truth-Making Principle

Let us start with a strict interpretation of **Grounding**, that is, **TSB**:

TSB For any proposition p and any worlds w_1 and w_2, if p is true in w_1 but not in w_2, then either something exists in one world but not the other, or else some object instantiates a property or a relation in one world but not the other.

As we have seen, Ockhamism is compatible with **TSB** if it embraces an eternalist metaphysics. In this case, only the **TRL** consists of actual facts; the other histories are made of merely possible facts. The future tensed sentences are evaluated on the actual history of the world. As these sentences are grounded on actual future states of affairs, **TSB** is respected.

Molinists, however, cannot rely on such a metaphysics. In the Molinist framework, there is not a unique **TRL** but many local **TRLs**. A possible metaphysics that might seem *prima facie* attractive for the Molinist is the following: the normal **TRLs** of all the worlds are actual, whereas the histories that branch from these are only possible. This is a curious metaphysics that mixes elements of concretism and actualism about possible worlds. There are at least two reasons why the Molinist cannot accept it, however. Firstly, the normal **TRLs** are all actual, and this is in contrast with the idea that God actualizes one of the possible worlds by His creative activity. Classical theism seems to require that the various possible worlds are only possible before creation and that God creates just one of these possible worlds. Secondly, this metaphysics does not account for the non-normal **TRL**s. Recall that for every fork, also for those external to the normal **TRL**s, there is a privileged history containing the choices that the agents would make in that situation. Now, a formula such as $\mathbf{F}\varphi$, when evaluated at a moment in the normal **TRL**, would be grounded on future actual facts; however, when this formula is evaluated at a moment external to the normal **TRL**, it is not easy to see what its grounding could be: the histories that pass through the time of evaluation have the same metaphysical "weight"—they are all possible, non-actual, histories—and so none of them is privileged over the others.

To solve the first problem, the eternalist Molinist might claim that only the normal **TRL** of the actual world is actual, while the other normal **TRL**s are only possible. However, this metaphysics exacerbates the second problem: the CFs that have situations of the actual world as their antecedents would be grounded, but all the other CFs would fail to be because the other normal **TRL**s would not be actual.

Then, in contrast to the Ockhamist, the Molinist cannot embrace an eternalist metaphysics, in which true future tensed sentences are grounded on the actuality of future histories.[26]

---

[26] The difference between the Molinist and Ockhamist positions is underlined by Cowan (2003), who writes:

Take, once again, the counterfactual of freedom,

(A) If David had remained in Keilah, then Saul would have besieged the city.

With this proposition, unlike our future contingent above, there is no state of affairs, past, present, or future, to which we can point in order to ground the counterfactual of freedom. That is, there is no time, past, present, or future, in which a present-tense version of (A) corresponds to an actual, present state of affairs. (pp. 96–97)

The Molinist might try to combine her theory with other metaphysics of time. She might accept Presentism. In this case, only the present instant of the actual world would exist, whereas everything else in the Molinist tree represents either non-existent future and past facts or merely possible histories. Alternatively, the Molinist might embrace the Growing Block view. In this case, only the present and past facts of the normal **TRL** of the actual world would be real, whereas the future of this **TRL** represents the facts that will obtain but that are not yet actual and the other histories represent only possible facts. Finally, the combination of Molinism with MST is puzzling. The Molinist MST theorist has two options: she can affirm that all the histories of the **TRL+** model are real and that the normal **TRL** of the actual world is distinct from the others because the light of the present travels along it; otherwise, she can affirm that only one of the possible worlds consists of real facts, that is, only one of the trees in $\mathfrak{U} = \{w_0, w_1, \ldots, w_n, \ldots\}$ is real. The normal **TRL** of this world is followed by the light. The other worlds are only possible. In the first case, the creation of the actual world by God would consist in putting the light of the present on one of the worlds of the set. One may doubt that this can be judged as "the creation of a world" at the expense of the others. More plausibly, in the second case, the creation of the actual world would consist in the actualization of one of the trees of $\mathfrak{U} = \{w_0, w_1, \ldots, w_n, \ldots\}$ and in putting the light of the present on the root of one of the histories of this tree.

Suppose that the Molinist accepts one of these metaphysics of time and a strict interpretation of **Grounding** such as **TSB**. Has this interplay of theories any chance of providing a coherent account? As we have seen, the Ockhamist who accepts this interplay in not in a good position. She must enrich the present with tensed facts or uninstantiated haecceities, which is very costly from the metaphysical point of view and too little explanatory. These problems are particularly acute in the case of future truths because the future, in contrast to the past, leaves no traces in the present. Therefore, the Ockhamist who accepts Presentism or the Growing Block view or MST and who sticks to **TSB** does not hold out much hope. The Molinist who accepts one of these metaphysics of time and **TSB** is in an even worse situation. She cannot enrich the present with tensed properties because the truth of CFs is independent of the existence of an actual world and, thus, of an actual present. It would be slightly better to accept the existence of uninstantiated haecceities, but also in this case the prospects are not good because these haecceities should instantiate very peculiar properties such as "being such that it would do φ if instantiated in the circumstances C", which do not seem genuine.

The incompatibility between Molinism and **TSB** *per se* does not falsify Molinism. As we will see in the next subsection, the Molinist can reject **TSB** and assume a more liberal interpretation of **Grounding**. However, the fact that the Ockhamist has no problem with **TSB**, provided that she accepts a certain metaphysics of time, whereas the Molinist is committed to a less restrictive theory of grounding, highlights the cost of Molinism.

5.3.2 Liberalizing TSB

As we have seen in Sect. 4.5.2, the presentist who does not wish to enrich the present can ground past tensed sentences liberalizing **TSB** and replacing it with **TSTB**:

TSTB Truth Supervenes on Tensional Being

However, we have seen in Sect. 4.5.4 that, if the future is open, **TSTB** does not seem sufficient for grounding future tensed sentences. But we have acknowledged that ours are not knock-down arguments and that Ockhamists can try to defend their position.

On the contrary, Molinists cannot hope to ground the truth of CFs on the basis of **TSTB**. At most, **TSTB** can provide a ground for the CFs that have as their antecedents situations belonging to the normal **TRL** of the actual world, but not for the other CFs. All the local **TRL**s but the normal **TRL** of the actual world do not represent past or present or future facts, but only possible facts; by consequence, the truths determined by these **TRL**s cannot be grounded by **TSTB**.

Which moves remain available for the Molinists? The only way seems to be to further liberalize **TSB**. This strategy is followed by Craig (2001), who considers these sentences:

(2) Emma drank a beer.
(3) Emma will drink a beer.

(4) All ravens are black.
(5) Torturing a child is wrong.
(6) If a rigid rod were placed in uniform motion through the aether, it would suffer a FitzGerald–Lorentz contraction.

He stresses that none of these propositions would be true in a strict interpretation of **Grounding** such as **TSB**. If one is presentist, then the past and the future are not real and, therefore, sentences (2) and (3) remain without truth-makers. Universally quantified sentences that express laws such as (4) do not refer only to the actual objects belonging to a class but also to the past, future and possible objects of that class. (4) generalizes not only on existing ravens, but also on past and future ravens and on merely possible ravens. Also in this case, then, a strict theory of truth-making fails. In the same way, moral truths such as (5) are not grounded in categorical facts of the reality. A counterfactual such as (6) has no direct truth-maker because it deals with a counterfactual situation in which something that does not actually exist—the aether—exists. As we consider these sentences true even though they do not have an existing truth-maker, **TSB** is an invalid principle. Why we not also think that CFs are true or false even though they lack an existing truth-maker?[27]

In light of these counterexamples, Craig proposes a complete liberalization of **Grounding**:

> For my part, I should say that if true counterfactuals of creaturely freedom have truth – makers, then the most obvious and plausible candidates are the

---

[27]The advocates of **TSB** have the resources to defend their principle against Craig's attack. For sentences (2) and (3), one can rely on an eternalist metaphysics in which past and future facts exist. As we have seen, within Presentism one can rely on *Lucretianism*, which takes the present world to exemplify primitive, unstructured properties such as "being such that Emma drank a beer at the party" or on uninstantiated haecceities of past and future objects. The sentences that express counterfactuals, such as (4) and (5), can be grounded on the essences of existing objects. For instance, a counterfactual such as "If I dropped the glass, it would fall to the ground" can be grounded in the fact that the glass has a mass and on the fact that the mass of the glass and that of the Earth are attracted by the force of gravity. The law of gravity, in turn, can be grounded in the essence of the objects that have mass. Finally, sentences expressing moral laws, such as (6), can be grounded in values, meant as abstract entities; alternatively, they can be grounded in laws of a different kind. However, here we do not explore the question of whether (2)–(6) are real counterexamples to **TSB** because this would take us too far afield from the topic of this book.

facts or states of affairs disclosed by the disquotation principle. Thus, what makes it true that "If I were rich, I would buy a Mercedes", is the fact that if I were rich I would buy a Mercedes. Just as there are tensed facts about the past or future which now exist, even though the objects and events they are about do not, so there are counterfacts which actually exist, even though the objects and events they are about do not. If counterfactuals of creaturely freedom require truth–makers, then it is in virtue of these facts or states of affairs that the corresponding propositions are true. (pp. 346–347)

Craig's proposal[28] is, then, to interpret **Grounding** in a very liberal way, by means of what we call here the *Maximally Liberalized Grounding Principle*:

MLGP Any proposition p is grounded on the fact that p

A CF such as

(7) If Emma had come to the party, she would have freely chosen to drink a beer.

is grounded simply on the fact that if Emma had been in a certain situation C, she would have brought about a certain state of affairs.

However, deflationary principles such as **MLGP** have raised several objections in literature. For instance, Baron (2015) maintains that

truthmaker theory is not obviously open to deflation. When we say that truth depends on ontology we mean something metaphysically robust by this claim […] If truthmaker theory is deflated then all of the substantive

---

[28] Craig's solution to the problem of grounding was foreshadowed by Freddoso (1988, p. 72). Also, Flint (2009) has suggested a solution similar to Craig's. He believes that many true sentences fail to have existing truth-makers, for instance, future tensed sentences, laws of nature and "would-probably conditionals", such as "If Emma went to the party, she would probably drink a beer". Flint adds that we do not

> start with a grounding principle and use it to decide whether or not the members of one of these classes of propositions are in fact contingent truths. Things work the other way around. [w]e'll start with the classes of propositions [w]e feels confident about and fashion a grounding principle that will (at a minimum) not rule any of them out. (p. 20)

issues in truthmaker theory seem either completely mysterious or else trivial to solve. It is, for instance, hard to see how we could have a substantive debate about the metaphysics of truthmakers – about what truthmakers really are – once the dependence of truth on ontology has been stripped of metaphysical import. Similarly, debates about the nature of the truthmaker relation – how exactly it is that we should understand the dependence at issue – appear just as pointless if truthmaking is metaphysically lightweight. (p. 930)

Therefore, there is space for those who hold that **TSB** should be liberalized but who do not accept deflationary principles such as **MLGP**. For instance, Davison (2004) believes that **TSB** should be liberalized, but he does not consider CFs as grounded. He argues that, *insofar as human beings are concerned*, a principle similar to **TSB** should be stated:

HB   The truth of a true proposition concerning a specific human person must be explained in terms of the actual situation of the person in question (p. 367)

Davison thinks that **TSB** should be liberalized, but not when it concerns human beings. CFs cannot be grounded through **MLGP**: according to **HB**, the sentences concerning human beings should be grounded on existing states of affairs, not on states of affairs that would obtain in certain circumstances.[29] Is this position reasonable? Which criterion can we offer for accepting only certain liberalizations? Is not this criterion arbitrary? Why should we say that **TSB** must be liberalized, but not in the case of human beings? Is not Craig's disquotational principle, according to which a sentence p is grounded exactly on p, more plausible?

Actually, we believe that we can find a criterion for distinguishing the various liberalizations of **TSB** and for excluding those that ground CFs. Molinists acknowledge that human decisions cannot be explained on the basis of the situation C in which they are taken. The context of the decision, the character, the tastes and the desires of the agent

---

[29] Cowan (2003) and Hasker (2011) express a similar position: even though they accept a liberalization of **TSB**, they do not believe that CFs can be grounded through **MLGP**.

can make a decision probable, but cannot imply it. The history of the world before the decision leaves it undetermined.[30] Let us consider a free action, Emma's drinking a beer. There is nothing that explains Emma's action according to libertarians: her action cannot be "deduced" by the circumstances, her character, her motivations and so on. So, the question is: what grounds a sentence such as the following?

(8) Emma freely chooses to drink a beer.

The only possible answer is: it is the decision that Emma *actually* has taken. It is precisely because Emma has chosen to drink a beer that (8) is true. Compare Emma's case with weather forecasts. What grounds the statement that it will rain tomorrow? The present circumstances and the laws that govern meteorology. By analysing the present weather conditions, the isobars, the high and low-pressure areas and so on, and by having an overall knowledge of the lines along which weather phenomena evolve, it is possible to ground the statement that it will rain tomorrow. But, by definition, (8) cannot be grounded on the circumstances previous to Emma's decision and on the laws that govern the world's evolution. Only Emma's positive and actual choice can ground the truth of this sentence. For this reason, we can propose a rather strict interpretation of the grounding principle for human free acts, along the lines of the following Free Actions Truth Maker Principle:

FATMP The truth of a true proposition concerning a specific free human act must be explained in terms of the actual decisions made by the person in question.

Notice that **FATMP** is weaker than **HB** because it does not require actual truth-makers for *every* proposition concerning human persons but only for those concerning free acts.

---

[30]We agree with Pruss and Rasmussen (2014), who say that there might be an explanation of CFs if there might be an explanation of free actions. Since in the libertarian view of freedom, free decisions lack explanations, CFs also do not need any explanation.

Craig (2006) attacks **HB** on the basis of the following examples:

(9) Napoleon lost the Battle of Waterloo.
(10) The US President in 2070 will be a woman.
(11) Torturing the Iraqi prisoners in Abu Ghraib is wrong.

Sentences (9)–(11) are or can be true even if they do not refer to actual states of affairs involving Napoleon, the US President in 2070 and Iraqi prisoners in Abu Ghraib. **FATMP** is more restricted than **HB** and, therefore, it is subjected to counterexamples such as (11) that concerns moral truths. However, one might propose examples analogous to (9) and (10):

(12) Caesar freely decided to cross the Rubicon river.
(13) Emma will freely decide to drink a beer at the party tonight.

As we have seen in Sect. 4.5, the trickiness of (12) and (13) for **FATMP** depends on the assumed metaphysics of time. If Eternalism is assumed, for instance, the state of affairs such that Caesar decides to cross the Rubicon river and the state of affairs such that Emma decides to drink a beer at the party tonight are actual and the truth of (12) and (13) does not conflict with **FATMP**. Things become more complex when the Growing Block view or Presentism are assumed: for the first view, only (12) is about an actual state of affairs; for the second view, neither (12) nor (13) is.

However, we have seen that the presentist can adopt different strategies for grounding the truth of (12): she can enrich the present or she can liberalize **TSB** and hold that past states of affairs can ground the truth of past tensed sentences. In the second case, **FATMP** should be replaced by **FATMP′**:

FATMP′   The truth of a true proposition concerning a specific free human act must be explained in terms of the actual or past decisions made by the person in question.

For the presentist, (12) does not represent a more difficult challenge than any other past tensed sentence.

As we have seen in the previous chapter, (13) represents a major problem for the presentists (and for Growing Block and MST theorists as well) who believe that such sentences have a truth value. The strategies that presentists can use for past tensed sentences are not suitable because it is indeterminate whether Emma will drink a beer at the party tonight. (At least) two different histories stem from the instant of evaluation: in the first one, the state of affairs such that Emma drinks a beer occurs; in the second one, this state of affairs does not occur. One of these histories grounds the truth of (13), the other one not. Therefore, it is indeterminate whether (13) is grounded or not. At the present moment, there is no state of affairs that *will* occur and, by consequence, no state of affairs that can ground the truth of (13). Ockhamists have some resources for contrasting this argument, but we have shown that they have a hard job to do. **FATMP** and **FATMP′** are compelling reasons for rejecting the idea that the truth of (13) is grounded on Presentism (and on the Growing Block view or MST).

The interesting point here is that Molinists make an even more dubious move because their view implies a greater distance from **FATMP** and from the actuality of the agents' choices. CFs state that an agent a would do φ if she were in circumstances C. These circumstances might never obtain. Ockhamists could claim that they keep a link with the actual world because they merely affirm that some states of affairs will *actually* obtain in the future. Molinists can say nothing like this. They claim that the agents would act in a certain way in certain circumstances even though they will *never* act in that way. No past, present or future states of affairs can be called for in order to ground the truth of CFs. The actual history of the world cannot offer a ground for them. This is in tension with **FATMP** and with the need to ground the sentences concerning the free decisions of the agents in their real and actual choices.

Again, we do not claim to have put forward a knock-down argument against Molinism. However, we believe that Molinists—as libertarian— have compelling reasons to accept **FATMP**, and this is in sharp contrast with the truth or falsehood of CFs. Since it is not easy to see how Molinists can solve this tension, they have a hard road to travel. We do not claim that it is impossible to travel; however, we believe we have provided sufficient reasons to show that it is a very rough road, even rougher than the Ockhamist's.

5.4 The Costs That the Molinist Does Not Have to Pay

In literature, another argument against Molinism, different from the grounding argument, circulates. It has been put forward by Merrihew Adams and William Hasker and aims to demonstrate that Molinism is a circular doctrine. In this section, we will demonstrate that this argument fails. In particular, if (and this is a big *if*) the Molinist is able to overcome the grounding argument and, thus, **TRL+** is a good model of the world, then Molinism is not a circular theory. In Sect. 5.4.1, we present Adams' and Hasker's arguments, while in Sect. 5.4.2, we outline our general objection to these arguments. In Sects. 5.4.3 and 5.4.4, we take into consideration more specifically Adams' and Hasker's arguments and their problems.

5.4.1 Adams' and Hasker's Arguments

The circularity argument was proposed for the first time by Adams (1991). Adams presents it as a new version of the argument advanced in Hasker (1998, ch. 2), but it is actually a new argument. It is based on the concept of "explanatory priority", which Adams does not define precisely but which he believes can be accepted by Molinists. The argument aims at demonstrating that Molinism is incompatible with a libertarian conception of freedom and can be summed up as follows (pp. 346–347):

1. The truth of all true counterfactuals of freedom is explanatorily prior to God's decision to create us. [Molinist premise]
2. God's decision to create us is explanatorily prior to our existence and to our choices and actions. [Premise]
3. The relation of explanatorily priority is transitive. [Premise]

4. The truth of all CF is explanatorily prior to all our choices and actions. [By 1–3]
5. Whatever we bring about is something to which some choices or actions of ours are explanatorily prior. [Premise]
6. We do not bring about the truth of any CF about us. [By 4–5]

This argument has provoked many criticisms focused on the notion of explanatory priority. Craig (1994) and Flint (1998, pp. 162–174) have argued that the expression *explanatory priority* is used in different senses within the argument. Craig, for instance, maintains that *priority* in premises 2 and 3

> is a sort of causal or ontic priority, but the priority in 1. is not causal or ontic, since the truth of all counterfactuals of creaturely freedom is neither a necessary nor a sufficient condition of God's decision to create us. At best, the truth of such counterfactuals is prior to His decision in providing a partial reason for that decision. (p. 859)

In the same way, Flint claims that "Adams's argument gains whatever plausibility it has from equivocating on the notion of explanatory priority" (p. 163). Hasker (1997) has responded to these criticisms by pointing out that there is a univocal sense of "explanatory priority" that can be used in the argument: x is explanatorily prior to y iff x must be included in a complete explanation of why y obtains (p. 390). Hasker explains that "an explanation of why y obtains" is to be understood in the sense that x contributes to y's obtaining; that is, it plays a role in bringing it about that y obtains (p. 391).

The argument of Hasker (1999b) is quite close to that of Adams and must be inspired by his response to Craig. This argument is based on the concept of "to bring about".[31] According to Hasker, on the one hand, the Molinist must say that the agent has the power to bring about the truth of CFs through free actions. On the other hand, he must say that

---

[31] This concept is defined by Hasker as follows: "A brings it about that Y iff: For some X, A causes it to be the case that X, and (X & H) $\Rightarrow$ Y, and $\sim$ (H =Y), where 'H' represents the history of the world prior to its coming to be the case that X" (p. 291).

the agent has no power to bring about the truth of CFs because "there are [...] compelling reasons for saying that such counterfactuals, were they to exist, would indeed be part of, or be entailed by, the world's past history" (p. 294). The reason provided for this thesis is that CFs have causal consequences on the actual world because "God's decision about which creative act of will to perform [...] is crucially guided by His middle knowledge" (p. 296), and then by CFs. Now, "*a fact is a part of the world's history if it has had causal consequences prior to the present time*. Facts that have such consequences are, so to speak, 'embedded' in the world's past, as part of the causal processes leading up to the present" (p. 294). However, since human beings have no power to change the past, they have not the power to bring about the truth of CFs.

How much the arguments of Adams and Hasker are similar depends on how we intend the concept of explanatory priority. There are many theories on what it means to give an explanation, but most of these are based on the idea that to explain something means to identify the causes (also partial or indirect) of the *explanandum*. If we intend Adams' notion of explanation along these lines, then his and Hasker's arguments are very similar. The statement that CFs are explanatorily prior to divine decisions would mean that CFs are partial causes of divine decisions. As divine decisions are in turn causes of the actual world, CFs have causal effects on the world and, in particular, on our actions. However, Molinists should, on the contrary, say that the truth of CFs is determined by our actions.

Molinists have used different strategies to answer Hasker's arguments. Flint (1999) has argued that the fact that something has had causal consequences on the present does not entail that agents do not have counterfactual power on that thing. For instance, Flint says, that Christ has predicted Peter's denial does not entail that Peter has no counterfactual power over what Christ predicted (if Peter had not denied, Christ would not have predicted it). However, Christ's prediction has had causal consequences on the present (e.g. Peter has a memory of Jesus' having uttered those words).

Hasker (2000) replies that these arguments can convince only the already convinced Molinist. In particular, according to Hasker, the Molinist is committed to the existence of alternative causal pasts, that is, to the idea that "at the time when I perform the action, there is some event in the causally relevant past that would have to be different than it is if I refrain from the action. In this case, it seems I am confronted with alternative causal pasts, either of which can be the actual past, depending on what I now decide to do. And that is a scary thought" (p. 104). Since the idea of alternative causal pasts should be rejected, Hasker believe that his anti-Molinist argument is sound. However, the cost charged to Molinism by this reply of Hasker is shared by Ockhamism. Moreover, it is a different cost from that originally charged by Adams' and Hasker's arguments, which aimed to show that Molinism is circular (agents' actions explain the truth of CFs and the truth of CFs explains their actions).

Flint (2011) and Cunningham (2016) have followed a different strategy in responding to Hasker's argument. Both their replies grant that CFs are part of the past history of the world and the agents do not bring about their truth. However, Flint states that the fact that the agent does not bring about the truth of a CF in any world does not imply that that agent has not the power to bring about the truth of that CF (cf. p. 42). This is a very controversial claim because, if an agent has a certain power, there should exist at least a possible world in which she exercises that power.

Cunningham, on the contrary, concedes that the agents have no power to bring about the truth of CFs because they are part of the past history of the world, which we cannot modify. However, Cunningham argues that the fact that the past history of the world *entails* the truth of certain CFs does not imply that the past history *causes* the actions of the agent and *forces* her to act along those CFs. According to Cunningham, this is the essential point for the libertarian: that the acts of the agent are not causally determined. Moreover, Cunningham argues that agents have the power to do differently from what they actually do. In a different world, in which they act differently, other CFs are true and are part of a different past history of the world. Such a history *entails* that agents act along a different CF—but, again, it does not cause them to do so. However, Cunningham's position also seems to be controversial. What is essential for libertarian freedom is the autonomy of the agents when they take decisions: such decisions must not be determined by external factors. However, Cunningham grants that the past history determines—broadly logically or metaphysically, not causally—our actions, and this does not seem to be entirely compatible with libertarian freedom.[32]

5.4.2 What Does Not Work in Adams' and Hasker's Arguments

Flint's and Cunningham's arguments concede that the truth of CFs are not determined by human beings. This is unconvincing: as we have seen, the fact that one of the histories stemming from a fork is privileged is determined by the fact that the agent would act in a certain way in a certain situation. It is because the agent would freely perform a certain action that a certain CF is true.

In this section, we will elaborate Flint's other line of defence, according to which human beings have counterfactual power over CFs and then over God's creative decision (cf. Flint 1999). However, we will refer to examples different from that of Flint because prophecies are a controversial matter. We will show that God's deliberative process when He decides which world to create is similar to some human deliberative processes. Such processes are common and familiar, so that they should not involve explanatory loops and impinge on the agents' freedom. This is also true for the divine deliberation about which world to create. We will show why the problems dreaded by Adams and Hasker do not arise in either divine or human cases. In what follows we will take for granted that God chose the actual world among a set of possible worlds $\mathfrak{U} = \{w_0, w_1 \ldots w_n\}$, each of which has a normal **TRL**.

---

[32]Hasker also expresses doubts about the compatibility of Cunningham's position with libertarian freedom:

> What matters most here is that, under the right circumstances, what an agent decides to do determines the direction of the world; events flow in one way or in another depending solely on that decision. It is important, to be sure, that the decision is not itself the necessary causal consequence of previous events. But the importance of this lies, not in the causation as such, but rather in the fact that such causation negates the genuine alternative possibilities with which the agent is confronted. (Hasker 2017)

Suppose that we are driving a car. We have to decide whether to push the accelerator or not in a certain situation. How do we decide what to do? We know that the following conditionals are true:

(14) If I pushed the accelerator, the car would speed up
(15) If I released the accelerator, the car would reduce speed

Our deliberative process will exploit our knowledge of these conditionals: we evaluate the road conditions and decide whether to increase or decrease speed. If we think that we can increase speed, we exploit the knowledge of the first conditional and push the accelerator.

Paralleling the anti-Molinist argument, one might argue that this situation is contradictory in some way. On the one hand, these conditionals are part of the deliberative process and thus are explanatorily prior to this process; on the other hand, they are the result of this process: it is because we push the accelerator that the car speeds up. It is possible to sketch an explanatory loop, similar to that through which Flint (1998, pp. 159–162) sums up Adams' argument (see Fig. 5.3).

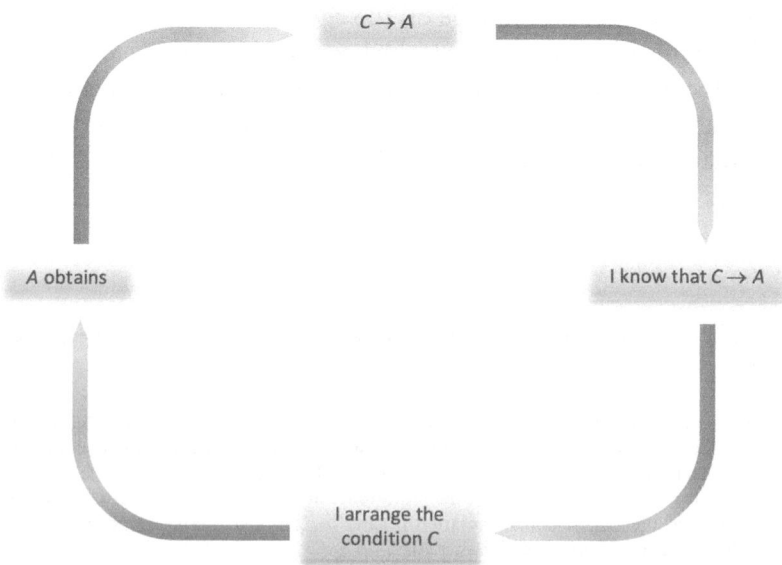

Fig. 5.3 Molinist loop

The loop would arise for the following reason. Some conditionals are true and some deliberative process is based on the knowledge of their truth. These conditionals are, therefore, explanatorily prior to the knowledge of the person who deliberates. On the basis of this knowledge, this person arranges condition *C* and thus the consequent of the conditional obtains. This arrangement is explanatorily prior to *C* and *a fortiori* to *A*. But the conditional is true precisely because in *C A* occurs, and then *C* and *A* are explanatorily prior to the conditional and this closes the loop.

We believe that there is something deeply wrong in this reasoning, but, before dealing with it, let us assess a possible objection. One might contend that the deliberative process is not based on conditionals such as (14) and (15) but on general laws as the following:

(16) Pushing the accelerator speeds up the car.
(17) Releasing the accelerator reduces the speed of the car.

There are two possible answers to this objection. Firstly, it is true that the knowledge of general laws (16) and (17) grounds the knowledge of conditionals (14) and (15), but it is also true that the conditionals, and not the general laws, are exploited in the deliberative process. The person who deliberates needs a *specific* knowledge about the particular pedal she must push and about the particular reactions of the car she is driving. The deliberative process of the agent needs these particular truths. Secondly, there are conditionals involved in deliberative processes that do not depend *directly* on general laws. Suppose that we have to evaluate whether to cross a river on a bridge formed by the trunk of a tree. Consider the following conditional:

(18) If I crossed on that trunk, the trunk would collapse.

Obviously, there are general laws that support the knowledge of this conditional: they involve the size of the trunk, its conditions, my weight and so on. But we cannot say that the conditional can be *directly* deduced by a general law.

Let us go back to the main question: why do examples (14) and (15) not give raise to an explanatory loop? These propositions are in fact conditionals: they say what will occur if some particular conditions obtain. But their truth is independent of the obtaining of these conditions and, therefore, of the consequent. Conditionals speak of what happens in possible worlds: if certain conditions occurred, then the consequent would also occur. They remain true if the antecedent obtains or does not obtain. It is therefore true that the person who drives and decides to accelerate makes the antecedent true and thereby, indirectly, brings about the consequent of the conditional. However, the driver does not make the *conditional* true, given that it is true independently of what the driver does. Accordingly, the conditional is explanatorily prior to the deliberation, but we cannot say that the deliberation is explanatorily prior to the conditional because it remains true whatever the outcome of the process of deliberation.

Let us now analyse some examples in which human deliberations exploit the truth of CFs (or at least of conditionals that are similar to CFs). Suppose that I have to entrust a job to either Emma or Thomas. Suppose also that Emma and Thomas will have to make some free choices during the performance of the work. I know that Emma is better than Thomas at this job and she will take better decisions than Thomas. Consequently, I know the following conditionals, very similar to the CFs on which divine creative deliberation hinges:

(19) If I entrusted the job to Emma, she would take good decisions.
(20) If I entrusted the job to Thomas, he would take bad decisions.

One might argue that these conditionals give rise to a loop similar to that involving the previous conditionals. Conditionals (19) and (20) are explanatorily prior to my decision to entrust the job to Emma or Thomas because I use them in the deliberation process. On the other hand, the situation in which Emma finds herself is arranged by my decision, which is therefore explanatorily prior to it. However, conditional (19) is true precisely because Emma decides in a certain way in that situation and this closes the loop.

However, this reasoning is deceptive for the same reasons explained above. The truth of the conditionals is one of the motives that leads me to entrust the job to Emma and so it is explanatorily prior to my decision. However, my decision is not explanatorily prior to the truth of the conditional. Certainly, it is explanatorily prior to the obtaining of the antecedent of the conditional, but not to the conditional itself. My decision to entrust the job to Emma explains why Emma and not Thomas will be placed in the condition to choose what to do, but it does not explain why conditionals (19) and (20) are true because they are true independently of my decisions. In other words, my decision to entrust the job to Emma explains why Emma and not Thomas will do the job, but it does not explain why Emma will decide *in that way*. This depends on Emma's free choices. The conditional would be true even though Emma had not been placed in the conditions to decide.

One might grant that my decision to entrust the job to Emma does not explain why Emma will choose in a certain way and then that it does not explain the conditionals, but might insist that this is the demonstration that conditionals (21) and (22) are true *before* Emma's choices. However, this is a cost that the Molinist *has already paid* insofar as she accepts that CFs are true and that **TRL+** is a good model of the world. According to Molinism, the truth of CFs is not detrimental to human freedom because the present truth of CFs is metaphysically determined by the future decisions of agents and not *vice versa*. Obviously, that the conditionals are exploited to entrust the job to Emma highlights that (19) and (20) are true *before* my decision and *a fortiori* Emma's decisions. However, one of the basic assumptions of Molinism is that the truth of CFs is independent of the obtaining of conditions C and, then, from the actual decision of the agent. According to Molinists, this is not at odds with libertarian freedom. As we have seen, one might object to these assumptions. However, while highlighting that the truth of CFs precedes Emma's decision *emphasizes* the troubled assumption of Molinism, it does not *add* new problems.

One might try to resist the argument and say that we cannot actually *know* conditionals such as (19) and (20). At most, we can *believe* that these conditionals are true: Emma and Thomas are free agents and they can always do something different from what we foresee they will do.[33] There

---

[33] A similar objection has been raised by Hasker (1997) to an argument of Craig (1994), which resembles that proposed here. Unfortunately, the CF chosen by Craig ("If children were born to us, they would come to love God") makes Hasker's critique more plausible. We consider our examples more effective.

are two possible answers to this objection. Firstly, we should not take for granted that we cannot know conditionals such as (19) and (20). Suppose that the world chess champion will play with an amateur and suppose that he is in his best conditions (he is rested, he does not get distracted during the match, he is motivated to win, for instance by a prize, etc.). Can we say that we do not *know* that the world chess champion will make better moves than the amateur during the match? Even assuming very high epistemic standards, this is completely implausible. Secondly, do things change substantially if instead of believing (19) and (20), one can know them? Even if we know (and do not simply believe) (19) and (20), our knowledge is explanatorily prior to our decision to entrust the job to Emma, but our decision is not explanatorily prior to the conditionals because they are true independently of our decision.

We believe that the analogy between our deliberation to entrust the job to Emma or Thomas and the divine deliberation about which world to create is clear. As we have seen in Sect. 5.2, God must choose among a set of possible worlds $\mathfrak{U}_0$, each of which has a normal **TRL** that makes some CFs true. Such CFs are explanatorily prior to the divine deliberation. However, the divine creation of a world does not ground or explain the truth of CFs. Certainly, God creates some agents and enables them to choose, that is, creates the conditions described by the antecedents of CFs. However, divine decision is not explanatorily prior to their truth because they are true independently of the world that God will decide to create. Moreover, that God's deliberation about the world to create is based on the truth of CFs highlights that CFs are true before and independently of the obtaining of the antecedent. However, this is the core of the Molinist doctrine. We have seen that the theory of the truth of CFs is controversial because it is difficult to ground it. Highlighting that they are true independently of the obtaining of their antecedent emphasizes this problem, but it does not add new difficulties.

5.4.3 Adams' Argument

Let us now see in more detail why Adams' argument does not work. The first premise—CFs are explanatorily prior to God's decision to create the actual world—is true: God uses His knowledge of CFs to deliberate about which world to create. Premise 2 of the argument states that God's decision to create this world is explanatorily prior to our existence and our choices. Clearly, if God had not created this world, we would not have existed and taken any decision. Therefore, God's deliberation explains our existence and the fact that we can act. However, again, the fact that we exist and the fact that we are in certain circumstances do not explain the truth of the CFs concerning our free action. These CFs are true independently of our existence and of our being in certain circumstances because they are conditionals that are true even though their antecedent is not actual. Therefore, God's creative decision explains why this agent exists and has to choose in conditions C but does *not* explain why the agent chooses in a certain way and, then, the truth of the CF. The explanation of why the agent acts in a certain way lies in the decision of the agent. As a CF is true in virtue of the fact that the agent would choose in a certain way, the truth of CFs, far from being explanatorily prior to the choice of the agent, is grounded on it. Since God's creative decision is not explanatorily prior to the particular decision of the agent (and only to the fact that she *can* decide), premise 4 of Adams' argument is false, that is, the truth of CFs is not explanatorily prior to the decision of the agent. The argument does not conclude.

One might try to improve Adams' argument using Hasker's notion of explanatorily priority, that is x è explanatorily prior to y if x is included in the complete explanation of why y obtains. The argument would be the following:

1. The truth of CFs is included in the complete explanation of God's decision to create the world. [Molinist premise]
2. God's decision to create the world is included in the complete explanation of our existence and our actions. [premise]
3. The relation of being included in the complete explanation is transitive. [Premise]

4. The truth of CFs is included in the complete explanation of our actions. [By 1–3]
5. If the truth of CFs is included in the complete explanations of our actions, we cannot do otherwise. [Premise]
6. Our actions are not free. [By 4–5]

However, this does not improve the argument. The truth of CFs explains why the agent finds herself in a certain situation where she has to decide what to do. This is also what happens in our examples: it is because Emma is better at this job than Thomas that Emma finds herself in a situation where she has to decide what to do. However, the truth of CFs does not explain, not even partially, why the agent will choose *in that way*. The particular choice that Emma will make does not depend on the truth of CFs, but on Emma alone. In fact, the opposite is true: it is because Emma will choose in that particular way that the CF is true.

One might contend that we are in the presence of a loop anyway. God's deliberation to create the world partially depend on CFs; then, that the agent is in C partially depends on CFs, and so that the agent will act in a certain way depends on CFs too. But CFs are true precisely because the agent will act in a certain way. However, we have already noticed that this loop does not exist because the truth of CFs is independent of the fact that the agent finds herself in conditions C. Certainly, given circumstances C, the agent will choose in a certain way, but CFs, being conditionals, are independent of the obtaining of C. And this breaks the loop.

5.4.4 Hasker's Argument

The fundamental thesis of Hasker's argument is that CFs are part of the past history of the world, that is of something that the agent cannot bring about. The reason supporting this thesis is that God relied on CFs to create the actual world and so CFs have causal consequences on the present. What has such consequences is part of the past history.

It is not entirely clear what Hasker precisely means when he says that CFs are part of the past history of the world. He cannot mean that CFs refer to past facts because they are conditionals concerning what would happen in certain circumstances. Therefore, they do not refer to past facts; in fact, if such circumstances will obtain in the future, they refer to future facts. On the other hand, if Hasker just means that the truth of CFs precedes the decisions of human beings, this is a cost that the Molinist pays as long as CFs are assumed to be true. As we have seen, the Molinist claims that human freedom is not compromised because CFs do not explain human decisions; on the contrary, the truth of CFs is grounded on the future or possible human decisions.[34]

However, Hasker means something more than this: he believes that CFs are facts that an agent cannot change because they have had an impact on the present and, since the present cannot be changed, also what has had an impact on the present cannot. However, it is not clear whether this argument adds something to the commitments of the Molinists. They grant that it is already true today that human agents will take some decisions tomorrow, but that they could have done differently. If they had done different things, the past would have been different from what actually is because God would have known different things. If the structure of the universe is **TRL+** and if human beings had done different things, then God would have decided to create a world by choosing from a set of worlds different from that from which He has actually chosen, namely, $\mathfrak{U}$. Indeed, if human beings had chosen differently, other CFs would have been true and, consequently, the normal **TRLs** of the worlds would have been different. God might have created a different world because one of the worlds of this new set might have been better than the actual world. This has already been noticed by Alvin Plantinga through his well-known example of the ant colony: God knew in advance that Paul will not mow his lawn this afternoon, but if He had foreknown instead that Paul would mow this afternoon, then God, who for reasons of His own wants to preserve a colony of ants, would have prevented the colony of ants from moving into Paul's lawn (Plantinga 1986, p. 254). This is

---

[34]Cunningham's response to Hasker's argument is particularly weak on this point. He maintains that the past history of the world, including CFs, metaphysically determines the agent's future decisions. However, the opposite is true: it is because the agent will choose in a certain way in the future that certain CFs are already true now, before the obtaining of conditions C. Human beings' future decisions make some past sentences true and not *vice versa*.

a direct consequence of the "butterfly" scheme: if the agents had acted differently in the future, the past also would have been different. In the Molinist framework, where every possible choice engenders a butterfly, this has dramatic effects: the possible choices of the agents determine which world is created. This may appear implausible, but it is part of the Molinist model of the universe and does not add further costs to it.[35]

Hasker's argument might seem plausible because Hasker ascribes to the Molinist the thesis that the past can be *altered*: "If we assume, as I think we must, that the past is inalterable, then it is out of the question to suppose that those causal processes could now be made different in any way" (Hasker 1999b, p. 294). However, we have seen in the previous chapter that this is not the case. As Craig (1986, 1991) repeatedly noted, to state that the past is determined by the future does not mean being committed to the view that we can change the past. By means of her future actions, the agent does not change but instead metaphysically determines what God believed in the past and partially contributes to His past decision. The past is not altered by the agents, but it is partially determined by the future acts of the agents. The future choices of the agents could have been different and, thus, the past also could have been different. However, this does not concern the actual world, but an alternative history of the world in which the agents make different choices. And that there is a possible history of the world in which the past is different from the actual past is something that Hasker can hardly deny.

5.5 Conclusion

In this chapter, three different topics have been tackled. Firstly, we have formalized the Molinist doctrine by means of the model **TRL+** and we

---

[35] One might contend that this situation is not exceptional and that we daily take decisions on the basis of our beliefs about what the other persons will do in the future. I believe that Emma is better than Thomas at this job and, therefore, I have decided to entrust the job to Emma. But if Thomas had been better than Emma, I would have entrusted the job to Thomas. So, what Emma and Thomas would do—a good or bad job—determines my choice and thereby whether they will be enabled to do the job or not. It is easy to see the similarities between this everyday situation and God's situation during the creative act.

have shown that this model does not incur the problems of the interpretation of CFs through Lewis' semantics. Secondly, we have faced the question of the metaphysical interpretation of **TRL+** and of its costs. We have seen that some solutions suitable for the Ockhamist are not open to the Molinist, who must fall back on more costly alternatives. In particular, CFs seem to remain groundless within these alternative interpretations. We have examined some Molinist responses to this problem, but we have concluded that there is a tension between **FATMP**, a principle that the Molinist, as libertarian, seems to be forced to accept, and the truth or falsehood of CFs. Thirdly, we have taken into consideration Adams and Hasker's circularity objection to Molinism. We have shown that this objection does not add further costs to the model: it may only emphasize some problematic features of the **TRL+** structure, without adding any further valid critique.

References

Adams, R.M. 1974. Middle knowledge. *The Journal of Philosophy* 70(17): 552–554.
Adams, R.M. 1977. Middle knowledge and the problem of evil. *American Philosophical Quarterly* 14(2): 109–117.
Adams, R.M. 1991. An anti-molinist argument. *Philosophical Perspectives* 5: 343–353.
Barcellan, B., and A. Zanardo. 1999. Actual futures in peircean branching-time logic. In *JFAK: Essays Dedicated to Johan van Benthem on the Occasion of his 50th Birthday*, ed. J. Gerbrandy, M. Marx, M. de Rijke, and Y. Venema. Amsterdam: Amsterdam University Press.
Baron, S. 2015. Tensed truthmaker theory. *Erkenntnis* 80(5): 923–944.
Basinger, D. 1993. Simple foreknowledge and providential control: A response to hunt. *Faith and Philosophy* 10(3): 421–427.
Braüner, T., P. Hasle, and P. Øhstrøm. 1998. Ockhamistic logics and true futures of counterfactual moments. In *Proceedings of Fifth International workshop on temporal representation and reasoning*, ed. L. Khatib, and R. Morris, 132–139. Piscataway: IEEE.
Cohen, Y. 2016. Counterfactuals of divine freedom. *International Journal for Philosophy of Religion* 79(3): 185–205.

Cowan, S.B. 2003. The grounding objection to middle knowledge revisited. *Religious Studies* 39(1): 93–102.
Craig, W.L. 1986. Temporal necessity; hard facts/soft facts. *International Journal for Philosophy of Religion* 20(2–3): 65–91.
Craig, W.L. 1991. *Divine foreknowledge and human freedom: the coherence of theism I: omniscience*, vol. 19. New York: Brill.
Craig, W.L. 1994. Robert Adams's new anti-molinist argument. *Philosophy and Phenomenological Research* 54(4): 857–861.
Craig, W.L. 2001. Middle knowledge, truth-makers, and the "grounding objection". *Faith and Philosophy* 18(3): 337–352.
Craig, W.L. 2006. Ducking friendly fire: Davison on the grounding objection. *Philosophia Christi* 8(1): 161–166.
Cunningham, A.J. 2016. Where Hasker's anti-molinist argument goes wrong. *Faith and Philosophy* 33(2): 200–222.
Davison, S.A. 2004. Craig on the grounding objection to middle knowledge. *Faith and Philosophy* 21(3): 365–369.
De Florio, C., and A. Frigerio. 2013. God, evil, and Alvin Plantinga. *European Journal for Philosophy of Religion* 5(3): 75–94.
Fischer, J.M. 2008. Molinism. In *Oxford studies in philosophy of religion*, ed., J. Kvanvig, vol. 1, 18–43. Oxford: Oxford University Press.
Flint, T.P. 1998. *Divine providence: The Molinist account*. Ithaca: Cornell University Press.
Flint, T. 1999. A new anti-anti-molinist argument. *Religious Studies* 35(3): 299–305.
Flint, T.P. 2009. Divine providence. In *The Oxford handbook of philosophical theology*, ed. T.P. Flint and M. Rea, 261–282. Oxford: Oxford University Press.
Flint, T. 2011. Whence and whither the molinist debate: A reply to Hasker. In *Molinism: The contemporary debate*, ed. K. Perszyk, 37–49. Oxford: Oxford University Press.
Freddoso, A. 1988. Introduction. In *On divine foreknowledge. (Part IV of the Concordia)*, 1–83. Ithaca: Cornell University Press.
Hasker, W. 1994. A philosophical perspective. In *The openness of God: A biblical challenge to the traditional understanding of God*, ed. C. Pinnock, R. Rice, J. Sanders, and W. Hasker, 126–154. Downers Grove: InterVarsity Press.
Hasker, W. 1997. Explanatory priority: Transitive and unequivocal, a reply to William Craig. *Philosophy and Phenomenological Research* 57(2): 389–393.
Hasker, W. 1998. *God, time, and knowledge*. Ithaca: Cornell University Press.

Hasker, W. 1999a. Book review: Divine providence: The molinist account. *Faith and Philosophy* 16(2): 9.
Hasker, W. 1999b. A new anti-Molinist argument. *Religious Studies* 35(3): 291–297.
Hasker, W. 2000. Are alternative pasts plausible? A reply to Thomas Flint. *Religious Studies* 36(1): 103–105.
Hasker, W. 2004. *Providence, evil and the openness of God*, vol. 3. Milton Park: Psychology Press.
Hasker, W. 2009. Why simple foreknowledge is still useless (in spite of David Hunt and Alex Pruss). *Journal of the Evangelical Theological Society* 52(3): 537—544.
Hasker, W. 2011. The (non-)existence of Molinist counterfactuals. In *Molinism: The contemporary debate*, ed. K. Perszyk, 25–36. Oxford: Oxford University Press.
Hasker, W. 2017. Molinism's freedom problem: A reply to Cunningham. *Faith and Philosophy* 34(1): 93–106.
Hunt, D.P. 1993a. Divine providence and simple foreknowledge. *Faith and Philosophy* 10(3): 394–414.
Hunt, D.P. 1993b. Prescience and providence: A reply to my critics. *Faith and Philosophy* 10(3): 428–438.
Hunt, D.P. 1996. The compatibility of omniscience and intentional action: a reply to Tomis Kapitan. *Religious Studies* 32(1): 49–60.
Hunt, D.P. 2004. Providence, foreknowledge, and explanatory loops: a reply to Robinson. *Religious Studies* 40(4): 485–491.
Jäger, C. 2011. Molina on foreknowledge and transfer of necessities. In *God, eternity, and time*, ed. C. Tapp, and E. Runggaldier, 81–96. Farnham: Ashgate.
Jäger, C. 2013. Molinism and theological compatibilism. *European Journal for Philosophy of Religion* 5(1): 71–92.
Kapitan, T. 1993. Providence, foreknowledge, and decision procedures. *Faith and Philosophy* 10(3): 415–420.
Lewis, D. 2013. *Counterfactuals*. New York: Wiley.
McDermott, M. 2007. True antecedents. *Acta Analytica* 22(4): 333–335.
Perszyk, K. 2011. *Molinism: the contemporary debate*. Oxford: Oxford University Press.
Plantinga, A. 1977. *God, freedom, and evil*. Grand Rapids: William B. Eerdmans.
Plantinga, A. 1986. On Ockham's way out. *Faith and Philosophy* 3(3): 235–269.
Plantinga, A. 2012. Replies. In *Alvin Plantinga*, ed. J. Tomberlin, and P. Van Inwagen, 313–396. London: Springer.

Pollock, J.L. 1976. *Subjunctive reasoning*, vol. 8. London: Springer.
Pruss, A.R., and J.L. Rasmussen. 2014. Explaining counterfactuals of freedom. *Religious Studies* 50(2): 193–198.
Robinson, M.D. 2004. Divine providence, simple foreknowledge, and the "metaphysical principle". *Religious Studies* 40(4): 471–483.
Sanders, J. 1997. Why simple foreknowledge offers no more providential control than the openness of god. *Faith and Philosophy* 14(1): 26–40.
Stalnaker, R. 1981. A defense of conditional excluded middle. In *IFS: Conditionals, belief, decision, chance and time*, ed. W.L. Harper, G. Pearce, and R. Stalnaker, 87–104. London: Springer.
Van Inwagen, P. 1997. Against middle knowledge. *Midwest Studies in Philosophy* 21(1): 225–236.
Walters, L. 2016. Possible world semantics and true-true counterfactuals. *Pacific Philosophical Quarterly* 97(3): 322–346.
Wierenga, E.R. 1989. *The nature of God: An inquiry into divine attributes*. Ithaca: Cornell University Press.
Wierenga, E. 2011. Tilting at Molinism. In *Molinism: The contemporary debate*, ed. K. Perszyk, 118–139. Oxford: Oxford University Press.
Zagzebski, L.T. 1991. *The dilemma of freedom and foreknowledge*. Oxford: Oxford University Press.
Zagzebski, L. 2017. *Foreknowledge and free will. Stanford Encyclopedia of Philosophy*. Accessed 4 July 2019.
Zimmerman, D. 2009. Yet another anti-Molinist argument. In *Metaphysics and the good: Themes from the philosophy of Robert Merrihew Adams*, ed. S. Newlands, and L. Jorgensen, 33–94. Oxford: Oxford University Press.

6

The Timeless Solution

In this chapter, we deal with a family of solutions to the dilemma of divine foreknowledge and human freedom based on the idea that God is a timeless entity. As said in Sect. 4.1, conceiving God as timeless implies various kinds of difficulties: metaphysical (the advocate of a tensed theory of time might affirm that all that exists, God included, is temporal), theological (one might argue that timelessness is in contrast with other divine attributes like being personal, or with some Christian doctrines, like Incarnation), and mixed (one might contend that a timeless entity cannot know temporal facts). In this chapter, we will disregard metaphysical and theological difficulties, which will take us too far afield from the topic of this book.[1] We will assume that it is possible to conceive God as timeless. Actually, as we have said in Sect. 4.1, we will restrict this assumption to divine knowledge: God's knowledge will be presupposed not to be located in time. On this view, it does not make sense to say that God *believed* or *will* believe something or that God believes something at time t. We can only say that God timelessly believes something.

---

[1] For a collection of papers that discuss the timeless and temporal conception of God, see Tapp and Runggaldier (2011).

In this chapter, some "mixed" difficulties of the timeless solution will be discussed because they directly concern the cognitive relations between God and the temporal world and affect the problem of the divine prescience of free human actions. This topic will turn out to be crucial for the timeless solution because its prospects change radically depending on the metaphysics of time that is assumed, in particular whether an A- or B-theory of time is presupposed. In Sect. 6.1, the fundamental tenets of the timeless solution will be surveyed, while in Sect. 6.2, some objections will be taken into consideration and discarded. The relations between a divine timeless knowledge and a static temporal reality are analysed in Sect. 6.3. We will see that in this case the timeless solution works very well and that there are no particular problems in assuming that a timeless God can know the block of events postulated by the B-theory. The relations between a timeless God and a dynamic temporal reality are examined in Sect. 6.4. In this case, the timeless solution is much more puzzling because, at least *prima facie*, a timeless God cannot capture the dynamic trait of the world postulated by the A-theory of time. We will see that the problem can be solved only by assuming a non-standard A-theory of time (Sect. 6.5). Section 6.6 contains some concluding remarks.

6.1 How the Timeless Solution Works

Let us consider again the theological fatalist argument:

1. Yesterday, God believed that p (divine foreknowledge).
2. If an event e occurred in the past, then it is accidentally necessary that e occurred then (necessity of the past).
3. It is now necessary that yesterday God believed p (1,2, *modus ponens*).
4. Necessarily, if yesterday God believed p, then p (infallibility of divine foreknowledge).
5. If r is accidentally necessary and if $\Box(r \to s)$, then it is accidentally necessary that s (principle of transfer of necessity).
6. So it is now necessary that p (3,4,5).
7. If it is now necessary that p, then you cannot do otherwise than p (definition of necessary).

8. Therefore, you cannot do otherwise than p (6,7,*modus ponens*).
9. If you cannot do otherwise when you do an act, you do not do it freely (Principle of Alternate Possibilities).
10. Therefore, when you do p, you will not do it freely. (8,9,*modus ponens*)

In Chap. 3, we have seen that open theists reject premise 1 of the argument because they do not believe that God foreknows human free acts. The advocates of the timeless solution also reject premise 1, but for another reason: they do believe that God knows human free acts, but they do not locate divine knowledge in time, as premise 1 does. Therefore, it is incorrect to state that God *believed yesterday* that p. In absence of a temporal collocation of divine knowledge, the argument cannot exploit the necessity of the past stated by premise 2 and cannot transfer this necessity to the future through premise 5. By consequence, the argument does not conclude.

The timeless solution has a venerable history. It dates back at least to Boethius,[2] who represents the relation between God and the world as a circle with a central point (cf. Fig. 6.1).

The point C represents God, whereas the circumference represents the sequence of events in time. The points of the circumference can have greater or shorter distances among them depending on the arc that separates them. Conversely, God is out of time and at the same distance from all the points of the circumference. For us the present is a privileged moment, whereas the other times are at greater or less distance. But for God no time is privileged because He has the same relationship with every time. This is represented by the fact that the radii of the circle all have the same length. The metaphor of the circle has some explicative advantages, but it is wanting on two important points. First of all, it seems to suggest a B-theory of time because there is no privileged present and all times are on a par. Secondly, the metaphor suggests a circular time, very far from our modern intuitions and from the topology of time assumed by the main metaphysical views. After all, if time were represented as a straight

---

[2] Boethius, *The Consolation of Philosophy*, IV, 6.

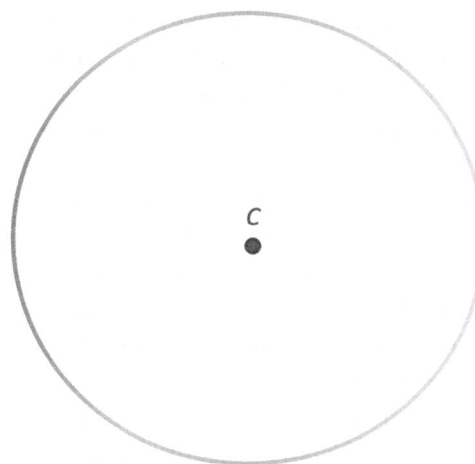

Fig. 6.1 Boethius picture of eternity

line, the idea of a central point (God) equidistant from all points would be missing.

Leaving metaphors aside, the main idea of the timeless solution is that it is inappropriate to say that God *fore*knows free human choices because God's knowledge is out of time; on the contrary, God timelessly sees free human choices. *Prima facie*, simply seeing what human beings choose to do does not damage human freedom. This applies to both God and human beings. For example, suppose one to be at the party and to see that Emma freely chooses to drink a beer rather than a Coke. The knowledge of this choice is clearly compatible with Emma's freedom and does not impinge upon it in any way. God is, in a certain sense, co-present with every time because He has the same relationship with all of them. He timelessly sees human free choices. However, since His relationship with these choices is similar to that of the participants in the party who see Emma decide to drink a beer, His knowledge is not in contrast with Emma's freedom: God timelessly knows that Emma drinks a beer at time t because He timelessly observes what happens at t and at every other time.

This point has been elaborated by Katherin Rogers,[3] who has shown that divine timeless knowledge can be easily married with historical necessity. Rogers claims that accidental necessity is a kind of consequent necessity: only when the agent has performed a certain act does it become necessary. Therefore, this necessity does not undermine the agent's freedom. It is the agent herself who, by choosing φ, makes φ necessary. God's timeless knowledge does not clash with the agent's freedom because it depends on the agent's choice. God eternally sees every point in time and thus He sees a performing φ at t. φ has a consequent necessity at t, but neither God's knowledge nor the consequent necessity of φ are in contrast with a's freedom because both depend on a's decision.

It is clear that the heart of the timeless solution is the relationship of co-presence between a timeless God and the temporal times. In our comparison, we are at the party with Emma at time t, so we are co-present with her choices. But how can a being that is out of time be co-present with something temporal like Emma's choice? It has been responded that the co-presence of God with a certain time is obviously not the particular kind of co-presence that two temporal beings—such as Emma and us—have. However, it is a *certain* kind of co-presence.

Stump and Kretzmann (1981) have tried to provide an analysis of the concept of timeless eternity in order to characterize more precisely the particular kind of co-presence existing between a temporal and a timeless reality, specifying analogies and differences with the co-presence between two temporal entities. They have argued that there is a generic concept of simultaneity according to which two entities are simultaneous if they exist or occur *at once* (i.e., *together*). There are many kinds of simultaneity but, as we will see shortly, they have in common the idea of existing or occurring at once. Stump and Kretzmann also believe that time and eternity are separate ontological dimensions. Eternal events cannot be temporal and, conversely, temporal events cannot be eternal. Since there are two categories of events (temporal and eternal), there must be two

---

[3] See, for example, Rogers (2007b).

simultaneity relations, one for temporal events and the other for eternal events:

(T) T-simultaneity = existence or occurrence at the same time within the reference frame of a given observer
(E) E-simultaneity = existence or occurrence with respect to the unique eternal frame (Stump and Kretzmann 1981, p. 435)

Reference to temporal frames arises from the fact that Stump and Kretzmann believe that there is no absolute notion of simultaneity. Einstein's Relativity theory teaches us that simultaneity is something relative to an inertial frame of reference. However, the eternal frame is a special one because it is not temporal. In the eternal frame, then, there is no past or future, no earlier or later; that is, the events in this frame cannot be ordered sequentially from the standpoint of eternity. Instead, all events happen at once in the eternal frame and, so, they are all E-simultaneous. In order to characterize the relationship between the timeless God and the temporal world, Stump and Kretzmann postulate a third type of simultaneity, called ET-simultaneity:

(ET) For every x and for every y, x and y are ET-simultaneous iff

1. either x is eternal and y is temporal, or vice versa; and
2. for some observer, A, in the unique eternal reference frame, x and y are both present—that is, either x is eternally present and y is observed as temporally present, or vice versa; and
3. for some observer, B, in one of the infinitely many temporal reference frames, x and y are both present—that is, either x is observed as eternally present and y is temporally present, or vice versa (cf. Stump and Kretzmann 1981, p. 439).

The relation of ET-simultaneity is symmetric (if x is ET-simultaneous with y, then y is ET-simultaneous with x), but also irreflexive and intransitive. If it were transitive, absurd conclusions would follow: since time t is ET-simultaneous with God and God is ET-simultaneous with another time t', it would follow that t and t' are ET-simultaneous.

A timeless God is ET-simultaneous with every time, and every time is ET-simultaneous with a timeless God. Although there are important differences between T-simultaneity and ET-simultaneity, if the analogy between T-simultaneity and ET-simultaneity is sufficiently strong, then the timeless solution offers an advantage with respect to Ockhamism and Molinism. As we have seen, these solutions suppose that past divine beliefs are determined by future human actions. This determination of a past fact by a future fact is metaphysically peculiar. However, if God, being out of time, is *in a certain sense* present to any time, the determination of divine beliefs by free human choices is less troublesome.

The concept of ET-simultaneity has drawn much criticism.[4] It has been noticed that timeless and temporal entities do not share any kind of present because *present* is meant in two different senses when applied to them. It is therefore difficult to see how, from these two different simultaneity relations, a third property of *being simultaneous* can arise, that is, the property that temporal and timeless entities have in common. What could then ground the relation of ET-simultaneity, given that E- and T-simultaneity cannot? According to Craig (1998), the relation of ET-simultaneity can be based on that of *both being real with respect to the same reference frame*:

> we must find some common property shared by God and temporal entities relative to either's "reference frame" which intuitively suffices to found a simultaneity relation. I think that the essence of the Stump-Kretzmann definition would be preserved if we state that relative to either frame "x and y are both real", one eternally real and the other observed as temporally real relative to the eternal "reference frame" or one temporally real and the other observed as eternally real relative to a moment of time. (Craig 1998, pp. 233–234)

Actually, in a later paper (Stump and Kretzmann 1992), Stump and Kretzmann grounded the relation of ET-simultaneity on those of cause and awareness: timeless and temporal entities are ET-simultaneous because they can enter into causal relationships and because they can

---

[4] See, for instance, Lewis (1984), Fitzgerald (1985), Leftow (1988), Craig (1998).

be directly aware of each other. These relations are exactly those needed by the timeless solution; in particular, it is sufficient that the following analogy between the relations of T- and ET-simultaneity exists:

Dependence If x is a free human action and y is the knowledge of x and if x and y are T- or ET-simultaneous, then y depends on x.

In other terms, admittedly there must exist at least this similarity between entities that are T-simultaneous and entities that are ET-simultaneous: if x and the knowledge of x are simultaneous, the knowledge of x depends on x. If we are at the party with Emma, our knowledge that she drinks a beer depends on the fact that she drinks a beer. In the same way, God's timeless knowledge that Emma drinks a beer depends on Emma's free choice because God's knowledge and Emma's choice are ET-simultaneous.

If **Dependence** is correct, we do not need to affirm that the past depends on the future, as in the Ockhamist and Molinist frameworks. It is God's timeless knowledge that depends on temporal facts, not the past on the future. Assuming **Dependence**, the dependence of a timeless fact on a temporal fact is less peculiar than the dependence of a temporal fact on another temporal fact.[5]

6.2 Some Objections

This section focuses on two objections against the timeless solutions that are independent of the assumed metaphysics of time. The first one aims to demonstrate that the timeless solution has no advantage over the

---

[5] This point is neglected by Cyr (2018), who alleges that the basic move to rebut the theological fatalist argument is to grant that divine beliefs depend on free human choices. For the sake of this rebuttal, it matters little whether divine beliefs are temporal or timeless. So, the timeless solution has no advantage over the temporal solution because the timeless solution also must grant this dependence. However, **Dependence** has a different cost than the temporal solutions: the latter must say that the past depends on the future, which is metaphysically peculiar. By contrast, on the timeless view, it suffices to say that a temporal fact depends on another fact that is *in a certain sense* simultaneous with it—in the sense of ET-simultaneity. Obviously, any advantage of the timeless solution would disappear if between divine timeless beliefs and times there were not a relation of ET-simultaneity but another relation in light of which it would be difficult to see how the timeless reality can be determined in some way by the temporal reality.

Ockhamist and Molinist views, in which God is in time. Conversely, the second objection acknowledges that the timeless solution presents some advantages over the temporal solutions but argues that these advantages are cancelled out by the existence of prophecies. We believe that the first objection fails to hit the mark and that the second is weaker than it could appear at first sight.

Let us start with the first objection, which is mainly due to Alvin Plantinga and Linda Zagzebski.[6] Zagzebski maintains that the fatalist argument can be reformulated, replacing premise 1 with premise 1′:

1′ God eternally believes that p

The crux of the objection raised by Zagzebski is that human beings can no more do anything about God's timeless beliefs than they can about His past beliefs. Timeless beliefs can no more be changed than past ones. If a timeless belief implies that p is true, then it seems that an agent cannot do otherwise than p. The fatalist argument can be formulated using premise 1′ thus:

1′ God eternally believes that p (divine omniscience).
2′ If an event e is out of time, then e is accidentally necessary [immutability of eternal things].
3′ It is accidentally necessary that God eternally believes that p (1′,2′,*modus ponens*).
4′ Necessarily, if God believes p, then p (infallibility of divine knowledge).
5′ If r is accidentally necessary and if $\Box(r \rightarrow s)$, then it is accidentally necessary that s (principle of transfer of necessity).
6′ So it is accidentally necessary that p (3′,4′,5′).

From this point, the argument goes on as usual. Note that the argument uses the concept of accidental necessity normally ascribed to past events. Why does Zagzebski believe that human beings cannot modify divine

---

[6]Plantinga (1986, pp. 239–240) and Zagzebski (1991, pp. 60–63).

timeless beliefs? In other terms, why should we think that timeless beliefs have the same type of necessity as past beliefs? We have the impression that Zagzebski tends to conceive a timeless belief as something that has always been so and will always be so, that is, as something everlasting. It is clear that a human being cannot modify something like this—and probably God cannot either. Divine beliefs are regarded as similar to laws of nature, in which a human agent has no possibilities of intervention. They have been so since the beginning of the universe and very probably they will be so until its end, and we can do nothing to determine or modify them.

However, if God is *out* of time, He is not an everlasting entity. His beliefs are not something that *have always been* and *will always be* so because they are not temporal. They are timelessly so, and if we accept **Dependence**, that is, the possibility that the timeless reality is determined by the temporal reality, we can say that God timelessly knows that Emma drinks a beer at t exactly *because* Emma drinks a beer at t. If Emma had chosen to drink a Coke instead of a beer at t, God would have timelessly believed that Emma drinks a Coke at t. God's timeless beliefs about what happens at a certain point of the temporal series counterfactually depend on what happens at that point of the temporal series.

One might then object that God's beliefs are immutable if they are out of time. God cannot acquire the belief that Emma drinks a beer at t. God has always had that belief. But, again, this objection locates what is out of time in time. In fact, this reply seems to postulate that God has the belief that Emma drinks a beer at t at times previous to t. However, this is impossible because there is no t at which God has a certain belief. Particularly, there is not a time at which God did not have the belief that Emma drinks a beer at t and a subsequent time at which God has this belief. God does not acquire this belief, but He has it timelessly. However, this does not mean that God has this belief *necessarily*: a timeless belief is not a necessary belief if it depends on what happens in time.

A similar but more refined version of Zagzebski's argument is offered by Alvin Plantinga. The argument proceeds as follows (cf. Plantinga 1986, p. 239). Suppose that God timelessly believes that Emma drinks a beer at t. But it has always been true that God timelessly believes that Emma drinks a beer at t, also at the times previous to t. Since divine beliefs are infallible, then it has always been true that Emma drinks a beer at t. In particular, this was true at the times previous to t. So, if Emma decides not to drink a beer, she has to change the past. As Stump and Kretzmann (1991) have noticed, there is an illegitimate premise in this argument. Generally, temporal specifications are not applicable to timeless states of affairs. Hence, it is not possible to say that it is true at a time previous to t that God timelessly believes that Emma drinks a beer at t. There is not a time at which God timelessly believes some proposition because this would locate within time something out of time.

To better see this point, let us formulate Plantinga's argument using the concept of ET-simultaneity. Emma's drinking a beer at t is ET-simultaneous with the divine timeless belief that Emma drinks a beer at t. Suppose that time t' precedes t. Since God is ET-simultaneous with every time, God's belief that Emma drinks a beer at t is also ET-simultaneous with time t'. Then, the fact that Emma drinks a beer at t is already true at time t', that is, a time previous to t. In a slightly more formal way, the argument proceeds as follows:

1. Emma chooses to drink a beer at t.
2. Emma's choice to drink a beer at t is ET-simultaneous with God's belief that Emma drinks a beer at t.
3. God's belief that Emma drinks a beer at t is ET-simultaneous with time t'.
4. It is true at t' that Emma will drink a beer at t.

However, this argument is invalid because the relation of ET-simultaneity is not transitive:

> From the facts that some past or future state of affairs is ET-simultaneous with the eternal present and that the eternal present is ET-simultaneous with the temporal present, it does not follow that that past or future state of affairs is ET-simultaneous (or simultaneous in any other respect) with the temporal present. (Stump and Kretzmann 1991, p. 411)

Again the argument locates divine timeless beliefs in time. This family of arguments cannot worry the advocates of the timeless solution because they are based on misconceptions about the notion of timeless belief. They tend to treat, one way or another, timeless beliefs as immutable temporal entities.[7]

The second objection that we will examine in this section is due to Winderker (1991). He acknowledges that the timeless solution need not postulate that the past is determined by the future, but he argues that this advantage is cancelled by prophecies. If God announces to a prophet what will happen in the future in virtue of His foreknowledge, then the prophecy of the prophet is a temporal fact that depends on what will happen in the future. Although divine beliefs are timeless, the announcement by the prophet is a temporal fact that depends on what some human beings will freely choose to do in the future. This is exactly what the timeless solution wishes to avoid.

This critique hits the mark. However, we do not believe that the advantage of the timeless solution over the temporal solution is completely nullified. First of all, prophecies are a controversial phenomenon. In Sect. 3.1.4, we have seen that open theists even deny the existence of the prophecies as they are usually understood, that is, as true predictions of the future. And they interpret the Biblical passages accordingly. Therefore, the advocate of the timeless solution also might deny the existence of prophecies to respond to Winderker's objection.

Secondly, even though classical prophecies exist, within the timeless framework there is still no *direct* dependence of the prophecies on free human actions. This dependence is mediated by divine timeless beliefs. God timelessly sees what occurs at t and at a time previous to t reveals to the prophet what will occur at t. In a strict sense, there is not direct dependence of a past event on a future event, but a dependence of a timeless fact (divine knowledge) on a temporal fact (human free action) and of a temporal fact (revelation to the prophet) on a timeless fact (divine will of revealing the future of a certain point of the temporal series). The first dependence relation, that is, that between free human choice and God's timeless view, *must* be granted; else God's knowledge would not

---

[7]For some support for this thesis, see the careful scrutiny of Plantinga's objection contained in Leftow (1991b).

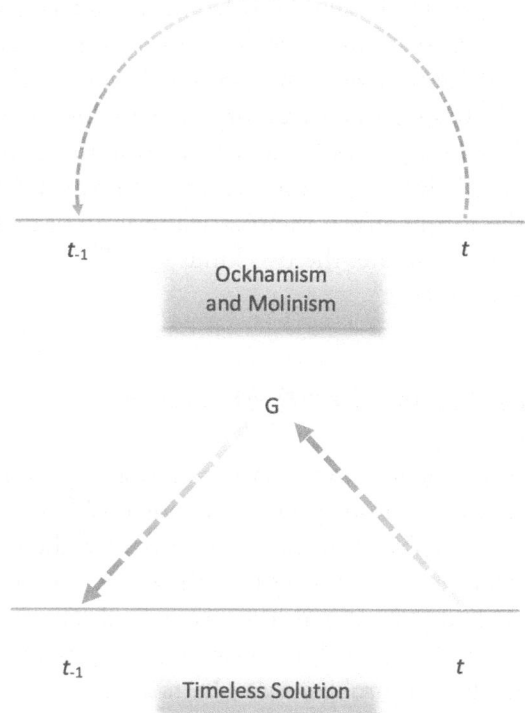

Fig. 6.2 Foreknowledge and prophecy

be grounded on the agents' free decisions. But the second dependence relation, that is, that between divine timeless will and the display of its effects in time, also must be admitted by the advocate of the timeless view, independently of the prophecy; else a timeless God could not intervene in the temporal world. We can sketch out the two situations as in Fig. 6.2.

Ockhamism and Molinism postulate that an event at time t determines another event at a previous time t_{-1}. Instead, the timeless solution postulates that a temporal event at t determines God's timeless belief (in the drawing God is represented as a point external to the temporal series); in turn, God determines another event at a previous time. The result is the same, but in the second case the determination is indirect and mediated by divine timeless knowledge. If it is taken for granted that temporal events can determine timeless events and *vice versa*, then from the metaphysical point of view, the timeless solution is less peculiar than the temporal solutions. Moreover, it offers an *explanation* of how a future event can determine a past event, an explanation that calls into question divine timeless beliefs. On the contrary, Ockhamism and Molinism must just say that the future affects the past without any explanation of how this can happen. Therefore, the two kinds of solutions are not on a par, even regarding prophecy.[8]

6.3 Timeless God and Eternalism

The objections considered in the last section are not very worrying for the timeless solution. In our opinion, major problems arise in relation to the assumed metaphysics of time. In particular, the timeless solution can be easily combined with a static B-theory of time (Eternalism) but not with an A-theory. In this section, we will discuss the combination between a timeless God and Eternalism, showing that it does not have particular metaphysical problems. In the next section, we will focus on the relation of the timeless solution with the A-theory of time, showing that it is very intricate. We will defend the thesis that only by adopting a non-standard A-theory, like Fragmentalism, is it possible to keep God out of time together with a dynamic conception of time.

The combination among a timeless God, Libertarianism and Eternalism has been championed by Katherin Rogers (see, especially, Rogers (2007a) and Rogers (2008, ch. 8-9)).[9] She believes that this combination of theories was defended by St. Anselm of Canterbury and, thus, she calls it Anselmianism. Rogers accepts the timeless conception of God and

---

[8]The different positions of timeless and temporal solutions regarding the determination of the past have been acknowledged by Widerker himself in a later paper: see Widerker (1994).

[9]The combination between timeless God and Eternalism has also been advocated by Paul Helm in Helm (1988) and MacBeath and Helm (1989). However, Helm rejects Libertarianism and embraces a compatibilist conception of freedom. For the aims of this essay, Rogers' position, which tries to reconcile human freedom in strong sense and divine omniscience, is more interesting.

argues, against other interpretations of this view,[10] that it entails that God has no duration:

> The temporal phenomenon with which we are familiar which is most like eternity is the present, durationless, instant. The difference being [...] that God's 'present' does not move, change, come into being or pass away. (Rogers 1994, p. 15)

Moreover, she advocates a strong conception of freedom, according to which the agents are not determined to make certain choices. Libertarianism implies that God's knowledge depends on human actions and not the reverse:

> It is the fact that the agent actually chooses what he chooses that produces God's knowledge of the choice, and so the consequent necessity involved in divine knowledge is ultimately produced by the agent making the choice. (Rogers 2008, p. 175)

Rogers then accepts the principle that we have called here **Dependence**, according to which divine timeless beliefs are dependent on facts occurring in time. Rogers maintains that this view about God and His relationship with human actions entails Eternalism about time. She refers to the two metaphors used during the Middle Age for clarifying the relation between God and the temporal world: the first one is that of the circle with a point in the middle that we have seen above, while the second one is that of

> the observer on the highest peak who sees all the objects and events in the plain below. Those below can perceive only what is in their immediate environs. They do not have cognitive or causal access to all the objects and events in the plain because most are too distant spatially. But the keen observer above, because of his unique perspective, can perceive each and every one of them equally. (Rogers 2007a, p. 8)

---

[10]For instance, those of Stump and Kretzmann (1981) and Leftow (1991a).

Both these metaphors suggest an Eternalistic metaphysics of time:

> the analogies suggest four-dimensionalism. All the points of the circle are equally real. They must be since each stands in the same relationship to the center which is its source. All the objects and events on the plain are equally real. They must be, else the observer on the height could not perceive them all at once. (*Ibidem*)

A timeless God has the same relationship with all the points of the temporal series so that none of them is privileged for Him. This is a distinctive feature of the B-theory, for which the present has no ontological privilege and every instant is present to itself. By contrast, A-theories state that the present has an ontological feature that distinguishes it from any other time.

In consequence, Rogers accepts Eternalism. She believes that Presentism is a metaphysics that appears natural to us only because we have a limited perspective on the reality:

> The more obvious view of time, what could be called the "common-sense" view, is presentism [...] This is how time appears, but appearances are deceiving. The commonsense view, on the Anselmian understanding of things, is the result of the very limited perspective of temporal perceivers. In fact time is essentially tenseless. What we temporal perceivers call present and past and future are relative to a given perceiver at a given point in time. What any given perceiver at any given time perceives as present is not ontologically privileged over what that perceiver holds to be past or future. In fact all times exist equally. (Rogers 2007a, p. 7)

The combination of a timeless God and Eternalism has no particular internal tensions. The most natural metaphysical interpretation of this solution is the postulation of a series of actual facts, none of which is temporally privileged with respect to the others (B-series). As we have seen in the previous chapters, it is possible to combine Eternalism and open future—and, then, also Eternalism and human freedom—stating that a stage of the world at a certain time together with natural laws does not determine the subsequent temporal stages. Moreover, Eternalists usually hold that we know our present better than our past and future not in virtue of certain ontological features that would distinguish our present but in virtue of our temporal collocation. It is because we are located at t that we know t better than other times. Hence, this is a limitation due to our particular perspective on the temporal block. Being all actual, temporal facts are *in themselves* knowable in the same way. Since God is not located at any particular point of the temporal series, He does not have our limitations: He has the same relationship with every time. Being omniscient, He knows every stage of the world and, then, the choices of every agent. This does not damage human freedom, just as seeing Emma who chooses to drink a beer at the party does not harm Emma's freedom.

As we have seen in Sect. 4.5.3, this combination of theories (Eternalism and indeterminism) is also the most suited metaphysical option for the Ockhamist. However, the Ockhamist locates God in time, while the friend of the timeless solution locates Him out of time. In consequence, the Ockhamist is forced to say that some events located at point t of the temporal block determine other events located at points previous to t. This can be a problem because, at least *prima facie*, future events cannot affect past events. The timeless solution has no problems of this kind, if temporal events can determine divine timeless beliefs.

The combination of a timeless God and Eternalist metaphysics is internally coherent. Its difficulties regard the content of the various positions that it combines. Firstly, as has been noticed in Sect. 2.2, many scholars do not believe that the B-theory of time is the best description of temporal reality: it cannot account for the flow of time, which is a feature too deep, too close to common sense to be branded as cognitive illusion. Secondly, from the theological point of view, the idea of a God out of time has often been considered a legacy of Greek philosophy rather than of the Biblical tradition. It may also be doubted of the very coherence of this idea and of the possibility of combining it with other divine attributes such as the fact that God is a loving Person. However, if the B-theory and the idea of a timeless God are believed acceptable, then this combination of theories provides an excellent solution to the problem of theological fatalism.

6.4 A-Theory and Timeless God

In this section, the combination of a timeless view of God and the A-theory is examined. We will see that the relationships between these two theories are more complex and intricate than those between the B-theory and the timeless God. Every A-theory—Presentism, Growing Block view, MST—holds that the present is an ontologically privileged time. However, the present changes. The relation between such a present and a timeless God, who does not change by definition, is problematic. As we will see, the A-theory of time, divine timelessness and divine omniscience are hardly reconcilable. There are some attempts to show that it is not so, but we will demonstrate that a coherent view that includes all these assumptions is possible only at the price of accepting a non-standard A-theory of time.

One of the clearest arguments for demonstrating that divine omniscience and a timeless conception of God are in contradiction is by Kretzmann (1966)[11]:

1. An omniscient entity knows what time it is (premise).
2. An entity that knows what time it is is subject to change (premise).
3. An omniscient entity is subject to change (1,2).
4. An entity that is subject to change is not timeless (premise).
5. An omniscient entity is not timeless (3,4).

The basic idea of this argument is that a timeless God cannot "follow" the flow of time because of His immutability. He can know the whole temporal series without knowing which point of the series is the present, because the present flows and a timeless God cannot capture this flow. To clarify this point, Kretzmann makes use of a metaphor:

> According to this familiar account of omniscience, the knowledge an omniscient being has of the entire scheme of contingent events is in many

---

[11]Kretzmann's argument is foreshadowed by Prior (1962), who states that a timeless God cannot "know that the 1960 final examinations at Manchester are now over; for this isn't something that He or anyone could know timelessly, because it just isn't true timelessly" (p. 116).

relevant respects exactly like the knowledge you might have of a movie you had written, directed, produced, starred in, and seen a thousand times. You would know its every scene in flawless detail, and you would have the length of each scene and the sequence of scenes perfectly in mind. You would know, too, that a clock pictured in the first scene shows the time to be 3:45, and that a clock pictured in the fourth scene shows 4:30, and so on. Suppose, however, that your movie is being shown in a distant theater today. You know the movie immeasurably better than do the people in the theater who are now seeing it for the first time, but they know one big thing about it you don't know, namely, what is now going on on the screen. (p. 414)

Notice that, although Kretzmann seems to presuppose an A-theory of time, he never states this. As we will see in the next section, this has engendered a semantic debate on the (in)dispensability of indexicals; in Sect. 6.4.2, it is shown that this debate has led the discussion astray because the problem is, instead, of metaphysical nature, as demonstrated in Sect. 6.4.3.

6.4.1 The Semantic Debate

One might object to Kretzmann's argument as follows. The argument aims to prove that a timeless God cannot know propositions such as (1):

(1) Now it is 11 a.m.

However, in order to know this proposition, one need not be temporally located at the time of the utterance of (1). It is possible to know this proposition even though one is located at other times provided that one know at which time (1) has been uttered. To demonstrate this point, Helm (1988) compares spatial and temporal indexicals[12]:

---

[12] A similar view has been defended by Wierenga (2002, 2004), and it is already foreshadowed in Castañeda (1967).

(s) Suppose Thomas says: "It is raining here". Then, a non-spatial being can know the truth value of the proposition expressed by Thomas if she knows both (1s) Thomas' spatial location and (2s) the weather conditions at that place when the sentence is uttered. In fact, it seems that an omniscient being need not know anything else to know the truth value of the proposition expressed by Thomas. Hence, since it is possible to know (1s) and (2s) without being located in space, the knowledge of the proposition expressed by Thomas is not barred for a non-spatial being.

(t) Suppose Thomas says: "It is raining now". Then, a timeless being can know the truth value of the proposition expressed by Thomas if she knows both (1t) Thomas' temporal location and (2t) the weather conditions at the time at which the sentence is uttered. In fact, it seems that an omniscient being need not know anything else to know the truth value of the proposition expressed by Thomas. Hence, because it is possible to know (1t) and (2t) without being located in time, the knowledge of the proposition expressed by Thomas is not barred for a timeless being.

This intuition can be justified on the basis of Kaplan's treatment of indexicals (Kaplan 1989). Kaplan regards indexicals as functions from contexts to referents and maintains that it is possible to know the referent of an indexical, and then its meaning in a context, if the context in which the indexical is uttered is known. Kvanvig (1986) clearly advances such an idea, distinguishing between the meaning of the sentence containing indexicals and the proposition expressed by that sentence in a context: two indexical sentences, such as "It is raining now" and "It was raining then", can both express the proposition that it is raining in London on 1 January 2010, even if they have different meanings, provided they are uttered in different contexts.[13]

---

[13] See Kvanvig (1986, p. 158):

> The sentences "It is now raining" and "It was then raining" have different meanings, but we have already noted that the proposition expressed by a sentence ought not be confused with the meaning of that sentence; we should not infer that there are different propositions that are the objects of belief when one person (today) believes what is expressed for him by "It is

Kvanvig, then, defends the idea that God can have access to the same propositions to which human beings have access, although from a different perspective: whereas human beings have direct acquaintance with the present moment only, God has direct acquaintance with every temporal moment.[14]

Some scholars try to resist the previous argument by insisting on the *indispensability* of indexicals and assuming that propositions like

(2) It rains today [uttered on 1 January 2010]
(3) On 1 January 2010, it rains

are not equivalent. Thus, Grim (1985) advances the classical argument in favour of the essentiality of indexicals to the effect that whoever knows (2) knows that she must take her umbrella, if she goes out, but whoever knows (3) might not know this unless she knows that *today* is 1 January 2010, that is, unless she knows a proposition containing an indexical. Thus, whoever knows (2) knows something more, meaning that the two propositions are not equivalent.

6.4.2 Assessing the Semantic Debate

The debate on the (in)dispensability of indexicals engendered by Kretzmann's argument risks being a red herring. In fact, it neglects the metaphysical question, which is crucial here. Suppose that we embrace Eternalism. In this case, indexicals such as "now" and "today" are in all

---

now raining", and another person (tomorrow) believes what is expressed for him by "It was then raining".

[14] Zagzebski (1991, pp. 52–56) similarly distinguishes between the content of knowledge and the mode of knowledge. Indexical sentences express both a propositional content and a certain perspective. She argues that God, being infinite, cannot have the same perspective that finite beings have and concludes that if God is not required to assume a certain spatial perspective on the world to know the truth of spatial propositions, then He is also not required to assume a certain temporal perspective on the world to know what time is.

respects similar to indexicals such as "here" and "there". They express a subjective perspective on an objective reality given by the particular collocation of the utterer in time or space. Since one is located at a certain point of space, one has a particular perspective on the spatial reality in virtue of the fact that some points are closer to the utterer, while other are farther. In the Eternalist framework, the same goes for time. Since one is located at a certain instant of time, one has a particular perspective on the temporal reality in virtue of the fact that some temporal stages are closer to the stage of the utterer, while other are farther. However, these subjective perspectives are not relevant when the omniscience of a knower is to be evaluated. We propose the following principle, inspired by Zagzebski (1991, pp. 52–56):

Omn In describing omniscience, the perspectival aspects of the modality of knowledge are not relevant; only what is known is relevant.

Omn is based on the fact that all perspectives, being pure perspectives, are on a par: no perspective is privileged over the others. Thus, the perspective one has on reality by being located at a certain spatial point has no priority over the perspectives one has by being located at other points. Based on **Omn**, we reject the idea that a subject cannot be omniscient because she knows only that it rains in London but not that it rains *here*.[15]

On Eternalism, no privileged instant exists. This parallels the spatial case, in which there is no privileged point, so temporal indexicals would simply express the relationship of the subject with a certain time in the way in which spatial indexicals express the relationship of the subject with a certain spatial point. In both cases, we have a subjective perspective that is not relevant when we evaluate the question of omniscience. On the Eternalist view, in light of **Omn**, we can reject the idea that a subject cannot be omniscient because she knows only that it rains on 1 January 2010 but not that it rains *now*. If we opt for Eternalism, tense turns out to be a linguistic aspect that does not concern propositional contents.

---

[15] It might be argued that the perspective one has on one's own thoughts and states of mind is privileged over the perspectives the other subjects can have on these mental contents. A complete analysis of this problem should investigate the nature of mental contents, the way through which we have access to these contents, and the question of whether there are first-person facts. This is beyond the scope of this book, but see Zagzebski (2013).

Things change considerably if we opt for an A-theory of time. In this case, times are not all on a par and the present is not just a subjective perspective on time, but something ontologically relevant: it is an *objective* feature of temporal reality. If God does not grasp which is the present instant, he does not grasp something real. Even if **Omn** is assumed, God cannot be considered omniscient if He is not able to know which is the present because the present, in this case, is not part of the *way* in which the world is known, but part of the world itself. Delmas Lewis is especially clear on this point:

> My claim is that there is an objective feature of reality (namely, the A-actuality of some temporal [...] entities and events) of which an eternal entity, who is supposed to know all of temporal reality *by direct acquaintance* [...], is ignorant. It is not that an eternal entity can't know that I am at one location and my birth or death is at another location in the temporal series. Rather, there is an important ontological feature – A-actuality – which we know I now possess and which my birth and death don't and, moreover, which talk of locations on a linear continuum neither reflects nor captures. (Lewis 1984, p. 79)

In assessing Kretzmann's argument, what matters is not whether indexicals are indispensable or not, but if an A- or a B-theory or time is accepted. One might also believe that indexicals are dispensable in a B-theory and indispensable in an A-theory. However, we do not commit to this thesis because **Omn** is sufficient for our point: assuming a B-theory, indexicals do not express a structural feature of the world but a perspective of the subject on the temporal series, and such a perspective should not be taken into consideration in evaluating God's omniscience. This thesis remains true even though indexicals are indispensable.

6.4.3 The Metaphysical Debate

Some scholars, while being aware of the relevance of the difference between A- and B-theory for the assessment of the debate about the compatibility between timelessness and omniscience, believe that a timeless God can be regarded as omniscient even though an A-theory of time is assumed. In this section, we will take this position into consideration and find it wanting. In our view, William Craig has advanced very convincing arguments aimed to show that these attempts to reconcile timelessness, omniscience and an A-theory of time do not work.[16] Here, we will just repeat his criticisms.

Some of these scholars, despite claiming that they reject the B-theory, in fact join it. For instance, Kvanvig (2001) admits no tensed facts and maintains that time concerns sentences and not facts. Moreover, he also submits that propositions are tenseless and their truth value cannot change through time. However, if time concerns only sentences and not facts or propositions expressed by sentences, it is difficult to see how the B-theory of time can be rejected. In the same way, Diekemper (2013) asserts to be an A-theorist but holds that the world is entirely described by tenseless propositions that are true at some time or other and that God timelessly knows these propositions. But this is something that even the fiercest advocate of the B-theory would be prepared to accept: the view that the world is described by tenseless propositions that are true at some time does not cause any trouble to the B-theorist.

Another example is Stump and Kretzmann (1981). They argue that to know what time it is now means to know all the events actually occurring at the time at which the sentence "it is now five o'clock" is uttered, as well as its being experienced as present by the utterer of the sentence. But this is in line with a B-theory of time, for which the present is just the perspective of a temporal subject on the series. Stump and Kretzmann acknowledge that this might not satisfy the A-theorist, who considers the present as absolute. They respond that

> the only way in which an eternal entity can be aware of any temporal event is to be aware of it as it is actually happening. And from the eternal viewpoint every temporal event is actually happening. There is no single temporal viewpoint; even when the temporal present is taken to be absolute, the temporal viewpoint that is correctly designated as now is incessantly changing. (p. 357)

---

[16] See, for instance, Craig (1998, 2000, 2001a,b, 2004).

The idea seems to be that the A-theorist must say that sooner or later every time will be present so that none of them is privileged from this point of view. God simply sees them as all present at once and not in sequence. However, that times are all present and none is privileged is the central claim of every B-theory. This becomes particularly clear if we consider the most radical A-theory: Presentism. On this view, only the things that are present at t exist at time t. The reality, *as a whole*, is constituted by the entities present at t. Now, suppose we follow a reasoning analogous to that of Stump and Kretzmann: since time flows, every instant is sooner or later present and none of them is privileged. God sees them all as present and, therefore, as existent. So, every instant exists. However, this is no more an A-theory of time: Presentism has become a B-theory. Stump and Kretzmann fail to take seriously enough that for presentists what exists at the present is the reality *tout court* and not a piece of reality. What exists *changes* and the reality is never the same. And it is this change of the reality that a timeless entity cannot follow.

The most elaborate attempt to defend the compatibility between an omniscient and timeless God and the A-theory of time is due to Brian Leftow.[17] He exploits even more thoroughly than Stump and Kretzmann the conceptual resources offered by the Theory of Relativity, for both polemic and positive aims. Concerning the negative aspect of this theory, he dismisses Stump and Kretzmann's notion of ET-simultaneity. Drawing on the Special Theory of Relativity, Leftow maintains that the relation of simultaneity is relative to an *inertial frame of reference*: only relatively to entities at rest with respect to each other does it make sense to speak of past, present and future. God also has His own inertial frame of reference, which is special, however, because every entity is present at once in that frame. Frames are incommensurable each other: the relationships of simultaneity and sequence are possible only within the various frames, not *between* frames. It does not make sense to speak of relationships of simultaneity and sequence between what exists in the various inertial frames and what exists in the timeless frame. These

---

[17] See, for instance, Leftow (1990), Leftow (1991a, ch. 10–11). For a similar position, see Robinson (1995).

entities are neither simultaneous nor subsequent to each other: they are temporally incommensurable. As a result, the concept of ET-simultaneity does not make sense.

So, how can God be in relation with the world? For the positive aspect of his theory, Leftow also builds on the Special Theory of Relativity. The simultaneity between two events e' and e'' is relative to a frame of reference: the fact that e' and e'' are simultaneous in a certain frame of reference does not entail that they are simultaneous in other frames. Events can exist in different frames and have different temporal relations in different frames. According to Leftow, temporal events also exist in God's timeless frame, but they too are timeless:

> [...] all temporal events occur at once for God and really do occur at once—that their being related to God places them in a new relation of simultaneity in which they would not stand if (*per impossibile*) there were no eternal being. Now there is no temporal reference frame in which all events occur at once [...] So if there is a simultaneity relation linking all actual events, this relation exists in an atemporal reference frame: if all events really occur at once, they occur at once in an atemporal reference frame. [...] then, temporal events occur and temporal entities exist all at once in eternity. [...] So rather than defining eternal simultaneity as the relation in which two *eternal* events stand if they occur at the same "eternal present", as Stump and Kretzmann do, on this view we should define it as the relation in which any entities stand if they occur at the same "eternal present". (Leftow 1991a, p. 161)

How can a temporal entity occur also in God's timeless frame? According to Leftow, this is a natural consequence of the Theory of Relativity, in which an element can be simultaneous with another event in a frame and not simultaneous with the same event in another frame. If simultaneity varies from one frame to another, why cannot a frame in which all events are simultaneous be possible?

> [I]f a frame of reference is a system of objects at rest relative to one another, then it appears that God and all spatial objects share a frame of reference, one in which nothing changes. Now if an event occurs in one frame of reference, it occurs in all, albeit simultaneous with different

groups of events. So all events which occur in other reference frames occur in the frame at rest relative to God. But how can this be, if nothing changes there? The answer, I think, is that relative to God, the whole span of temporal events is always actually there, all at once. Thus in God's frame of reference, the correct judgment of local simultaneity is that all events are simultaneous. But all events are simultaneous in no temporal reference frame. Therefore the reference-frame God shares with all events is atemporal. (Leftow 1991a, p. 164)

The *same* event can be simultaneous or not with other events in the various temporal frames, but in the timeless frame all events are simultaneous with God. Therefore, God can know all events because they are co-present in the same timeless frame. God is not simultaneous with all times; rather, all temporal events are co-present in the same timeless frame. God's knowledge of human free acts does not damage freedom because God knows all free acts in the timeless frame in which all events are simultaneous. Since free choices and divine knowledge of free choices occur at once, there is no conflict between them.[18] Being that the choice and its knowledge are simultaneous in the timeless frame, we could say that the former produces the latter or, at least, that the latter depends on the former. However, this is not the route followed by Leftow. He believes not only that God is timeless but also that He is simple. Leftow demonstrates that the knowledge of a simple God cannot be a causal consequence of anything created. Although the free choices and their knowledge are simultaneous in the timeless frame, the latter cannot be a consequence of the former. Leftow, then, tries to provide an account of how God can know human free choices without either causing them or being affected by them. Such an account has some points in common with Molinism (see Leftow 1990, pp. 255–265). Here we will leave aside these complications, arising from divine simplicity and impassibility, and we

---

[18] Using this framework, Leftow can hinder the arguments in favour of the thesis that the timeless view does not present any advantage over the temporal views (Ockhamism and Molinism) more effectively than Stamp and Kretzmann. Indeed, it is untrue in 1995 that God timelessly believes that Emma drinks a beer at the party in 2019. A sentence like this states that in a certain temporal frame it is the case that a certain event occurs in the timeless frame. Being that the frames are incommensurable, this sentence is obviously untrue. See Leftow (1991b).

will focus on the question of whether Leftow's solution is able to reconcile the omniscience of a timeless God with an A-theory of time.

It is difficult to assess Leftow's theory because it is based on a certain interpretation of the Theory of Special Relativity, whose philosophical exegesis is, as is well known, a controversial matter. For example, as we have seen in Sect. 2.4, the Theory of Relativity is one of the arguments brought by B-theorists against the A-theory of time. The fact that the present is dependent on the inertial frame seems to count in favour of the thesis that the present is not an absolute trait of reality, as supposed by A-theorists. According to this interpretation, reality would be a block of events, none of which is absolutely present and each of which is present relatively to itself and to what is at rest relatively to itself. If we opt for this metaphysical interpretation of the Theory of Relativity, which seems to prevail in literature, the Theory does not to provide any help for Leftow's attempt to conciliate timeless omniscience and an A-theory of time.

As we have seen in Sect. 2.4, A-theorists have followed two routes to avoid this unfavourable conclusion. The first one is that the Theory of Relativity is a physical theory that does not grasp everything. For instance, one of the inertial frames could be privileged, but our scientific tools would not be able to detect it. This interpretation, however, is not suitable for Leftow's attempt because it reintroduces an absolute present as a metaphysical trait of the world. Following this interpretation, Leftow might say that actually there is a metaphysically privileged frame, that is, the divine one. But, since there is no change and dynamism within this frame, it would follow that change is not a fundamental trait of reality. Therefore, this interpretation would also end up corroborating a B-theory against Leftow's intentions.

A second path that A-theorists have followed in dealing with the problem of relativity takes more seriously the interplay between science and metaphysics. Some A-theorists point out that the Theory of Relativity does not deny the dynamics of the world; certainly, it puts into question the idea of an absolute present, but it seems to be consistent with the view that every entity has its own particular dynamics and present. Or better: the objects that share the same inertial frame have their own present. In other words, the concepts of dynamics and present are not set aside by the physical theory; rather, they must be relativized to the various observers and to their inertial frames. Although Leftow is not particularly explicit about this topic, he seems to assume this interpretation of the Theory of Relativity. Answering to the objection that the Theory of Relativity would make the distinction among past, present and future illusory, he says:

> The slip in this argument, a defender of tensed time can say, is that it does not take the framework-relativity of actuality seriously enough. It presumes that there is just one attribute (or whatever), actuality-*simpliciter*, and that things simply either have this or do not. A tensed theory of time can deny this, and hold instead that a distinction between present (and perhaps past) events and future events is real but framework-relative. If present actuality is ontologically special, then as there is no absolute simultaneity and so no absolute, framework-independent now, there is no absolute present actuality. (Leftow 1991a, p. 167)

The present is a real feature, but relative to the different frames of reference. This interpretation can save Leftow's solution, even though it does not prevail in literature. We will see in the next section that this is indeed the only way to conciliate the A-theory with a timeless and omniscient God: to hold that reality is fragmented and that every fragment has its own present.

However, this realist interpretation of the present of every frame brings up new issues for Leftow's theory. The various presents of the different frames are objective traits of the reality, but God does not seem to have access to them because He is in contact with the world in His own frame, where events obtain all at once. Again, God cannot grasp the dynamics of the world and, especially, the dynamics of the different inertial frames. Leftow responds to this objection by arguing that:

> That in God's frame of reference all events occur at once does not entail that God does not know all the facts about simultaneity which obtain in temporal reference frames. God's being located in just the eternal frame of reference does not put a limit on what He knows. From any reference frame, one can extrapolate what judgments of simultaneity would be correct in other reference-frames. Leftow (1990, p. 235)

However, as God has no access to the temporal frames, given that the frames are incommensurable each other, one may wonder whether God can really grasp the present time of every frame. William Craig points out that:

> God could know the appropriate simultaneity classes relative to every reference frame and still not have any idea which class of events is occurring now with respect to any frame. This can be easily seen by reflecting on the fact that appropriate lines of simultaneity can be drawn on a Minkowski diagram through any point on the inertial trajectory of a hypothetical observer connected to that frame. (Craig 2001a, p. 106n)

Given the movement of an observer connected to a frame, it is possible to know the events that are simultaneous to that observer at every point of her trajectory, but it is not possible to establish which point is the present of that observer. Therefore, even though this interpretation of the Theory of Relativity is consistent with an A-theory of time, a timeless God is not able to know the present of the objects connected to the temporal frames. The problem noticed by Kretzmann about a non-relativistic theory of time arises anew within the Theory of Relativity: for every frame, a timeless God can extrapolate the sequence of the events and their relations of simultaneity, but He cannot know which events are happening *now* for the different observers.

There is another problem for Leftow's theory. In the divine timeless frame, events obtain all at once. The temporal order among the events is lost within this frame: no event precedes or follows any other event. One may wonder how God can know that the death of Caesar precedes the defeat of Napoleon at Waterloo. In the timeless frame, these two events obtain at once and it is not possible to determine which precedes which. To fix this problem, Leftow assumes that the whole block of events with their relationships of precedence and succession exists in the timeless frame. This is the block postulated by Eternalism: "In eternity events are in effect frozen in an array of positions corresponding to their ordering in various B-series" (Leftow 1990, p. 237). In the timeless frame, this block obtains at once with God. Instead, in the temporal frames only some of the events of the block are present, while others are past or future. However, since the relationships of simultaneity, precedence and succession are relative to an inertial frame, in a footnote Leftow is forced to point out:

> Every temporal frame of reference generates its own unique B-series. This is a consequence of the relativity of simultaneity to reference-frames. Thus it is oversimple to say that God, in eternity, sees all events spread out in their temporal order. Events have many temporal orderings. If God is omniscient, He must be aware of all of them. (Leftow 1990, p. 239n and Leftow 1991a, p. 179)

Many aspects of this theory are problematic. Firstly, if the B-series is produced by the relationship of succession among the events in the different frames, how can a B-series exist in the timeless frame where the events are all co-present? No B-series can be produced in the timeless frame. Secondly, suppose that in frame R, two events e' and e'' are simultaneous and occupy the same place in the B-series. Suppose that in frame R^*, e' precedes e'' and they occupy different places in the B-series. In the timeless frame, do e' and e'' occupy the same place or different places in the B-series? Since neither of the frames R and R^* is privileged over the other, there seems to be no reason why they should be simultaneous or not in that frame.

Although Leftow's theory offers interesting suggestions, the difficulties that it must overcome are considerable. For many aspects, it seems to go in the right direction: only if it is assumed that the present is an actual but relative trait of the world, it is possible to reconcile the A-theory with an omniscient and timeless God. Yet, the fact that God has no cognitive access to the temporal frames and the fact that God knows events only within His timeless frame where there are no relationships of temporal succession and precedence are remarkable limits of this view. In the theory we will propose in Sect. 6.5.4, God has cognitive access to the different fragments of the world and can know them directly. This avoids many of the problems of Leftow's theory. However, before explaining this fragmentalist view, we will offer a logical framework able to account for the flow of time. This framework will be useful for depicting more precisely the relations between a timeless God and a temporal universe.

6.5 Fragmentalism and Timeless God

Is it not possible then to reconcile A-theory with a timeless and omniscient God? Let us recapitulate the ingredients needed by our framework. The future must be open to guarantee the possibility of doing otherwise, which is at the base of the libertarian concept of freedom. Moreover, we have to combine this topological feature with an objective dynamics of the passage of time. Finally, these two ingredients must interact with divine timeless knowledge.

Our first step is to introduce a framework able to characterize the first two aspects, which uses the concept of *perspective* (Sect. 6.5.1). The evaluation of a proposition in this framework depends on two parameters: the point at which a formula is evaluated and the perspective from which it is evaluated. This logical framework has many possible metaphysical interpretations: it can serve as a model of the B-theory of time (Sect. 6.5.2), but the most natural interpretation is by means of the A-theory in both its standard and non-standard versions. In particular, in Sect. 6.5.3, we will introduce a non-standard version of the A-theory, Fine's Fragmentalism. Finally, in Sect. 6.5.4 it is shown that a perspectival semantics can model Fragmentalism and that a timeless God can know every true proposition in this semantics.

6.5.1 Perspectival Semantics

In agreement with the basic assumptions of this work, we will presuppose an indeterministic view of the world, in which the past does not determine the future and many possible future histories are open. In this framework, a natural effect of the flow of time is the progressive closure of possibilities: Emma can decide at time t_0 whether to go to the party and, once at the party, she can decide whether to drink a beer. Suppose that Emma chooses to go to the party, which occurs at time t_1. At this time, Emma cannot decide whether to go to the party or stay at home any more. One possibility—to stay at home—is closed. However, she can still decide whether to drink a beer or a Coke. Suppose that she chooses to drink

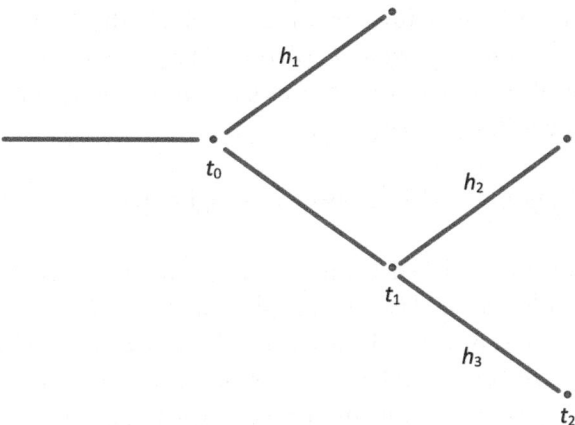

Fig. 6.3 The closure of possibilities

a beer and that this occurs at time t_2. At t_2, Emma cannot decide to drink a Coke any more: this possibility is also closed.

This progressive closure of possibilities is well illustrated by the tree diagram. Many histories can pass through every point t_i of tree. If we do not allow branching towards the past, every history that passes through t_i also passes through the times preceding t_i, but not every history that passes through t_i passes through the times subsequent to t_i. In other terms, the histories that pass through the times subsequent to t_i are always a subset of the histories that pass through t_i. This illustrates how, as the time flows, the number of histories that pass through the present decreases and, therefore, the number of the possibilities that remain open shrinks. Figure 6.3 depicts this situation.

Three histories pass through t_0 (suppose: the history in which Emma stays at home, that in which she goes to the party and drinks a Coke, and that in which she goes to the party and drinks a beer); two histories pass through t_1 (suppose: the history in which Emma goes to the party and drinks a Coke, and that in which she goes to the party and drinks a beer); just one history passes through t_2 (suppose: the history in which she goes to the party and drinks a beer).

However, there is a further sense in which the flow of time closes possibilities. From the *perspective* of today, the past is closed, but the future of yesterday also seems closed. Let us explain this point with an example. Consider the following sentence:

(4) Emma is going to drink a beer at tonight's party.

According to the open future assumption, the truth value of (4) is genuinely undetermined (we assume the supervaluationist semantics here, see Sect. 2.6.3). Emma will be able to make up her mind and to get a beer or a Coke or whatever. But let us reflect on the just-described situation and add some details. It is 6 p.m. and Emma is getting ready for the party. It is, by assumption, ontologically indeterminate whether Emma will drink a beer at the party. At 10 p.m., halfway through the party, Emma is thirsty and decides to have a beer, and therefore, it becomes true that Emma drinks a beer at the party. Now, the question is whether (4) is a sentence with a determinate or indeterminate truth value. Well, *prima facie* the answer might be that it depends on the instant at which we evaluate it. (4) is indeterminate at 6 p.m., but it is true at 10 p.m. But this answer is troublesome. In fact, *because* Emma decides to have a beer at 10 p.m., it is true at 10 p.m. that it was *already* true at 6 p.m. that Emma *would* decide to have a beer. Therefore, its truth value seems perfectly determinate.

In order to realize how deeply rooted the intuition of the retrogradation of truth is, let us suppose that Thomas and George make a bet at 6 p.m.: Thomas bets on the truth of (4), that is, on the fact that Emma is going to have a beer at the party. George bets against (4). If Emma drinks her beer, Thomas can ask for the payment of the bet by saying that he *was right* and he *stated* the truth when he said that Emma would have a beer. If George replied that, after all, it was indeterminate at 6 p.m. what Emma was going to do and that, therefore, what Thomas *said* was neither true nor false, so that he has no right to request the payment of the bet, his argument would seem totally captious. Therefore, from the 10 p.m. perspective, (4) is true at 6 p.m. But, on the other hand, Emma is still undecided at 6 p.m., and it is plausible to regard, from the 6 p.m. perspective, the future tensed sentence as indeterminate. Then, the ascription of indeterminateness to a future tense sentence depends not only on the instant at which it is evaluated but also on the *perspective* from which it is evaluated. This fact is deeply connected with the question of the open future; the future is open when we put ourselves, so to speak, in the present. But, retrospectively—when we look at the future of a certain moment from the future of that moment—the future appears to be determinate.

To account not only for the openness of the future and the closure of the past but also for the closure of the future of the past, some amendments to the usual indeterminist semantics are needed. In fact, a normal indeterminist framework cannot account for the retrogradation of truth. To better see this point, let us see what happens in such a framework. Let us assume the usual branching time structure and the following semantics:

$$M, t \vDash p \Leftrightarrow t \in V(p)$$
$$M, t \vDash \neg \varphi \Leftrightarrow M, t \nvDash \varphi$$
$$M, t \vDash \varphi \wedge \psi \Leftrightarrow M, t \vDash \varphi \text{ and } M, t \vDash \psi$$
$$M, t \vDash \mathbf{P}\varphi \Leftrightarrow \exists t'(t' < t \wedge M, t' \vDash \varphi)$$
$$M, t \vDash \mathbf{H}\varphi \Leftrightarrow \forall t'(t' < t \wedge M, t' \vDash \varphi)$$

For the future, we will assume here the supervaluationist clauses, according to which the formula $\mathbf{F}\varphi$ is true when φ is true in every future history, false when φ is false in every future history and indeterminate otherwise:

$$M, t \vDash \mathbf{F}\varphi \Leftrightarrow \forall h \exists t'(t' > t \wedge t' \in h \rightarrow M, t' \vDash \varphi)$$
$$M, t \nvDash \mathbf{F}\varphi \Leftrightarrow \forall h \exists t'(t' > t \wedge t' \in h \rightarrow M, t' \nvDash \varphi)$$

Let us hypothesize that we are in the following situation (see Fig. 6.4): φ is true at t_1 in history h_1, whereas it is false at t_2 in history h_2. According to the previous semantics, this means that at t_0, $\mathbf{F}\varphi$ is neither true nor false. But let us hypothesize that time flows and that φ obtains (the world "takes" the road h_1). We have that at t_1 φ is true. But then we must claim that *because* at t_1 it is true that φ, then it has always been the case that it would be true that φ. In other words, since Emma, at the end of the day, decides to have a beer, it has always been true that Emma would have her

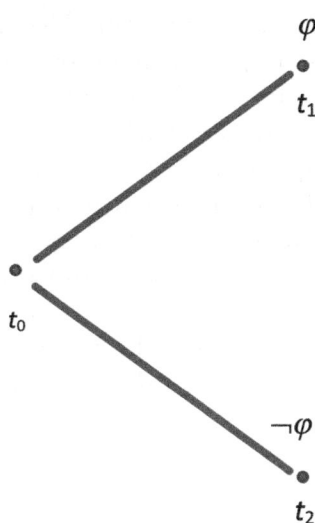

Fig. 6.4 The failure of retrogradation

beer. In formal terms, the conditional $\varphi \rightarrow \mathbf{HF}\varphi$ must hold. However, in the indeterminist framework we have just presented, this formula *does not* hold, and it is not difficult to see why. Look at Fig. 6.4 again.

Clearly, φ holds at t_1. Now, let us determine whether $\mathbf{HF}\varphi$ holds. Accordingly, $\mathbf{F}\varphi$ must always be true in the past of t_1. So, the question is whether $M, t_0 \vDash \mathbf{F}\varphi$ holds. However, as we have seen, the existence of a history in which $\neg\varphi$ is true entails that $\mathbf{F}\varphi$ is untrue at t_0.

Let us see now how perspectival semantics solves this problem. The basic idea of perspectival semantics is that formulas are evaluated in a model, at a time t, from a certain perspective or context.[19]

---

[19] The idea of a perspective or context of evaluation circulates in the branching time semantics in very different forms. The model of Belnap et al. (2001) uses the parameter of the context, and that of Malpass and Wawer (2012) employs the parameter of the context of use. Here we adopt a notion of perspective close to that of MacFarlane (2003, 2014). According to MacFarlane, every proposition must be evaluated at two different times, which he calls the context of assessment and the context of evaluation. In our proposal as well, the evaluation occurs at two different times. In De Florio and Frigerio (2019), we consider the differences between these approaches and ours.

Let us take into account the closed formula φ. φ has a certain truth value at t. As noted above, our semantic framework introduces another ingredient: we evaluate φ at t from the temporal perspective t' (which, of course, might coincide with t). Roughly, the idea is to consider the perspective t' as the point at which the world has arrived, that is, the present moment. As we will see shortly, the advocates of a dynamic and realist metaphysics of time can construe the idea of perspective we are presenting in a strong sense. However, our semantics also allows for an indexical reading according to which the perspective indicates the instant we consider as our "now", without any metaphysical privilege.

Let $H_t = \{h | t \in h\}$ be the bundle of histories at t, that is, the set of histories that pass through t. Our model is, then, constituted by the branching structure **BT**, the evaluation function V and two temporal indexes: the instant of evaluation and the perspective from which one evaluates. We sharply distinguish two kinds of propositions: *factual* propositions, which concern things that happen at the present, in the past and in the possible futures of a given perspective, and *counterfactual* propositions, which concern not what is happening, what happened or what will happen from the given perspective, but what could happen or could have happen from that perspective.[20]

The evaluations of factual propositions in our model are always relativized to the *intersection* of the (bundle of) histories that pass through the moment of evaluation t and the histories that pass through the perspective t'. As we are evaluating factual propositions, we suppose that this intersection is never empty, that is, that the moment of evaluation is connected with the temporal perspective (viz. $(t > t') \vee (t' > t) \vee (t' = t)$). This seems a reasonable condition, because factual propositions concern what happens at a certain time or in the past or in the possible futures of that time (the perspective). Because the histories on which we evaluate must pass through the perspective, certain branches are *pruned*. Let us consider the example represented in Fig. 6.5.

---

[20] Developing this interpretation of counterfactual propositions seems to be a very fecund path of inquiry. Here, however, we do not take that into account. See De Florio and Frigerio (2019) for a proposal for the treatment of counterfactual propositions.

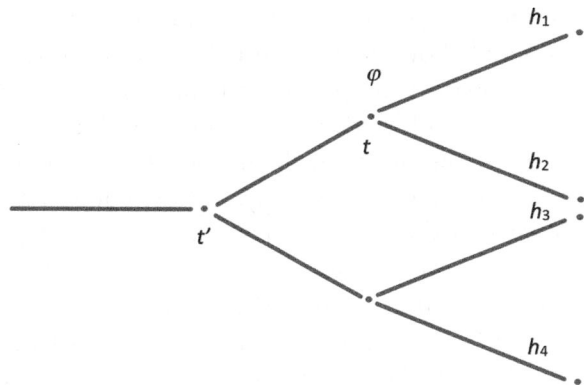

Fig. 6.5 Evaluation of φ at t from perspective t'

In this schema, we have four histories; let us suppose we evaluate the formula φ at t, from the perspective t': $M, t, t' \vDash \varphi$. We consequently have the following truth conditions:

$M, t, t' \vDash p \quad \Leftrightarrow \forall h \in H_t \cap H_{t'}, t \in V(p)$
$M, t, t' \vDash \neg \varphi \quad \Leftrightarrow \forall h \in H_t \cap H_{t'}, M, t, t' \nvDash \varphi$
$M, t, t' \vDash \varphi \wedge \psi \Leftrightarrow \forall h \in H_t \cap H_{t'}, M, t, t' \vDash \varphi$ and $M, t, t' \vDash \psi$
$M, t, t' \vDash \mathbf{P}\varphi \quad \Leftrightarrow \forall h \in H_t \cap H_{t'}, \exists t'' < t, M, t'', t' \vDash \varphi$
$M, t, t' \vDash \mathbf{H}\varphi \quad \Leftrightarrow \forall h \in H_t \cap H_{t'}, \forall t'' < t, M, t'', t' \vDash \varphi$

Notice that our evaluation at times and perspectives is analogous to a standard evaluation as far as evaluations not regarding the future are concerned. Things change when we consider the evaluation of the future tense. The idea is, in a nutshell, the following.

In Fig. 6.6, we have a branching structure in which there are four histories: in the first two, it is true that φ; in the second pair, it is true that $\neg \varphi$. Now, let us hypothesize that we want to evaluate $\mathbf{F}\varphi$ at t from the perspective t. We then have

$$M, t, t \vDash \mathbf{F}\varphi \Leftrightarrow \forall h \in H_t \cap H_t \exists t' > t, M, t', t \vDash \varphi$$

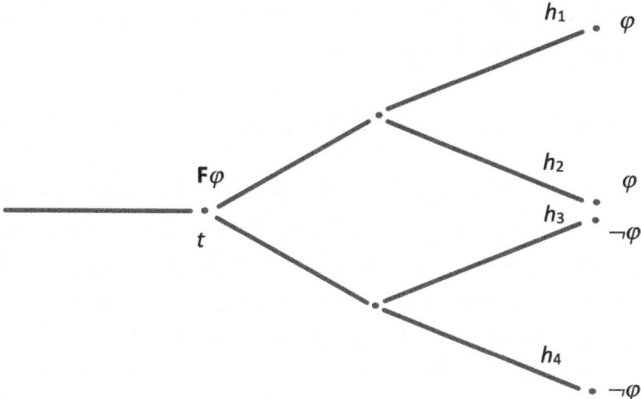

Fig. 6.6 Evaluation of Fφ at t from perspective t

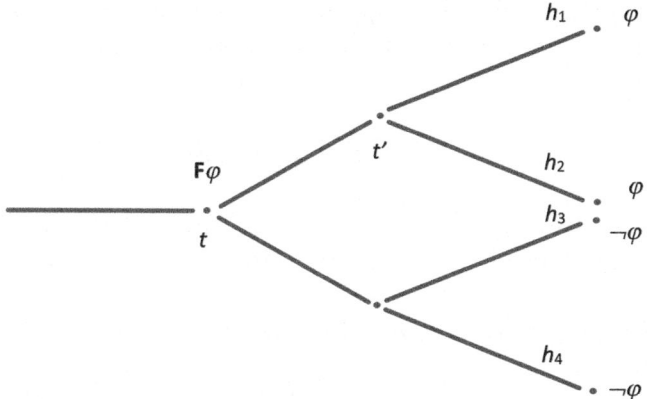

Fig. 6.7 Evaluation of Fφ at t from perspective t'

Obviously, this does not hold, because there exist two histories in the intersection in which $\neg\varphi$ is true. But let us now suppose that the perspective changes (i.e. that time flows); the schema becomes that represented in Fig. 6.7.

This schema is identical to the previous one, except for the perspective of the evaluation, which is now t'.

$$M, t, t' \vDash \mathbf{F}\varphi \Leftrightarrow \forall h \in H_{t'} \cap H_t \exists t'' > t, M, t'', t' \vDash \varphi$$

Time flowed—so to speak—and number of histories into the intersection decreased. From the perspective of t', therefore, φ will happen in the future of t. So, for example, whereas from the perspective of 6 p.m., it is not true that Emma will drink a beer at the party, from the perspective of 10 p.m., when Emma has already decided to drink a beer, it was true at 6 p.m. that Emma would drink a beer. So, our framework incorporates MacFarlane's intuition that the evaluation at a certain time of a formula containing a future operator changes depending on the perspective that is assumed.

Let us now observe what happens to the crucial principle $\varphi \to \mathbf{HF}\varphi$. Let us assume that we evaluate at t' from the perspective of t'; we have, then, that

$$M, t', t' \vDash \varphi \to \mathbf{HF}\varphi$$

So, let us assume $M, t', t' \vDash \varphi$; hence, it must always have been true in the past that $\mathbf{F}\varphi$. Let us consider the instant t previous to t':

$$M, t, t' \vDash \mathbf{F}\varphi \Rightarrow \forall h \in H_{t'} \cap H_t \exists t'' > t, M, t'', t' \vDash \varphi$$

Of course, this holds because φ holds in every history that passes through t'. In particular, it holds at t' itself. Because the evaluation is always restricted to the histories in the intersection $H_{t'} \cap H_t$, if φ holds at t', then it is true at every moment in the past of t' that φ will hold in the future. Thus, the principle $\varphi \to \mathbf{HF}\varphi$ is vindicated in this semantics.

As we will see, perspectival semantics is especially apt to account for the flow of time because perspectives can be naturally interpreted as "the moment at which the flow of time has arrived". However, this logical framework does not have a single metaphysical interpretation. In the next section, we will show how to combine perspectival semantics with Eternalism and a timeless God.

6.5.2 Perspectival Semantics and Eternalism

Even though perspectival semantics is especially apt to model the flow of time, it does not necessarily have an A-theoretical interpretation. This semantics presupposes nothing about the nature of the perspectives. They can be interpreted just as indexicals and therefore seen as the stage of the world with respect to which a formula is evaluated. On this view, there is no privileged stage of the world: all of them are on an equal footing.

If the semantics described in the previous section is interpreted along these lines, we are led to Eternalism: all the stages of the world are on a par because they are all actual. Therefore, all the branches of the tree are actual. As we have seen in Sect. 2.5, this metaphysics encounters troubles because, for instance, both the Emma who drinks a beer at the party and the Emma who does not drink a beer are real in the same way. This is due to the fact that both the branch in which Emma drinks a beer and the branch in which she does not drink it are actual. There are, then, many problems with the identity of the objects, which must be conceived as split. However, we will not discuss these problems here because our aim is just to show that perspectival semantics can be combined with Eternalism.[21]

If this metaphysical interpretation of perspectival semantics is taken on board, it is easy to conceive an omniscient and timeless God. In any case, and in some sense independently of the metaphysical construal adopted, God is omniscient not only because He knows the truth value of each proposition at each time but, crucially, because He also knows the truth value of each proposition at each time from each perspective. Omniscience is, then, omni-perspectival knowledge. Looking back at our example, we have that God knows that at t_0 from the perspective t_0, it is indeterminate whether Emma will drink a beer at the party. However, God also knows that at t_0 but from the perspective t_1, it is true that Emma

---

[21] Alternatively, and more plausibly, eternalists can maintain that one of the branches of the tree is the actual world, while the other branches are not real, but only representations of possible alternative scenarios. In Sect. 6.3, we have adopted this solution. However, this view is at odds with perspectival semantics, according to which all future contingents are indeterminate. If there is an ontologically privileged future, then future tensed sentences are not indeterminate, but have a truth value: $\mathbf{F}\varphi$ is true if φ is true in the unique existing future.

will drink a beer at the party. All these sentences are formally coherent, and both God's omniscience and Emma's free will are preserved.

Knowing all the details of every stage of the tree, God knows the truth value of propositions with respect to the "context" of every stage of the tree. On the one hand, this preserves the agents' freedom because Eternalism is not tied to a determinist conception of the world. At time t, it is genuinely indeterminate whether Emma will drink a beer or not because both a branch in which Emma drinks a beer and a branch in which she does not drink it stem from t. In the particular metaphysical interpretation we are examining, both of these branches exist and neither of them is privileged. Then, it is ontologically and semantically indeterminate what Emma will do.

On the other hand, divine knowledge *depends* on Emma's choices. As we have seen in Sect. 6.2, the advocate of the timeless solution must crucially assume that timeless divine knowledge depends on the arrangement of the world. It is because Emma chooses to drink a beer at t_1 that God knows that Emma drinks a beer at t_1, not the other way around. To preserve human freedom, it is necessary to accept **Dependence**.

This interpretation of perspectival semantics is coherent. However, one could find it more natural to interpret perspectives not as pure indexicals but as objective features of the world, that is, as the present in an ontologically relevant sense. In the next section, we will take into consideration this interpretation, investigating whether it is possible to combine it with a timeless God.

6.5.3 Fragmentalism

Suppose we assume an A-theory of time. In this case, the present is something that distinguishes some facts from others—either it is all that exists (Presentism) or it is the border between an existing past and a non-existing future (Growing Block view) or it is a feature that only some facts possess (MST). In this case, then, the index of the perspective indicates something metaphysically relevant.

In all A-theories, the present is something that continuously moves: some facts that are now present will be confined to the past and other facts that are now future will become present. The perspective must be a mobile index, that is, something that moves forward in the tree. If we evaluate formulas from perspective t, we are modelling the world as it is when the present has arrived at t. But the present is something that moves forward. If we move the index of the perspective to a time subsequent to t, we will model the world as it is when the present has moved forward from t and has become a time subsequent to t. Therefore, we have as many representations of the world as perspectives. Each of them models the world when a certain instant of time is the present, that is, when the world "has arrived" at that instant. For instance, the structures represented in Figs. 6.6 and 6.7 are two images of the world: in the first one, the present is t; in the second one, it is t', a time subsequent to t.

One might believe that a timeless God has no problem of omniscience in this case either. He can know all the models of the world and then He can evaluate every proposition with respect to every perspective and time of evaluation. In this respect, the metaphysics of time would make no difference if we assume that God's knowledge is *omni-perspectival*. However, things are not quite so simple because Kretzmann's objection we have examined at the beginning of this chapter re-emerges.

Suppose that God has an omni-perspectival knowledge and that He knows, for instance, the truth value of every proposition when the present (i.e. the perspective) is the Ides of March 44 BC, that is, the day of Caesar's death. He also knows the truth value of every proposition when the present (i.e. the perspective) is 18 June 1815, that is, the day of the Waterloo battle. In spite of having a complete knowledge of the world from both perspectives, God could not know which perspective is *now* present, that is, if Caesar will die today or if Napoleon will be defeated (while Caesar was murdered 19 centuries ago). In other terms, God cannot distinguish, among the various configurations of the world in each of which the present is located at a different time, which is the configuration that describes the world as it is now. In fact, the perspective moves from one point to another in the tree, but a timeless God cannot follow this movement step by step. He can know which trajectory the perspective will follow because, in a sense, He sees the trajectory as already drawn, but He cannot know at which point the perspective has arrived *now*, that is the present configuration of the world.

Suppose, however, that the configurations of the world—differing with each other for the instant that is present—are all actual. In such a case, having an omni-perspectival knowledge, God would know the whole reality. But to assume that all the configurations of the world are actual is inconsistent with one of the basic assumptions of an A-theory of time, that is, that the present is something absolute, which different instants possess as time flows. If all these configurations of the world were actual, then we would have as many absolute presents as configurations. But this is not possible: if t_1 is today, tomorrow t_2 will be today. But two different times t_1 and t_2 cannot both be today simultaneously.

The standard A-theorist cannot say that all the configurations of the world are actual. However, as we have seen in Sect. 2.2, Kit Fine has proposed, for reasons entirely independent of the question of divine prescience, a non-standard A-theory of time, in which all the configurations of the world are actual. Fine acknowledges that this leads to an incoherence. This view is called Fragmentalism[22] because Fine believes that the reality is constituted by fragments that contain tensional facts incompatible with each other. A single fact can be past in a fragment and future in another fragment.

Obviously, Fragmentalism is a very costly theory, but according to Fine this cost is balanced by the considerable advantages that Fragmentalism has over the standard A-theories. We will briefly mention two of them. Firstly, Fragmentalism can better account for the passage of time. Fine points out that the standard realist considers the present as a metaphysical trait that objectively discriminates past, present and future facts. But this simple division still does not account for the passage of time, because this passage requires different moments of time to be successively present and more than the presentness of a single moment of time is needed for this. The realist at this point might appeal to the fact that every particular future time will be present and that every particular past time was present.

---

[22] See Fine (2005, 2006). For discussions of Fine's theory, see Correia and Rosenkranz (2012) and Lipman (2015).

However, the future presentness of a time t_1 subsequent to the present time t_0 amounts to no more than t_0 being present and t_1 being later than t_0 and, similarly, the past presentness of a time t_{-1} previous to the present time t_0 amounts to no more than t_0 being present and t_{-1} being earlier than t_0. But then how can the passage of time be seen to rest on the fact that a given time is present and that various other times are either earlier or later than that time? In fact, this is something that also can be accepted by the B-theorist interpreting the present as an indexical.

Fine believes that Fragmentalism is able to overcome this problem in a better way than standard realism. On Fragmentalism, *every* time is present in a certain fragment of the reality. Although the present is a metaphysical trait, it is spread on every time in different fragments. Fine recognizes that this still does not explain the *passage of time*, but it is at least a beginning of an explanation:

> Clearly, something more than the equitable distribution of presentness is required to account for the passage of time. But at least, on the current view, there is no obvious impediment to accounting for the passage of time in terms of a successive now. We have assembled all the relevant nows, so to speak, even if there remains some question as to why the relationship between them should be taken to constitute a genuine form of succession. (Fine 2005, p. 288)

The second reason why Fine considers Fragmentalism preferable to the standard A-theories of time has to do with the Theory of Special Relativity. On Fragmentalism, tensional facts can be relativized to the various inertial frames. Every inertial frame could be regarded as a fragment of an incoherent reality:

> The resulting metaphysical view is quite remarkable. The usual view is that Special Relativity shows space-time to be Minkowskian rather than Newtonian; physical processes are to be seen as taking place within a physical space-time with the structure of Minkowskian rather than Newtonian space-time. But the present view is that what Special Relativity shows to be mistaken is not that space-time is Newtonian but that there is a single space-time. Thus we should picture physical processes as taking place within a plurality of physical space-times, each of them enjoying a common

ontology of space-time locations and each of them Newtonian in structure, and yet differing in the spatial and temporal relationships that hold among the space-time locations. (Fine 2005, p. 306)

We will not discuss whether these reasons are sufficient for embracing Fragmentalism in place of a standard A-theory of time. It is sufficient to have shown that there are independent reasons for believing that Fragmentalism is a more explanatory theory than standard A-theories. The advocate of the timeless solution who rejects Eternalism has one more reason for accepting Fragmentalism: in contrast to standard A-theories, Fragmentalism can be married with a timeless and omniscient God. The next section is devoted to this topic.

6.5.4 God's Knowledge and Fragmentalism

Fine states that every fragment contains a privileged time (the present of that fragment), which determines the tensed facts of that fragment: the facts that obtain at that time are present, those that obtain before that time are past, and those that obtain after that time are future. Fine does not take into consideration branching structures, but the combination of Fragmentalism and the perspectival semantics that we have sketched out here is plausible. Consider a tree structure and the evaluations of propositions from the perspective t. This structure and this semantics can be easily interpreted as tools to model a fragment of the reality. It is natural enough to understand the perspective as the present of that fragment and all the propositions true from that perspective as descriptions of the tensional facts of that fragment.

Some propositions will have indeterminate truth values because the fragment contains "ontological holes", that is, it leaves some facts indeterminate. For instance, in some fragments it is indeterminate whether Emma will drink a beer at the party and, then, some propositions of the kind $\mathbf{F}\varphi$ are neither true nor false. However, there is a fragment in which the present is a time t' subsequent to the party, where the proposition that Emma will drink a beer at the party evaluated at t—a time preceding the party—is true and not indeterminate. The branching structure and the perspective indicating the present of the structure are apt to completely describe a fragment: the position of the present in the structure determines which facts are determinate and which facts are left indeterminate in that fragment and, accordingly, which propositions are true, which are false and which are neither true nor false. Generally, the earlier the point of the present in the structure, the higher the number of indeterminate facts. This accounts for the progressive closure of the possibilities with the passage of time.

Given this semantic framework and this metaphysics, a timeless God can be omniscient, since He can retain a constant epistemic relationship with all the fragments, thus knowing all the propositions that are true in them. God, for instance, knows that in a fragment in which the present precedes the party, it is indeterminate whether Emma will drink a beer. This guarantees Emma's freedom and the possibility of doing otherwise. Yet, God also knows that in a fragment in which the present is subsequent to the party, it is not indeterminate that Emma will drink a beer. This guarantees God's knowledge of free human acts. So, God's knowledge too is fragmented, but it cannot be otherwise, because the reality He knows is fragmented too. Here our thesis is conditional. We are not saying that Fragmentalism is the correct metaphysics of time, but that, *if* one wishes to maintain (1) God's omniscience, (2) God's timelessness and (3) an A-theory of time, then one must accept a non-standard A-theory such as Fragmentalism. Standard A-theories are not compatible with (1) and (2).

One may object that Fragmentalism is not a genuine A-theory of time because it does not entail a real dynamics: in every fragment, the present is frozen at a certain time, and there is not a real passage from one fragment to another. Certainly, the fragments can be ordered on the basis of the point on which the present is fixed, but the order of the fragments is not yet a dynamics. Fragmentalism would be a B-theory in disguise. This objection can be answered in two ways. Firstly, as we have seen, Fine believes that Fragmentalism is better equipped to describe the flow of time than a standard A-theory. The standard realist about time can only say that certain facts are past, others present and still others future; moreover, the future facts will become present and the present facts will become past. However, Fine points out that there is a sense in which the B-theorist can agree with all of this. Instead, Fragmentalism is better apt to describe the flow of time. Fine admits that Fragmentalism still does not describe a dynamics, but it is a better framework in which the dynamics can be described. Secondly, we need to understand what an A-theory of time is. Fragmentalism is a view in which some facts are *ontologically* privileged because they are present and in which some tensional facts determined by the position of the present in the fragments exist. These facts are ontologically relevant and not simply indexical. If we believe that an A-theory of time is a theory that states the existence of irreducible tensed facts, then it is undeniable that Fragmentalism is an A-theory.

6.6 Conclusion

In this chapter, we have looked through the timeless solution to the foreknowledge problem, which states that the argument for theological fatalism does not conclude because God's knowledge is not located in time. We have seen that, to be plausible, the timeless solution must embrace **Dependence**, that is, the possibility that some temporal facts (for instance, human free decisions) determine God's timeless beliefs. If **Dependence** is taken on board, many objections raised against the timeless solution turn out weak. Also, the objection that relies on the prophecy does not appear particularly serious.

The questions regarding the metaphysics of time are much more worrying. The timeless solution can be easily combined with a B-theory of time. It is easy to imagine how a timeless God can observe the entire temporal series and know the outcomes of free human decisions. Problems arise when a timeless and omniscient God is combined with an A-theory of time. To be omniscient, God should "follow" the flow of time, that is, change His beliefs about the present time. However, this is not allowed for a timeless God, who by definition cannot change. The most serious attempt to demonstrate the consistency between a timeless God and an A-world, that of Leftow, encounters many troubles.

Our main claim is that it is necessary to fall back on a non-standard A-theory such as Fragmentalism. We have proposed a perspectival semantic, which is neutral from the metaphysical point of view, but which can be easily interpreted as a model of a fragmented reality. In this framework, it can be proved that a timeless God can know tensed facts. Certainly, Fragmentalism is a very costly theory, but perhaps it is a cost worth paying given the advantages of Fragmentalism over standard A-theories of time.

Our journey through the theories that try to reconcile divine omniscience and human freedom is finished. Some closing words follow.

References

Belnap, N.D., M. Perloff, M. Xu, et al. 2001. *Facing the Future: Agents and Choices in Our Indeterminist World*. Oxford: Oxford University Press.

Castañeda, H.-N. 1967. Omniscience and Indexical Reference. *The Journal of Philosophy* 64(7), 203–210.

Correia, F., and S. Rosenkranz. 2012. Eternal Facts in an Ageing Universe. *Australasian Journal of Philosophy* 90(2), 307–320.

Craig, W.L. 1998. The Tensed vs. Tenseless Theory of Time: A Watershed for the Conception of Divine Eternity. In *Questions of Time and Tense*, ed. R. Le Poidevin, 221–250. Oxford: Clarendon Press.

Craig, W.L. 2000. Omniscience, Tensed Facts, and Divine Eternity. *Faith and Philosophy* 17(2), 225–241.

Craig, W.L. 2001a. *God, Time, and Eternity: The Coherence of Theism II: Eternity*. Berlin: Springer.

Craig, W.L. 2001b. Kvanvig No a-Theorist. *Faith and Philosophy* 18(3), 377–380.

Craig, W.L. 2004. Wierenga No a-Theorist Either. *Faith and Philosophy* 21(1), 105–109.

Cyr, T.W. (2018). Timelessness and Freedom. In *Synthese*, 1–15. Dordrecht: Springer.

De Florio, C., and A. Frigerio. 2019. Molinism and thin red line. *Journal of Logic, Language and Information*. https://doi.org/10.1007/s10849-019-09304-4.

Diekemper, J. 2013. Eternity, Knowledge, and Freedom. *Religious Studies* 49(1), 45–64.

Fine, K. 2005. Tense and Reality. In *Modality and Tense: Philosophical Papers*, ed. K. Fine, 261–320. Oxford: Oxford University Press.

Fine, K. 2006. The reality of tense. *Synthese* 150(3), 399–414.

Fitzgerald, P. 1985. Stump and Kretzmann on Time and Eternity. *The Journal of Philosophy* 82(5), 260–269.

Grim, P. 1985. Against Omniscience: The Case from Essential Indexicals. *Nous* 19(2), 151–180.
Helm, P. 1988. *Eternal God: A study of God Without Time*. Oxford: Clarendon Press.
Kaplan, D. 1989. Demonstratives. In *Themes from Kaplan*, ed. J. Almog, J. Perry, and H. Wettstein, 481–563. Oxford: Oxford University Press.
Kretzmann, N. 1966. Omniscience and Immutability. *The Journal of Philosophy* 63(14), 409–421.
Kvanvig, J.L. 1986. *Possibility of an All-Knowing God*. Berlin: Springer.
Kvanvig, J.L. 2001. Omniscience and Eternity: A Reply to Craig. *Faith and Philosophy* 18(3), 369–376.
Leftow, B. 1988. The Roots of Eternity. *Religious Studies* 24(2), 189–212.
Leftow, B. 1990. Time, Actuality and Omniscience. *Religious Studies* 26(3), 303–321.
Leftow, B. 1991a. *Time and Eternity*. Ithaca: Cornell University Press.
Leftow, B. 1991b. Timelessness and Foreknowledge. *Philosophical Studies* 63(3), 309–325.
Lewis, D. 1984. Eternity Again: A Reply to Stump and Kretzmann. *International Journal for Philosophy of Religion* 15(1–2), 73–79.
Lipman, M.A. 2015. On Fine's Fragmentalism. *Philosophical Studies* 172(12), 3119–3133.
MacBeath, M., and P. Helm. 1989. Omniscience and Eternity. *Proceedings of the Aristotelian Society, Supplementary Volumes* 63, 55–87.
MacFarlane, J. 2003. Future Contingents and Relative Truth. *The Philosophical Quarterly* 53(212), 321–336.
MacFarlane, J. 2014. *Assessment Sensitivity: Relative Truth and Its Applications*. Oxford: Oxford University Press.
Malpass, A., and J. Wawer. 2012. A Future for the Thin Red Line. *Synthese* 188(1), 117–142.
Plantinga, A. 1986. On Ockham's Way Out. *Faith and Philosophy* 3(3), 235–269.
Prior, A.N. 1962. The Formalities of Omniscience. *Philosophy* 37(140), 114–129.
Robinson, M.D. 1995. *Eternity and Freedom: A Critical Analysis of Divine Timelessness as a Solution to the Foreknowledge/Free Will Debate*. Lanham: University Press of America.
Rogers, K. 2008. *Anselm on Freedom*. Oxford: Oxford University Press.
Rogers, K.A. 1994. Eternity has No Duration. *Religious Studies* 30(1), 1–16.
Rogers, K.A. 2007a. Anselmian Eternalism: The Presence of a Timeless God. *Faith and Philosophy* 24(1), 3–27.

Rogers, K.A. 2007b. The Necessity of the Present and Anselm's Eternalist Response to the Problem of Theological Fatalism. *Religious Studies* 43(1), 25–47.

Stump, E., and N. Kretzmann. 1981. Eternity. *The Journal of Philosophy* 78(8), 429–458.

Stump, E., and N. Kretzmann. 1991. Prophecy, Past Truth, and Eternity. *Philosophical Perspectives* 5, 395–424.

Stump, E., and N. Kretzmann. 1992. Eternity, Awareness, and Action. *Faith and Philosophy* 9(4), 463–482.

Tapp, C., and E. Runggaldier. 2011. *God, Eternity, and Time*. Farnham: Ashgate Publishing, Ltd.

Widerker, D. 1994. Providence, Eternity, and Human Freedom: A Reply to Stump and Kretzmann. *Faith and Philosophy* 11(2), 242–254.

Wierenga, E. 2002. Timelessness Out of Mind: On the Alleged Incoherence of Divine Timelessness. In *God and Time: Essays on the Divine Nature*, ed. G.E. Ganssle, D.M. Woodruff, pp. 153–164. Oxford: Oxford University Press.

Wierenga, E. 2004. Omniscience and Time, One More Time. *Faith and Philosophy* 21(1), 90–97.

Winderker, D. 1991. A Problem for the Eternity Solution. *International Journal for Philosophy of Religion* 29, 87–95.

Zagzebski, L.T. 1991. *The Dilemma of Freedom and Foreknowledge*. Oxford: Oxford University Press.

Zagzebski, L.T. 2013. *Omnisubjectivity: a Defense of a Divine Attribute*. Milwaukee: Marquette University Press.

Conclusions

As we said in the preface of this book, this is not a long argument to solve (or "dissolve") the dilemma of divine omniscience and human freedom. We have, on the contrary, tried to map the territory of thousands of years of philosophical answers, clearly in an incomplete and tentative way. It seems to us, however, that some conclusions can be drawn according to what was said in the previous chapters. One of the theses, maybe *the* main thesis, of this book has, actually, a meta-philosophical flavour: we think that the philosophy of time (better, the metaphysics of time characterized through systems of temporal logic) is not merely tangent to the foreknowledge dilemma but, quite the opposite, it is an essential part. In other terms, we believe that any solution to the *conundrum* presupposes a precise stance about temporal reality. This result is not trivial; for many centuries, great philosophers faced with this problem have simply ignored the question of the ontology of time. And yet, time matters. Moreover, in the light of previously discussed various solutions, it matters still more.

Indeed, there are three views which—according to us—show the best internal theoretical stability.[1] The first is *Open Theism* (see Chap. 3). It is an extreme solution—as you recall—since it deeply revises one of the two concepts at play, that of divine omniscience. However, from the philosophical point of view, Open Theism is a convincing and robust position. The second view is that we can call *Timeless Eternalism*, advocated, for instance, by Katherin Rogers and that maybe dates back to Anselm.[2] The third view is *Perspectival Fragmentalism*, our original contribution to the debate.

It is interesting to notice how the first approach, namely, Open Theism, has a robust conception of time: temporal reality is intrinsically dynamic and the future structurally open. The dynamic feature of the reality is so strong that even God, in some way, must face it: the metaphysical indeterminateness of the future—which, according to open theist, is precondition for human free will—is such that it carves the cognitive power of God. Although immensely superior, even God cannot know what a free agent will decide in the future.

Specularly, Timeless Eternalism maintains God's complete omniscience at the price of buying a *deflationist* (so to speak) conception of time: all the temporal reality exists, extruded as a block of metal. For sure, its topology is ramified, and this allows us to admit free agents who decide which branch of the tree to take. But from a timeless point of view, there is (already) the choice of constructing Martian colonies in 2070. Here, there is all the oddity of a B-theory of time. But once this statical metaphysical picture is accepted, it is not hard to suppose that God eternally observes reality all at once. One could say that the *true* dimension of time is eternity. Nothing properly flows, and God knows that very well.

We are, thus, between Scylla—a God who takes some risks (maybe unacceptable, from the theological point of view)—and Charybdis—a frozen Universe where the flow of time is, at the end of the day, a mere

---

[1] Someone could not be satisfied with a philosophy which looks for "internal cohesion" and avoids "conceptual tensions"; he could want the truth about the world. We'll give him that; but we do not know any other path for the summit but that through the difficult and dangerous rock face.

[2] Or, at least, this is Katherin Rogers' opinion.

illusion. Is it possible to reconcile these two views by creating a third one able to account for all the desirable features? Is it possible, in other terms, to provide an account that brings together the genuine, libertarian, free will, the dynamic view of time and God's absolute omniscience? This is the challenge we tried to take up by formulating Perspectival Fragmentalism. The ingredients of this view are three: one logical, one metaphysical and the last one, maybe, theological.

From the logical point of view, the truth conditions of the propositions are based on *two* parameters: the *instant* at which one evaluates the proposition and the *perspective* from which one evaluates it. Our semantic framework, then, accounts for not only truth, but also *truth cum point of view*. The second ingredient is that the perspectives receive a robust metaphysical construal: they are not mere evaluation contexts but, on the contrary, they indicate the point at which the world has arrived. The perspective of evaluation changes because the world goes on, so to speak. This allows us to say that it is true that Emma was free to choose to go to the party and it is true that Emma chose to go to the party. The third point on which Perspectival Fragmentalism hinges has to do with its theoretical costs: is it defensible? We have seen, in the previous chapter, that the perspectives are incompatible with each other; the solution (or, at least, one possible solution) must be investigated within the metaphysics of time. However, we cannot adopt the stable proposals on the market: we had to exploit Kit Fine's intuition (which owes it to the philosophical sensitivity of his teacher, Arthur Prior) and to assume a non-standard A-theory of time.

As we have seen, according to Fragmentalism, reality is originally constituted as fragmented. God's point of view, then, is not simply timeless but is a form of *omni-perspectival timelessness*. That is, God sees everything from every point of view. After all, if we construe perspective as the metaphysical "now", the present moment, God's knowledge is "located" at every present, each with its distinct perspective on the world. Clearly, all that has a high theoretical cost, maybe too high. If reality—which is originally fragmented—were given as a whole, it would bring about contradictions. Thus, if God's epistemic status were given as a whole, it would be contradictory.

But maybe, this is a not such a hard limitation. We should never surrender—and this book seems to us the best proof—to the flattery of some theologians and philosophers who take refuge in a too-comfortable *mysterium*: whenever the investigation is hard, it is too easy to declare that it is a mystery. However, and we are really at the end, we could concede that the ultimate constitution of God's mind is beyond our philosophical efforts. But it does not matter; there still is a lot to do, down here.

Index

Page numbers followed by 'n' refer to notes.

A
Accidental necessity, 12, 20, 121, 213, 217
  necessity of the past, 9, 11–13, 17–19, 22, 23, 70, 92, 111, 121, 171, 172, 210, 211
A-theory of time, 33, 210, 222, 226, 231–233, 236, 238, 250, 252, 254–256

B
Backward causation, 132, 133, 150
Bivalence, 9–11, 15, 15n15, 16, 20, 22, 24, 59, 62
Block Universe view, 38, 40, 41, 44
Branching time, 50–53, 78n8, 81, 129, 243, 244n19
Branching towards the past, 241
B-theory of time, 33, 38, 210, 211, 222, 225, 232, 262
Butterfly schema, 129, 130, 132, 145

C
Circularity argument, 191
Closed universe/closed future, 48–50, 52, 59, 64, 65
Compatibilism (free will), 82, 93–96, 104, 105
Conditionals of divine freedom (CDFs), 167, 168n10

Conditionals of Freedom (CFs), 155–162, 164, 167, 168, 172–174, 176–178, 177n20, 178n21, 186, 192, 194, 195, 199n33, 201, 202
Counterfactual dependence of the past on the future, 150

D

Dependence principle 216, 216n5, 218, 250, 256
Determinism, 3–6, 13, 24, 44, 44n19, 77, 82, 92–111, 146n30, 148
Divine providence, 105, 160
Divine simplicity, 235
Divine sovereignty, 100, 155, 159
Dynamics of time, 32–38

E

Endurantism, 40, 41
Erosionism, 78n8
Eternalism, 30, 30n6, 31, 38–40, 44–46, 78n8, 79n9, 81, 116n2, 134–136, 140, 144, 144n29, 151, 189, 222–225, 229, 230, 238, 248–250, 254, 262
ET-simultaneity, 214–216, 216n5, 219, 233, 234
Excluded middle, 10, 52, 54, 55, 57, 59
Explanatory priority, 191–193

F

Four-dimensionalism, 30n6, 40
Fragmentalism, 36, 37, 222, 240–257, 263

Free Actions Truth Maker Principle (FATMP), 188–190, 205
Freedom of self-determination, 97–100, 103, 104
Freedom of self-realization, 97, 98, 104, 110
Free knowledge, 158, 159, 167
Future contingent(s), 2, 2n1, 8, 21, 22, 51–53, 56, 57, 83–85, 120n5, 150, 182n26, 249n21

G

God's inertial frame, 233, 237
Grounding intuition/grounding principle, 44, 136, 141
  Maximally Liberalized Grounding Principle (MLGP), 186, 187, 187n29
Growing Block view, 31, 39n13, 44, 78n8, 148, 183, 250

H

Hard determinism, 102, 108–110
Historical compatibilism, 107
Historical connectedness, 50, 51
Human responsibility, 108

I

Immutability of the past, 15
Incompatibilism (free will), 14, 20, 84, 102, 108
Indexicals, 36, 46, 227–231, 229n14, 245, 249, 250, 253, 256
Inertial frame of reference, 214, 233
Infallible knowledge, 2, 18, 167

L

Leibniz' Lapse, 159n2
Lewis' semantics of counterfactuals, 174, 176, 176n18, 179
Libertarian freedom–Libertarianism, 93, 176, 194, 195, 195n32, 199
Linear time, 49–50
Logical fatalism, 3, 6–15, 20–24, 126, 130, 131

M

Metaphysics of time, 15, 24, 25, 27–29, 39, 41, 42, 47, 64, 78n8, 80, 93, 116n2, 120, 134–150, 183, 184, 189, 210, 216, 222, 224, 245, 251, 255, 256, 261
Middle knowledge, 83, 157–159, 161, 171n12
Might-counterfactuals, 175, 178n21
Molinism, 23, 24, 64, 81–83, 88, 111, 116, 117, 151, 155–205, 215, 221, 222, 235, 235n18
Molinist loop, 196
Moving Spotlight Theory (MST), 39, 78n8

N

Natural knowledge, 158
Necessitism, 5, 24, 44
Non theological compatibilism, 94–99, 110

O

Ockhamism, 23, 24, 47, 52, 52n20, 53, 53n21, 54, 80, 111, 115–151, 155, 160, 162, 173, 179, 181, 194, 215, 221, 222, 235n18
Omniscience, definition, 18, 23, 100
Ontology of time, 5, 13, 16, 25, 27–32, 78n8, 149, 261
Open Theism, 23, 70–94, 115, 262
Open universe/open future, 44, 48–51, 65, 77, 78n8, 125, 151, 242, 243

P

Peircean semantics, 53–58, 65
Perdurantism, 40, 41
Persistence, 28, 39–42, 116
Perspectival semantics, 64, 240–250, 254
Presentism, 29, 30, 30n5, 31, 37, 39, 43, 44, 78n8, 80, 134, 136–141, 143, 146n30, 147, 183, 185n27, 189, 190, 224, 226, 233, 250
Prophecy, 86–88, 220–222, 256

S

Shrinking Block view, 32, 43–45, 65
Simple foreknowledge, 83, 160, 160n3
Soft facts
    epistemic soft facts, 127, 173
    semantic soft facts, 126, 127, 130
Special Relativity (Theory of), 41, 42, 45, 236
Supervaluationism, 17, 56

T

Temporal logic, 25, 28, 47–65
Temporal operators, 48–50

Tensed properties, 32, 33, 146, 183
Tenseless properties, 32, 33n9
Theological compatibilism, 100–111
Theological determinism, 82, 92–111
Theological fatalism, 2, 3, 14, 15, 21–25, 130, 131
Thin Red Line (TRL)
   local TRL, 62, 63, 162–166, 169, 173, 181, 184
   normal TRL, 165–171, 173, 181–184, 195, 200, 203
   TRL+, 62–64, 64n25, 155, 162, 164–166, 168, 179, 183, 191, 199, 203–205
Timeless God, 117, 119, 210, 213–215, 221–256
Timeless solution, 209–257
Topology of time, 24, 25, 28, 39, 42–47, 93, 124, 129, 211
Transfer of necessity principle, 93, 172n13
Transworld depravity, 89, 162n5
True future, 56, 60, 115–151, 160n3, 162, 182
Truth-making
   truth-making maximalism, 137
   tensed truth-making, 142
Truth supervenes on being (TSB), 80, 137–139, 141–147, 181, 183–191
Truth Supervenes on Tensional Being principle (TSTB), 142–148, 184